FASCINATING MAMMALS

FASCINATING MAMMALS

Conservation and Ecology
in the Mid-Eastern States

RICHARD H. YAHNER

University of Pittsburgh Press

Manufactured in the United States of America

Printed on acid-free paper

10 9 8 7 6 5 4 3 2 1

Library of Congress Cataloging-in-Publication Data
Yahner, Richard H.
    Fascinating mammals : conservation and ecology in the mid-eastern states /
Richard H. Yahner.
       p.   cm.
    Includes bibliographical references (p.   ).
    ISBN 0-8229-4158-9 (cloth : alk. paper) — ISBN 0-8229-5765-5 (paper : alk. paper)
      1. Mammals—Middle Atlantic States. 2. Wildlife conservation—Middle Atlantic
States. I. Title.
   QL719.M54 Y35 2001
   599'.0974—dc21

00-013224

To my wife, Darlinda, and my sons, Rich and Tom

CONTENTS

Contents

Contents

Contents

PREFACE

Mammals have fascinated humans since the earliest of times, perhaps in part because we also are mammals. Our ancestors, known as Cro-Magnon man, had a rich admiration of mammals, as witnessed by their beautiful drawings of real and imagined mammals that can be seen today in caves of southern France. Native Americans have always respected and revered mammals, such as the grizzly (brown) bear for its strength and the coyote for its cunning. Today, our fascination with mammals often begins in early childhood. Pick up any children's book of animals, and you will find it filled with information and pictures of charismatic mammals, such as elephants, giraffes, and bears.

Besides their aesthetic value, mammals have many other values, including economic, recreational, ecological, and scientific. For thousands and even millions of years, mammals have been a source of food, clothing, and energy (as labor and farm animals). Beginning in the latter decades of the twentieth century, recreation associated with hunting of the white-tailed deer alone has added millions of dollars to our regional and national economies. As recreational opportunities become more accessible to us in future decades, viewing of mammals and other wildlife will certainly be an increasingly important leisure activity.

From an ecological perspective, mammals represent a very important component of the biodiversity of any woodlot or old field and are important links in the food chain of many ecosystems. From a scientific perspective, mammals, like birds, have been intensively studied, yet we have much to learn about the natural history, behavior, and ecology of this interesting taxon. In turn, mammals can have some negative attributes—for instance, deer can have a major effect on forest regeneration and farm crops, and some rodents cause considerable damage to foodstuffs. Our generation and future generations must learn to live compatibly with mammals in this ever-shrinking world, with its changing land uses, and we must work collectively to ensure the conservation of mammals in our region and throughout the world.

Ever since I was a child, mammals have always been interesting to me in both my readings and outdoor activities. I recall reading over and over a book entitled *American Wild Life Illustrated*, which was published initially in 1940 by the City of New York. This book helped shape my love for mammals and other wildlife at an early age. I also vividly remember the thrill of encountering mammals, such as gray foxes and gray squirrels, as I sat or walked quietly during a midsummer morning in the woodlands behind my childhood home in western Pennsylvania. My fascination continued into adulthood as a teacher and researcher.

In this book, I discuss selected aspects of the conservation and the ecology of mammals, which, I hope, has stimulated a lifelong interest in mammals in nearly 150 undergraduate and graduate students per year who have enrolled in my mammalogy or conservation biology classes at the Pennsylvania State University since the mid-1980s. Since the mid-1970s I have conducted extensive research on the ecology, conservation, and behavior of many mammal species, ranging from shrews to white-tailed deer. Hence, my interest in mammalian conservation and ecology will undoubtedly continue throughout my life.

My goal here is to provide an in-depth understanding of contemporary topics in mammalian conservation and ecology, with a particular focus on mammals in eight mid-eastern states: Delaware, Maryland, New Jersey, New York, Ohio, Pennsylvania, Virginia, and West Virginia. This book is intended for a general outdoors-oriented audience, which includes college students, upper-level high school students, high school teachers, professionals in the environmental or natural resource disciplines, and persons simply interested in the many fascinating mammals in our region.

I begin with a general introduction to mammalian characteristics, history, and conservation status (e.g., numbers of federally and state endangered species). The next nineteen chapters present selected families of terrestrial mammals, given in taxonomic order; aquatic mammals in waters adjacent to the eight states are not included. Each chapter begins with a brief introduction to the family, including general morphological, ecological, and behavioral characteristics of the family and the number of species found in the eight states. General information on each family is principally taken from Burt and Grossenheider (1976), Whitaker and Hamilton (1998), and Nowak (1999), and from published information on the status of mammals available from wildlife agencies in each of the eight states. Common and scientific names of mammals are taken from Jones et al. (1997).

Each chapter concludes with one or more in-depth essays covering significant and interesting aspects of the conservation and the ecology of species in that family. Information on these topics is mainly based on scientific publications. Thus, this book is not designed as a field guide to mammals; many fine field guides are already available on the market. Instead, my hope is that the topics in this book will give readers a better appreciation of mammals in our region, as they have to me and my students over the years. Perhaps this book also will be an impetus for some young person to become a leading mammalogist or conservationist in the decades to come.

ACKNOWLEDGMENTS

My research on mammals has been funded by several agencies and organizations during my career: the Hammermill Paper Company, the Max McGraw Wildlife Foundation, the National Park Service, the Pennsylvania Game Commission, the Pennsylvania State University, the Pennsylvania Wild Resource Conservation Fund, the University of Minnesota, the U.S. Environmental Protection Agency, and the U.S. Forest Service. I am very grateful to the personnel in these agencies and organizations for their cooperation and interest in my research and that of my graduate students. I thank Rick Sharbaugh for assistance with the graphics. I especially appreciate the support and patience of my family, Darlinda, Rich, and Tom, during the time I spent writing this book.

FASCINATING MAMMALS

1

Introduction to Mammals

What Is a Mammal?

Mammals occur in all environments—on land from desert to tundra, and in water from a small mountain stream to the deepest ocean. Only Antarctica has no land mammals. Mammals feed on every conceivable food item; some are specialized to feed solely on blood (e.g., vampire bats), whereas others are omnivores (black bears), which feed on a variety of plant and animal food items. Yet despite the widespread distribution and our familiarity with many mammals, they are not well represented (in terms of the number of species) compared to most other taxonomic groups. For example, a conservative estimate of the number of extant species is about 12 million (Cox 1997), with at least 75 percent of these being arthropods. Fewer than 4 percent of the total extant species are plants, and only about 0.5 percent are vertebrates. Of the estimated 55,500 vertebrate species, most are fish (54%; 30,000 species), followed by birds (18%; 9,800 species), reptiles (12%; 6,700 species), mammals (9%; 4,800 species), and amphibians (8%; 4,200 species).

The success of mammals largely stems from their evolution of remarkable structural, behavioral, and physiological adaptations, allowing them to exist in a variety of environments. Bats, for example, which represent about 20 percent of the extant mammalian species, have evolved flight and typically use an interesting type of communication known as echolocation. The blue whale is one of the many truly aquatic mammals and is the largest animal ever to live on earth. Conversely, many shrews live a relatively fossorial way of life and weigh only a few grams as adults. The ability of mammals to inhabit a variety of environments is mainly attributed to their ability to maintain a relatively constant body temperature, known as endothermy, and, hence, deal with temperature extremes—a characteristic found also in birds. In addition, many mammals hibernate, exhibit torpor, or migrate to avoid harsh environmental conditions caused by changes in seasonal or daily weather conditions.

Besides endothermy, all mammals share four important and unique characteristics: mammary glands, a muscular diaphragm, hair, and three small bones in the inner ear (Vaughan, Ryan, and Czaplewski 2000). Mammary glands provide milk, which is an energy-rich source of food for developing young. The muscular diaphragm in the thoracic cavity helps draw air into the lungs, thereby increasing air capacity—a feature vital in maintaining the high metabolism of mammals. A coat of hair, termed the pelage, serves to insulate most mammals but also acts to conceal or advertise a mammal. Birds and reptiles have a single inner-ear bone (stapes); on the other hand, mammals have two additional bones (malleus and incus) in the inner ear. These three mammalian bones increase hearing ability by magnifying sounds and reduce damage to the inner ear by cushioning loud sounds entering the ear canal.

Origin of Mammals

The first mammals arose from mammal-like reptiles in the Triassic period of the Mesozoic era about 230 million years ago. Later, about 65 million years ago in the Cenozoic era, they rapidly diversified into a variety of species representing ancestors of modern mammals. At least three factors helped ancestral mammals to flourish in early geologic time and shape the spectrum of modern mammalian species in today's world. First, the earliest mammals were relatively generalized in body plan and habits. They were nocturnal and mouse-like in size, which enabled them to be less conspicuous and better able to escape predation by juvenile dinosaurs. These mammals also had good climbing ability, in part to flee from predators but also to prey on insects in trees and other vegetation; insects flourished in the late Mesozoic era and were important pollinators of flowering plants.

Second, mammals evolved mammary glands, which provided energy-rich milk for their young. Lactation enables juvenile mammals to attain rapid body and brain growth and early sexual maturity compared to other coexisting taxa, such as reptiles. Because juvenile mammals depend on the mother for food, the growing young experience an extended period of parental care (typically solely maternal care occurs in mammals), which allows young to learn foraging techniques and predator-avoidance tactics. In contrast, parental care is virtually nonexistent in reptiles.

Third, the earth's land masses were in a state of flux, a phenomenon called continental drift. In the late Triassic period, a single land mass, termed *Pangea*, began to split into northern (Laurasia) and southern masses (Gondwana). By the end of the Cretaceous period, corresponding to the demise of the ruling dinosaurs about 65 million years ago, Gondwana continued to split to form what we recognize as continents. For example, in Gondwana, South America moved west and away from Africa, and Australia moved further north and became isolated from Antarctica. This separation of land masses led to the isolation of mammals, thereby facilitating the evolution of a greater diversity of mammal species adapted to regional or local environmental conditions.

Many species of mammals common to our region originated in North America, while others migrated to our region via various land bridges connecting North America with Europe, Asia, and South America at various times in geologic history (Vaughan, Ryan, and Czaplewski 2000). For instance, horses and leporids (hares and rabbits) evolved in North America. In contrast, moles and shrews initially evolved in Europe, cats and deer (with the exception of white-tailed and mule deer) in Asia, and porcupines and armadillos in South America.

Classification and Conservation Status of Regional Mammals

Mammals are placed in the class Mammalia within the phylum Chordata. Two subclasses of mammals exist today: Protheria, which contains fewer than 1 percent of extant mammals, including platypus and echidna, and Theria, which includes all other mammalian species. The therians are subdivided into the infraclass Methatheria (or "marsupials"), comprising about 6 percent of today's mammals, and the infraclass Eutheria (or "placentals"), encompassing the remaining extant mammalian species.

According to Nowak (1999), 4,809 extant mammalian species exist worldwide. The American Society of Mammalogists recognizes nearly 450 extant mammalian species in North America (and its adjacent waters) north of Mexico; of these, about twenty-five (or 5%) are exotic species (Jones et al. 1997). Approximately 20 percent (96 species) of these North American species occur in the eight states focused upon in this book, and thirteen of the regional mammalian species are exotic (see Table 1). Most species in our region are rodents (31 species), followed by bats (16 species), and shrews (10 species). The number of species per state ranges from eighty in Virginia to only thirty-five in Delaware.

We should jointly share, scientists and nonscientists alike, a worldwide concern for the conservation of mammals because of the following alarming statistic. Of the 4,809 extant species, nearly one-half are in jeopardy with classifications of critically endangered, endangered, vulnerable, conservation dependent, or near threatened (Nowak 1999). Many species in our region are of conservation concern in at least one state, ranging in status from endangered to rare. Notably, eight of the ninety-six species are of conservation concern in at least two states. These species include three shrews (long-tailed, water, and least), two bats (gray and Indiana myotis), a lagomorph (Appalachian cottontail), and a rodent (Appalachian woodrat).

Table 1. Order, family, and status of extant mammalian species in each of the eight mid-eastern states based primarily on checklists obtained from state wildlife agencies. Dashes (—) indicate that a given mammal species is presumed extirpated or absent from the state; other designations indicate that presence of a species is confirmed in the state. Common and scientific names are taken from Jones et al. (1997); scientific names are given in appendix A.

Order/Family/Species	State Status[a]							
	DE	MD	NJ	NY	OH	PA	VA	WV
Didelphimorphia: Opossums								
Didelphidae: American Opossums								
Virginia Opossum	S5	S3+	S	GA	X5	C	P	C
Insectivora: Insectivores								
Soricidae: Shrews								
Masked Shrew	S5	S3+	S	UN	X5	C	P	C
Long-tailed Shrew	—	S2-I	U	UN	—	I	P	R
Maryland Shrew	—	S3+	—	—	—	C	—	—
Smokey Shrew	—	S1S2-T	U	UN	X5	C	P	U
Pygmy Shrew	—	S2	U	UN	X1-SI	C	P	U
Southeastern Shrew	—	S3S4	—	—	—	—	P	U
Water Shrew	—	S1-E	U	UN	—	T	E	R
Northern Short-tailed Shrew	S5	S3+	S	UN	X5	C	P	C
Southern Short-tailed Shrew	—	—	—	—	—	—	P	—
Least Shrew	—	S3+	U	UN	X5	E	P	R
Talpidae: Moles								
Hairy-tailed Mole	—	S3+	U	UN	X5	C	P	C
Eastern Mole	S5	S3+	S	UN	X5	C	P	U
Star-nosed Mole	S4	SU	U	UN	X5-SI	C	P	U
Chiroptera: Bats								
Vespertilionidae: Vespertilionid Bats								
Southeastern Myotis	—	—	—	—	—	—	P	—
Gray Myotis	—	—	—	—	—	—	E	R
Eastern Small-footed Myotis	SU	S1-I	U	UN-SC	X1-SI	T	P	R
Little Brown Myotis	S5	S3+	S	UN	X5	C	P	C
Northern Myotis	—	S3+	U	UN	X5	R	P	U
Indiana Myotis	—	S1-E	E	E	X5-E	E	E	R
Eastern Red Bat	—	S3+	S	UN	X5	U	P	U
Hoary Bat	—	S3+	U	UN	X5	U	P	U

Table 1.

Order/Family/Species	State Status[a]							
	DE	MD	NJ	NY	OH	PA	VA	WV
Northern Yellow Bat	—	—	—	—	—	—	P	—
Seminole Bat	—	—	—	—	—	U	P	—
Silver-haired Bat	—	S3+	U	UN	X5	R	P	—
Eastern Pipistrelle	S5	S3+	U	UN	X5	C	P	C
Big Brown Bat	S5	S3+	S	UN	X5	C	P	C
Evening Bat	—	S3+	—	—	X3	R	P	R
Rafinesque's Big-eared Bat	—	—	—	—	X2-SI	—	E	R
Townsend's Big-eared Bat	—	—	—	—	—	—	P	R

Lagomorpha: Lagomorphs

Leporidae: Rabbits and Hares

Eastern Cottontail	S5	S3+	S	GA	X5	C	P	C
New England Cottontail	—	—	—	GA-SC	—	—	—	—
Appalachian Cottontail	—	S1-I	U	—	—	A	P	U
Marsh Rabbit	—	—	—	—	—	—	SC	—
Snowshoe Hare	—	—	—	GA	—	A	P	U
Black-tailed Jackrabbit (exotic)	—	—	—	EX	—	—	—	—
White-tailed Jackrabbit (exotic)	—	—	EX	—	—	—	—	—
European Hare (exotic)	—	—	EX	EX-GA	—	—	—	—

Rodentia: Rodents

Sciuridae: Squirrels

Eastern Chipmunk	S5	S3+	S	UN	X5	C	P	C
Woodchuck	S5	S3+	S	UN	X5	C	P	C
Thirteen-lined Ground Squirrel	—	—	—	—	X5	I	—	—
Gray Squirrel	S5	S3+	S	GA	X5	C	P	C
Fox Squirrel	S1	S3+	—	GA	X5	C	P	C
Red Squirrel	S5	S3+	S	UN	X5	C	P	C
Northern Flying Squirrel	—	—	U	UN	—	I	E	R
Southern Flying Squirrel	S5	S3+	U	UN	X5	C	P	C

Castoridae: Beavers

American Beaver	—	S3+	INC	GA	X5	C	P	C

Muridae: Mice, Rats, and Voles

Marsh Rice Rat	S3	S3+	S	—	—	—	P	—
Eastern Harvest Mouse	—	—	—	—	X3	—	P	R
Cotton Mouse	—	—	—	—	—	—	P	—

Table 1.

Order/Family/Species	State Status[a]							
	DE	MD	NJ	NY	OH	PA	VA	WV
Muridae: Mice, Rats, and Voles (cont.)								
White-footed Mouse	S5	S3+	S	UN	X5	C	P	C
Deer Mouse	—	S3+	—	UN	X5	C	P	C
Golden Mouse	—	—	—	—	—	—	P	U
Hispid Cotton Rat	—	—	—	—	—	—	P	—
Appalachian Woodrat	—	S1-E	E	E?	X2-E	T	P	U
Norway Rat (exotic)	EX	EX-S3+	EX	EX-UN	EX-X5	EX-C	EX	EX
Black Rat (exotic)	EX	EX-S3+	EX	EX-UN	—	—	EX	EX
House Mouse (exotic)	EX	EX-S3+	EX	EX-UN	EX-X5	EX-C	EX	EX
Southern Red-backed Vole	—	S3+	S	UN	X1-SI	C	P	C
Rock Vole	—	S1-E	—	UN	—	A	E	U
Prairie Vole	—	—	—	—	X5	—	—	R
Meadow Vole	S5	S3+	S	UN	X5	C	P	C
Woodland Vole	S4	S3+	S	UN	X4	C	P	C
Common Muskrat	S5	S3+	S	GA	X5	C	P	C
Southern Bog Lemming	—	S3+	U	UN	X5	I	P	U
Zapodidae: Jumping Mice								
Meadow Jumping Mouse	S5	S3+	U	UN	X5	C	P	U
Woodland Jumping Mouse	—	S3+	U	UN	X2-SI	C	P	C
Erithizontidae: New World Porcupines								
Common Porcupine	—	S1S2-I	INC	UN	—	C	P	—
Family Myocastoridae: Myocastorids								
Nutria (exotic)	—	EX	EX	—	—	—	EX	—
Order Carnivora: Carnivores								
Family Canidae: Canids								
Feral Dog (exotic)	EX	EX	EX	EX	EX	EX	EX	EX
Coyote	P	S3+	INC	GA	X5	C	P	R
Red Fox	S5	S3+	S	GA	X5	C	P	C
Gray Fox	S5	S3+	S	GA	X5	C	P	C
Family Ursidae: Bears								
Black Bear	—	S3	INC	GA	X?-E	C	P	U
Family Procyonidae: Procyonids								
Common Raccoon	S5	S3+	S	GA	X5	C	P	C

Table 1.

Order/Family/Species	State Status[a]							
	DE	MD	NJ	NY	OH	PA	VA	WV
Family Mustelidae: Mustelids								
American Marten	—	—	—	GA	—	—	—	—
Fisher	—	S3+	—	GA	—	A	P	R
Ermine	—	S3+	U	GA	X1	C	—	—
Long-tailed Weasel	S5	S3+	S	GA	X5	C	P	U
Least Weasel	—	S3+	—	UN	X5	U	P	U
Mink	S5	S3+	S	GA	X5	C	P	U
American Badger	—	—	—	—	X5	—	—	—
Northern River Otter	—	S3+	S	GA	X2-E	A	SC	R
Family Mephitidae: Mephitids								
Eastern Spotted Skunk	—	S3+	—	—	—	A	P	U
Striped Skunk	S5	S3+	S	GA	X5	C	P	C
Family Felidae: Cats								
Feral Cat (exotic)	EX	EX	EX	EX	EX	EX	EX	EX
Lynx	—	—	—	GA	—	—	—	—
Bobcat	—	S3	E	GA	X2-E	A	P	U
Order Perissodactyla: Odd-toed Ungulates								
Family Equidae: Equids								
Feral Horse (exotic)	—	EX	—	—	—	—	EX	—
Order Artiodactyla: Even-toed Ungulates								
Family Suidae: Pigs								
Feral Pig (exotic)	—	—	—	—	EX	—	EX	EX
Family Cervidae: Deer								
Elk	—	—	—	GA	—	A	—	—
Sika Deer (exotic)	—	EX	—	—	—	—	EX	—
White-tailed Deer	S5	S3+	DEC	GA	X5	C	P	C
Moose	—	—	—	GA	—	—	—	—
Caribou	—	—	—	GA	—	—	—	—
Family Bovidae: Bovids								
Feral Goat (exotic)	—	—	—	—	—	—	—	EX
Total Number of Species	35	68	60	69	60	67	80	69

aState status designations—Delaware (DE): S1 = extremely rare (<5 occurrences) or that some factor immediately threatens the future existence of the species, S3 = rare to uncommon (21–100 occurrences), S4 = apparently secure under present conditions, S5 = very common, P= present, and EX = introduced into the state as an exotic species; Maryland (MD): S1 = highly rare (<5 occurrences) or some factor(s) makes it vulnerable to extirpation, S2 = very rare (6–20 occurrences) or some factor(s) makes it vulnerable to extirpation, S3 = rare to uncommon (21–100 occurrences), S3+ = at least a ranking of S3 or higher (e.g., S4), E = endangered, T = threatened, I = in need of conservation because limited or declining, and EX = introduced into the state as an exotic species; New Jersey (NJ): E = endangered, DEC = decreasing, S = stable, INC = increasing, U = undetermined, and EX = introduced into the state as an exotic species; New York (NY): GA = game species, UN = unprotected, E = endangered, SC = special concern, and EX = introduced into the state as an exotic species; Ohio (OH): X1, X2, . . . X5 = known to occur in one to five of the regions in the state, respectively, E = endangered, SI = special interest, and EX = introduced into the state as an exotic species; Pennsylvania (PA): C = common, I = restricted distribution, R = rare, A = at risk, T = threatened, E = endangered, U = status undetermined, and EX = introduced into the state as an exotic species; Virginia (VA): P = present, SC = special concern, E = endangered, and EX = introduced into the state as an exotic species; and West Virginia (WV): C = common, U = uncommon, R = rare, and EX = introduced into the state as an exotic species.

Introduction to Mammals

2

American Opossums

Family Didelphidae

Description of the Family Didelphidae

The American opossums are in the family Didelphidae and the order Didelphimorphia (formerly Marsupialia), which is a different order from the metatherians of Australia. The didelphids include sixty-three species but only the Virginia opossum is found in North America; the other sixty-two didelphid species occur in Central and South America (Vaughan, Ryan, and Czaplewski 2000). Some authors, however, have adopted a different classification system for didelphids, which considers only eight species in Didelphidae (see Nowak 1999).

American opossums are medium-sized mammals (18–104 cm in total length, 0.2–5.9 kg in weight). Our Virginia opossum is a grayish, relatively large member of this family (61–102 cm, 4–5.9 kg), being about the size of the feral (domestic) cat.

The tail of American opossums is usually long, relatively hairless, and prehensile. Most species have a distinct marsupium (or pouch) within which to raise the young. The muzzle is usually long and pointed, and the thumb on the hind foot is opposable.

Didelphids are usually omnivorous and are active in the evening and at night. Gestation in didelphids is only twelve to thirteen days. In the Virginia opossum, one or two litters are produced, with up to fourteen young per litter. Compared to the body weight of the mother, young Virginia opossums are very small (2 g) at birth. After climbing to the pouch soon after birth, the young remain within the pouch for about two months and later travel on the back of the mother for another month. With the exception of this association between mother and young, Virginia opossums are solitary.

American Opossums

Misconceptions about the Virginia Opossum

Many of us have driven down a country road or looked out into our back-yard at dusk to see a lumbering, slow-moving gray animal that we recognized as a Virginia opossum. The opossum's appearance, its ability to feign death by "playing possum," and the fact that it has a pouch give us the impression that this mammal is a relict species of some earlier age. Indeed, historically, the Virginia opossums and other metatherians have been viewed as "inferior" and primitive compared to eutherians. Even the early biologists, including Charles Darwin and Thomas Huxley, regarded the metatherians as taxonomically intermediate between the protherians and eutherians (Kirsch 1977).

A characteristic shared by the Virginia opossum, some extant meta-therians, and fossil mammals is a primitive tribosphenic molar, which has three rather than four cusps on its cutting surface. Metatherians, however, are distinguished from eutherians by some other features (Nowak 1999; Vaughan, Ryan, and Czaplewski 2000). For instance, with few exceptions, metatherians tend to have more than forty-four teeth in the dentition, whereas eutherians typically have forty-four or fewer teeth. The Virginia opossum has fifty teeth; in our region, the mammals with the next highest number of teeth are some moles, for example, the hairy-tailed mole, with forty-four teeth (Burt and Grossenheider 1976). Females of most metatherians have an abdominal marsupium or pouch, which is used to carry young during lactation; eutherians do not have pouches. The presence of a pouch in metatherians is believed to be an advanced characteristic in this infraclass; hence, a pouchless metatherian species is considered to be more primitive than one with a pouch (Kirsch 1977).

Metatherians also have an incomplete placenta, which is a structure that permits the exchange of nutrients from the mother to young and

Family Didelphidae

waste materials from young to the mother; on the other hand, eutherians have a complete (and more efficient) placenta. Compared to eutherians of comparable size, the gestation for metatherians is considerably short. For example, the gestation is twelve days in Virginia opossums, whereas it is twenty-eight to thirty days in common muskrats, which are eutherian counterparts of roughly the same size (Gardner 1982; Perry 1982). However, the lactation period in Virginia opossums is fifty to sixty days compared to only fifteen to sixteen days in common muskrats. Thus, many scientists now contend that, from a reproductive perspective, female metatherians may not be primitive relative to eutherians because total energy expended in raising young by metatherians may actually exceed that required by a similar-sized eutherian (Kirsch 1977; Morton, Recher, Thompson, and Braithwaite 1982).

The Virginia opossum is unique among our resident mammals by being the only metatherian in the mid-eastern states and throughout North America (Hall 1981). This is surprising because most scientists believe that metatherians evolved in North America and were later eliminated by competition with the more successful eutherians, which colonized North America from Eurasia (Vaughan, Ryan, and Czaplewski 2000). Moreover, only two families of metatherians remain today in South America, with the stronghold of metatherian families found in Australia. The diversity of metatherians in Australia may be attributed to continental drift (see chap. 1), such that the movement of Australia northward rapidly changed the environment of Australia from a temperate forest to a tropical rainforest (Dixon, Cox, Savage, and Gardiner 1988). As a result, metatherians in Australia had to evolve continuously in order to adapt to changes in environmental conditions. In contrast, South America remained stationary or moved westward during the period of continental drift with little change in climate or other environmental conditions.

For a variety of reasons, our Virginia opossum should not be viewed as a "living fossil" or "second-class citizen." In fact, it is a relatively new species, having evolved only two million years or less ago from a species known as the common opossum, which can still be found from eastern Mexico to northern Argentina (Gardner 1973; Nowak 1999). Hence, the Virginia opossum evolved much later than the great apes and ancestors of early humans. Moreover, based on some learning and discrimination tests, some scientists go as far as to contend that the intelligence of Virginia opossums is higher than that of dogs and equal to pigs (Kirkby 1977).

From an ecological perspective, we have to look far and wide to find a more successful mammal than the Virginia opossum. It feeds on a variety of foods from plant to animal (living and dead) and occurs in habitats ranging from forest to farmland (Gardner 1982). Prior to European settlement in North America, the northern range of the Virginia opossum extended only into Indiana, Kentucky, and Ohio (Guilday 1958). Today this marsupial has extended its range throughout the eight states in our region because of human activities and introductions (Hall 1981; Seidensticker, O'Connell, and Hohnsingh 1987). The northern limit of opossums probably will be restricted eventually to about the United States–Canada border (below the −7°C or 19.4°F January isotherm) because of cold temperatures and excessive snowfall (Brocke 1970; Tyndale-Biscoe 1973).

In summary, our Virginia opossum is the sole survivor of ancestral metatherians that once occurred throughout much of North America. Yet, this interesting mammal is by no means primitive or a living fossil. Instead, it represents one of the most successful mammals in the mideastern states in terms of abundance, distribution, and adaptability.

3

Shrews

Family Soricidae

Description of the Family Soricidae

The family Soricidae is the largest family in the order Insectivora, containing about 322 species of small mammals referred to as shrews. Shrews are found on all continents except Australia, but are absent from all but the northernmost portions of South America and from many islands, like Iceland and the West Indies. In a sense, the worldwide distribution of the shrew family is nearly opposite to that of the metatherians (see chap. 2). Ten species of soricids occur in our region, ranging from nine in both Maryland and Virginia to two in Delaware (see table 1). The most ubiquitous species in the eight-state region are masked and northern short-tailed shrews.

A beginning naturalist can easily confuse shrews with mice, particularly voles. Shrews are about the size of mice

(9–120 mm in total length) and are among our smallest mammals in body weight (2–35 g). Unlike most mice, shrews have a pointed snout, reduced pinnae, and very small eyes (see fig. 1). The pelage is short and dense, ranging from gray to brown in color. Teeth vary in number from twenty-six to thirty-two and usually have brown pigmentation at the tips; the first incisor is large and hook-like.

Shrews in our region are typically found in moist woodlands or grasslands. The water shrew, however, is often associated with cold, mountainous streams. Shrews are active day and night while foraging for food in leaf litter or burrows. They are insectivorous or carnivorous but may also consume plant material.

Northern Short-Tailed Shrew

Hairy-Tailed Mole

Meadow Vole

Figure 1. A northern short-tailed shrew, a hairy-tailed mole, and a meadow vole.

Family Soricidae

17

Shrews can produce more than one litter of two to ten young over a breeding season that often extends from March through November, depending on latitude and species. Gestation varies from seventeen to twenty-eight days or about twice that of didelphids (see chap. 2); the young are weaned within two to four weeks.

Many shrews, like the northern short-tailed shrew, have well-developed flank glands that produce a powerful odor. In males of some species, these glands may attract females during the breeding season. Shrews generally are solitary, with the exception of the gregarious least shrew.

Shrews

ESSAY 2

The Role of Venom in Mammals

When we think of venomous animals, bees, wasps, and other inverte-brates with poisonous stings or bites come to mind. Stinging insects, such as yellow jackets, can become a bother at an outdoor summer picnic. An-other familiar group of poisonous animals are snakes in the pit viper and coral snake families. Approximately 540 species of the world's snake species, or about 13 percent of the total species, are venomous (Behler and King 1995). In some areas of the mid-eastern states, we have to be cautious because of the presence of timber rattlesnakes and copperheads. Two additional reptilian species, both known as Gila monsters, are ven-omous lizards in deserts of the southwestern United States. Snakes and Gila monsters use their venom for defense and immobilizing prey.

Compared to reptiles, however, venom has rarely evolved in mam-mals. Only three types of mammals have evolved venom: a few species of shrews, the solenodons, and the duck-billed platypus (Whitaker and Hamilton 1998; Vaughan, Ryan, and Czaplewski 2000). Of these three poisonous mammals, venom use has been best studied in shrews, partic-ularly in the familiar northern short-tailed shrew (Tomasi 1978; Martin 1981). Here, poison is produced in submaxillary glands, which are located at the base of the incisors, and is transmitted in saliva as the shrew bites its prey. In the late 1940s and early 1950s scientists suggested that short-tailed shrews used venom to overcome relatively large vertebrate prey, such as mice, or to aid in the digestion of prey (Pearson 1942; Lawrence 1945). However, venom by the short-tailed shrew is not very effective in killing vertebrates, except very small individuals, such as young mice (Tomasi 1978). Wounds inflicted by the bites of shrews, rather than the action of venom per se, seem to be the major cause of mortality in vertebrate prey, although the venom may act to stun the prey.

Family Soricidae

A very plausible and interesting role of venom in the short-tailed shrew is related to three aspects of its way of life. First, shrews have high metabolic rates compared to other mammals of similar body size, thereby requiring considerable amounts of food (Platt 1974). Second, shrews cache (or hoard; see chap. 7) most prey instead of immediately consuming it (Robinson and Brodie 1982). Third, the short-tailed shrew relies extensively on invertebrates as food (Hamilton 1930). Hence, the most recent hypothesis for the evolution of venom in shrews is that it is used to immobilize insects and other invertebrates, thereby providing shrews with a ready source of fresh food (Martin 1981). Because insects often exhibit dramatic irruptions in population numbers, an individual shrew can quickly exploit many insects within a short time by biting through the exoskeleton of each insect and injecting its venom. Insects poisoned by shrew venom remain alive as a fresh source of food for up to ten days, resulting in a cache or "refrigerator" full of comatose insects for the shrew to fulfill its future metabolic requirements.

The solenodons comprise two species in the order Insectivora, which are endemic to Hispaniola and Cuba (Nicoll 1984). These mammals resemble large shrews with a very elongated snout. Limited evidence suggests that the poison of solenodons is transmitted via saliva by a bite to the victim and acts to paralyze relatively large prey. Before the arrival of Europeans, solenodons were the principal carnivores on these islands. Europeans, however, introduced more efficient predators, like feral cats and dogs, which preyed on solenodons to the point of near extinction.

The duck-billed platypus and two species of echidnas (or spiny anteaters) are the sole representatives of the order Monotremata and occur only in the Australian region (Grant 1984). Monotremes are very different from other mammals in many ways; most notably, they are egg-layers rather than bearers of live young.

The platypus is principally aquatic and feeds on bottom-dwelling invertebrates in freshwater streams (Grant 1984). But only the male platypus possesses a venom-producing gland, which is positioned behind its knee. The gland is connected via a duct to a horny spur on the ankle, which is thrust toward the intended target. Because the gland occurs only in males and enlarges in the breeding season, poison in platypuses probably is used primarily in aggressive male-male encounters during the breeding season. The venom of platypuses also serves as a defense against enemies and may even kill large predators, like the Australian dog known as the dingo (see chap. 11). Hence, unlike shrews or solenodons, venom in the platypus is not used for food capture.

Family Soricidae

4

Moles

Family Talpidae

Description of the Family Talpidae

$\mathcal{A}$s with shrews (see chap. 3), the family Talpidae is placed in the order Insectivora. Forty-two species of talpids (commonly referred to as moles) are found in North America, Europe, and Asia. Three species of moles occur in each of the mid-eastern states, but the hairy-tailed mole is absent from Delaware (see table 1).

Like shrews, moles are mouse-like in size and can easily be confused with small rodents, such as voles (see fig. 1 in chap. 3). Moles are relatively small (63–215 mm in total length, 11–168 g in weight). They are cylindrical in shape, allowing them to move easily within a subterranean burrow system. Because moles live in a closed underground environment, they are very tolerant of high carbon-dioxide levels, with the ability to sense subtle changes in temperature and humidity in burrow systems.

The snout of a mole is typically long and naked. The star-nosed mole's snout, however, is unique; it consists of twenty-two "tentacles" or fleshy appendages radiating off the snout, which makes it an excellent tactile organ. This interesting snout also can detect minute levels of electrical current given off by the muscular contractions of prey, such as aquatic invertebrates (Gould, McShea, and Grand 1993).

The eyes of moles are very small, and no external ears are present. The pelage is soft and velvety, permitting the hair to lie flat in either direction as the mole makes its way through a burrow system. The front feet are distinctive—the "hand" is broad and turned permanently outward for digging into soil. Moles also have massive musculature in the forelimbs and chest for digging. Moles in the mid-eastern states have either thirty-six or forty-four teeth.

Talpids are insectivorous, feeding on insect larvae, earthworms, or other invertebrates, which they encounter in burrow systems or while digging in soil. Moles in our region generally produce one litter of three to seven young per year.

Talpids are solitary and spend virtually all of their time in an underground burrow system. They form two types of burrow systems, deep and shallow. Deep systems are relatively permanent, are located well below the soil surface (15–60 cm), and function as refugia and for raising young. The familiar "molehills" are associated with deep systems. These hills form as the mole pushes excess subterranean soil out the burrow system; a hill may be fifteen to thirty-five centimeters in height and eighteen to thirty-six centimeters in diameter. Shallow systems, on the other hand, are more temporary and are used by moles as runways while foraging just beneath the surface of the soil. Of the three mole species in our region, eastern moles are most responsible for damage to golf courses, lawns, and flower beds as they tunnel for food within shallow burrow systems. Not all surface tunnels can be attributed to moles, however, because some rodent species (e.g., woodland vole) also construct subterranean tunnels just below the soil surface.

Moles

The Evolution of a Subterranean Way of Life

Nearly 75 percent of all mammalian species are terrestrial or semiaquatic in their way of life, spending all or a large percentage of their time above ground. Another 20 percent or so of the total species are bats, which are aerial (see chap. 5). About 2 percent of the species are entirely aquatic, including mammals, like toothed whales, baleen whales, and manatees. Yet 4 percent of the world's mammals have opted for a way of life that is spent completely in a subterranean environment. Imagine living your entire lifetime in a windowless basement!

The 4 percent of mammals that have evolved this subterranean, or fossorial, way of life are not restricted to one or two families of mammals. Instead, this way of life occurs in ten families from three very different mammalian orders. These are the marsupial moles of Australia (order Notoryctemorphia), the golden mole of Africa and true moles (order Insectivora), and seven different rodent families (order Rodentia) from around the world (Nevo 1979).

Regardless of species, subterranean mammals share common characteristics. None has long appendages or protruding body parts, such as pinnae, that would make rapid back-and-forth movements in burrow systems difficult. Instead, these species are relatively small, sausage-shaped animals, with reduced appendages and eyes and no external ears. Olfactory, auditory, and tactile senses are well developed in subterranean mammals. Virtually all species are solitary and territorial, and few young are produced per litter. Compared to similar-sized terrestrial mammals, dispersal distances in subterranean mammals are considerably reduced (Williams and Cameron 1984).

Why did some mammals evolve a subterranean way of life? Throughout the world, as the climate became increasing arid from the late Eocene

Family Talpidae

to early Oligocene and later from the Pliocene to the Pleistocene, forests were converting to open-country habitats like savannahs and steppes. In these aboveground habitats, ungulate and kangaroo species flourished and perhaps competed for plant food resources. Food items, such as insects and plant roots, were available underground and free for the taking by species adapted to a subterranean way of life. Hence, ancestors of the three extant families of "moles" chose an underground insectivorous feeding strategy, whereas ancestors of the seven families of rodents selected an underground herbivorous strategy.

An underground environment provides conditions that are very different from those above ground or in water. It is a comparatively simple, sealed system. Temperatures are predictable and relatively constant; predation risks are low. Because the underground environment is typically stable and uniform in many ways, little genetic variation is found in subterranean mammals compared to their aboveground counterparts. Thus, in early evolutionary time, the subterranean environment represented an untapped resource for certain types of small, cylindrical mammals.

The subterranean environment has changed little over evolutionary time and continues to remain important to several families of small, sausage-shaped mammals that are perfectly adapted to a "basement without windows." Today, however, this underground environment may be impacted by habitat alterations, such as those created by tillage or other farming practices, which can influence the distributional patterns of subterranean mammals (Tucker and Schmidly 1981).

5

Bats

Family Vespertilionidae

Description of the Family Vespertilionidae

The family Vespertilionidae is one of eighteen bat families in the order Chiroptera. The term *Chiroptera* means "wing-handed," in reference to the unique ability of bats to sustain true flight. Bats have been regarded by some people and cultures as eerie animals full of superstition and folklore for many centuries. Yet, in reality, bats are vital components of our landscapes, serving as predators of insects and pollinators of plants. From a conservation perspective, many bat species have shown serious declines in population numbers (see table 1). Hence, these flighted mammals are of considerable concern to wildlife biologists in the mid-eastern states and elsewhere throughout the world.

About 977 extant species of bats are found in various tropi-

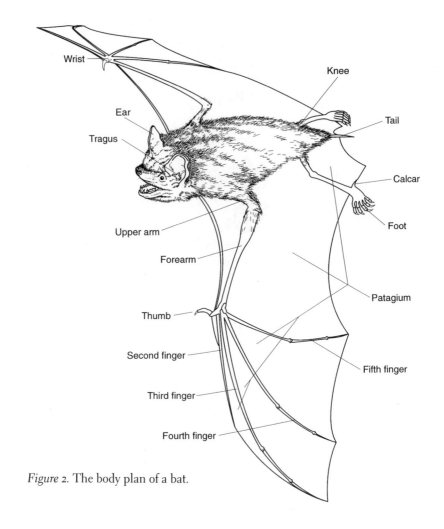

Figure 2. The body plan of a bat.

cal and temperate regions of the world. Along with rodents, bats are one of the most successful groups of mammals in terms of both number of species and geographic distribution. Bats are unique in that they have a flight membrane, termed a patagium, which extends from the body and hind feet to the forearm, between the digits of the hand, and often from the hind feet to the tail (see fig. 2). The bones of the forearm and hand are elongated for flight and result in a remarkable wingspan.

The order Chiroptera includes two suborders: Megachiroptera and Microchiroptera. The megachiropterans include about 150 species of large bats with wingspans sometimes exceeding one and a half meters. These megabats are often referred to as fruit bats because they eat fruit, nectar, and flowers; they occur in tropical and subtropical regions of the Old World.

The suborder Microchiroptera, on the other hand, consists of about 827 species of smaller bats from seventeen families. Microbats are more cosmopolitan than megabats in distribution, occurring in temperate, tropical, and subtropical habitats around the world. The microchiropterans usually feed on insects at night, using a system of ultrasounds, known as echolocation (see essay 5 below), to navigate and find food. In contrast, megabats usually navigate and forage during the day using large eyes.

The family Vespertilionidae, referred to often as vespertilionid or evening bats, is the largest bat family (342 species) and has a worldwide distribution. Sixteen of these species are found in the mid-eastern states, with the number varying from sixteen in Virginia to four in Delaware (table 1). Three of these sixteen species (little brown myotis, eastern pipistrelle, and big brown bat) are common in each mid-eastern state.

Vespertilionids are small to medium in body size (57–180 cm in total length and 4–50 g in weight). They range widely in color from blackish, gray, and brown to yellow, orange, and reddish. Most vespertilionids, particularly those from the mid-eastern states, feed exclusively on insects. Bats use echolocation at night to capture insects in flight. Gestation in vespertilionids is from forty to seventy days, and surprisingly few young are produced. The nonmigratory bat species, in particular, produce very small litters (one to two young per year), whereas the migratory species usually have slightly larger litters (two to four young per year). The larger number of young produced per litter by migratory bats perhaps evolved to help offset the hazards associated with migration. Many vespertilionids occupy caves, but mineshafts, tree cavities, crevices in tree bark, and buildings are among the sites used as daytime rest sites or as hibernacula (see essay 6 below).

ESSAY 4

Flight in Bats

On a warm summer evening after dusk, the sight of the big brown bat foraging around a streetlight (hence its nickname, the "streetlight bat") is common in the mid-eastern states.

Flight in some bats, like eastern pipistrelles, has been described as slow and erratic; in others, such as eastern red bats, flight is rapid and steady (Burt and Grossenheider 1976). The evolution of flight, echolocation, and the ability to reduce metabolism via entrance into hibernation or daily torpor as a means of saving energy have led to the success of this amazing group of mammals (Vaughan, Ryan, and Czaplewski 2000).

The evolution of flight is not restricted to bats, with many bird and insect species also exhibiting this means of locomotion. When extant bat, flying bird, and flying insect species are considered together, they outnumber the extant species of nonflying animals in the world. However, the wings of bats, birds, and insects are very different (Vaughan, Ryan, and Czaplewski 2000). Bat wings consist of sheets of skin attached to a complex skeletal pattern in the forelimb and digits, bird wings consist of feathers and a simplified forelimb, and insect wings are thin sheets of **chitin** supported by chitinous veins.

The remarkable adaptations of bats to an aerial way of life are obviously shown by their extremely elongated forelimbs and fingers on the wing (see fig. 2 above). Imagine standing in the middle of an average-sized room; if you were a bat, you would be able to extend your arms and touch both sides of the room with the tips of your fingers! The wings of bats also are characterized by patagia, which are wing membranes that extend between the forelimb and hindlimb, between the fingers, in front of the forearm, and between the hindlimb and tail. In addition, bat wings are relatively lightweight for better control and precision by large, powerful pectoral (chest) muscles. The thumbs on the bat's wings are reduced to claws, which are used to crawl over surfaces. The hindlimbs of bats are used to hang while inactive during the day or over winter. Bats have a pelvic (hip) joint that is modified to point laterally rather than forward as in other mammals.

The speed of flight in bats, birds, and other flying animals is determined by the aspect ratio of the wings (Stebbings 1984). This is measured as the ratio of the wingspan (from tip to tip) to average wing length. In bats the aspect ratio is determined by the length of the third digit (wing length) relative to that of the fifth digit (wing width; see fig. 2). Bats with a fifth digit longer than the third digit have a higher aspect ratio and fly rapidly (e.g., 36–55 kmh) but have reduced maneuverability around trees or other obstructions.

Bats in the family Molossidae are representative of species with high-aspect ratios; these bats often forage for insects at altitudes from 600 to 3,000 meters, which are devoid of ground-level obstructions (Williams, Ireland, and Williams 1973; Fenton and Griffin 1997). An example of a high-altitude, fast-flying molossid of the southeastern United States is the Brazilian free-tailed bat. Common vespertilionids in our area, like the big brown bat or the little brown myotis, have a third digit that is longer than the fifth, giving a relatively low-aspect ratio and slower flight (e.g., <30 kmh) (Stebbings 1984; Birch 1997). These vespertilionids have a slow, maneuverable flight, which adapts them to forage for insects at low altitudes in habitats with many obstructions (Stebbings 1984; Adams 1997).

The evolution of bats and their ability to fly are interesting and controversial subjects (Thewissen and Babcock 1992). Bats, like birds, have delicate bones that do not leave good fossil records. Some scientists have suggested that extant bats evolved from either a primate or an insectivore ancestor (e.g., Pettigrew 1986; Dixon, Cox, Savage, and Gardiner 1988). A more recent hypothesis, however, is that bats originated from extant mammals known as "flying lemurs," which can be found today on the island of Madagascar (Dixon et al. 1988). Flying lemurs consist of two species from the tropical forests of Myanmar (formerly Burma), Indochina, and surrounding areas. Ironically, flying lemurs once had a much broader geographic range, with some species occurring in forests of the mid-eastern states and throughout much of North America. The common name of flying lemur stems from the fact that these animals resemble primitive African primates known as lemurs.

Unlike the insectivorous bats in our region, flying lemurs are herbivorous and glide, rather than "fly," between foraging sites. In a single glide a flying lemur can traverse distances up to 130 meters, thereby exceeding the gliding abilities of flying squirrels from North America (see essay 11 in chap. 7). The evolutionary link between flying lemurs and bats is based on similar musculature in the "wings" of both mammalian taxa just anterior to the forelimb (Thewissen and Babcock 1992). Because of this similarity, bats and flying lemurs likely shared a common ancestor; hence, modern bats may have gone through a flying-lemur phase of gliding in their evolution before attaining the ability of true flight. This bat–flying lemur hypothesis will not be conclusively accepted by all scientists until further fossil evidence is obtained. Even if bats evolved from flying lemurs, the evolutionary story stops because the ancestry of flying lemurs is unknown.

Insects evolved flight sometime between 330 and 400 million years ago, which was well before the first appearance of mammals on earth (Vaughan, Ryan, and Czaplewski 2000). The possible evolution of flight in one group of extant aquatic insects, known as stoneflies (Marden and Kramer 1994, 1995), somewhat parallels the story given for the evolution of flight in bats. Stoneflies maintain close contact with the water surface by continuously flapping their wings, thereby allowing them to skim or "glide" over the water surface. Conceivably, ancestral stonefly-like insects used a similar form of water "gliding," which evolved later as true flight in other aquatic insects associated with ponds and other aquatic habitats in the mid-eastern states. In the flight evolution story the parallels are ancestral stonefly-like insects = a common ancestor to flying lemurs and bats, stoneflies = flying lemurs, and other extant aquatic insects = bats.

Why and how bats evolved flight will continue to be intriguing questions, with some scientists suggesting that flight evolved separately in megachiropterans and microchiropterans and for different reasons (e.g., Smith and Madkour 1980). For instance, flight in the megabats may have evolved to enable them to traverse considerable distances from roosts to foraging sites. These large bats typically are diurnal and rely on vision and olfaction to exploit fruit and other food resources at the foraging site.

Family Vespertilionidae

Microbats, on the other hand, have less acute senses of vision and olfaction. Instead, flight combined with echolocation permitted these nocturnal bats to orient and forage efficiently for insects with little competition from diurnal birds (Vaughan, Ryan, and Czaplewski 2000). Despite some unanswered questions regarding flight in bats, we can conclude this unique form of locomotion in mammals has been a very successful evolutionary strategy that rivals the locomotory abilities of two other very successful taxa, birds and insects.

ESSAY 5
___

Echolocation in Bats and Other Mammals

An *echo*—the reflection of sound—is a term rooted in Greek mythology (Dickey 1986). Echo was a mountain nymph whom Zeus persuaded to distract his wife, Hera, with constant talk to prevent Hera from spying on her husband. When Hera became aware of Zeus's plan, she eliminated Echo's ability to speak, except to repeat or "reflect" only the first syllable of every word that Echo heard.

Many of us have experienced hearing an echo as our shout is reflected from one ridgetop to another. Yet imagine using echoes constantly to walk or drive to and from work, to find food at the dinner table, or to communicate with family members and coworkers. Many mammals have evolved echolocation for one or more of these purposes, but its degree of sophistication and functions vary widely among species.

Echolocation and other sounds are measured in frequency or the number of vibrations per second, using a unit of measure called a hertz

(Hz). Echolocation has been best studied in bats; bats create these sounds through either the mouth or the nose, depending on the species. Signals emitted by bats can range between 100 and 200,000 Hz whereas those used for echolocation are generally between 25,000 and 140,000 Hz (MacDonald, Matsui, Stevens, and Fenton 1994; Vaughan, Ryan, and Czaplewski 2000). Because humans typically hear sounds between about 20 and 20,000 Hz (with higher frequencies becoming harder to hear with increased age), echolocation in bats is truly ultrasonic from a human standpoint.

Before addressing why ultrasounds produced by bats are beyond the hearing range of humans, let's examine the roles of echolocation in bats from a historic perspective. Nearly two centuries ago, in 1793, echolocation was strongly suspected as being important to the bat's way of life because individual bats who had been deliberately made deaf became disoriented, while those made blind were not disoriented (Stebbings 1984). Over a century later, in 1920, echolocation was believed to be important to foraging bats in capturing flying insects at night. Yet ultrasonic sounds produced by bats were not discovered until the late 1930s, when microphones capable of detecting high-frequency sounds were invented. Today, the general consensus among scientists is that the functions of bat echolocation are primarily to acquire food (e.g., flying insects), and secondarily as a means of orienting in darkness (Lawrence and Simmons 1982). Because of the nocturnal way of life of microchiropteran bats, echolocation has become the ideal communication system for this group of mammals that exploited the aerial environment in early mammalian history.

Why are ultrasonic signals produced by bats so high in frequency? Bats almost certainly did not evolve ultrasounds in order to fly undetected by humans and other potential predators; instead, that evolution probably had a lot to do with prey capture and navigation. A bat flying at 30 kmh in relative darkness is able to detect and capture flying insects several meters away that are about the size of a dime or smaller. Under these circumstances, a rapid series of signals of about 30,000 Hz allows the bat to produce dime-size wavelengths that match the body size of an eleven-millimeter flying insect. When the wavelength of the signals emitted by bats is the same size as the intended prey, a better "echo" returns to the bat, thereby giving the bat more precise information on the location of the

Family Vespertilionidae

prey. The detection of insects smaller than eleven millimeters would require bats to emit signals even higher than 30,000 Hz in frequency because wavelengths of echolocation signals are inversely related to frequencies.

A challenge for an echolocating bat in flight is to distinguish quickly between outgoing signals and incoming signals that "echo" off a flying insect or obstacle. Reflected incoming signals return to the bat in milliseconds, so signals emitted by the bat must be not only brief but also spaced often enough to detect immediate changes in the location of the intended object in the bat's echolocation field. The little brown myotis, for example, achieves this by using a normal rapid-fire series of pulses emitted approximately every twenty-five seconds when searching for prey (Suga 1990). When prey is detected, the pulse duration is shortened, and the pulse rate is increased to around 200 pulses per second as the bat closes in on the prey. This adjustment of pulse duration and rate also allows the bat to better determine the characteristics of a prey item, such as its size. Interestingly, the little brown myotis (and perhaps other bats) is capable of eavesdropping on the calls of conspecifics to locate better foraging areas (Barclay 1982).

The fleshy projection in the ear of bats, termed the tragus (see fig. 2 in chap. 5), plays an important role in echolocation. It functions as a reflecting surface for incoming signals, providing a second and slightly longer path for the sound to travel down the ear canal of a bat. This second, phased signal enables bats, such as the big brown, to distinguish very slight changes (3°) in the vertical positioning of an object, such as a flying insect or an inanimate obstacle to the bat's flight path (Lawrence and Simmons 1982).

Each species of bat produces a "vocal signature" when echolocating. For instance, the little brown myotis uses signals slightly below 40,000 Hz, the eastern red bat emits signals between 35,000 and 40,000 Hz, and the big brown bat echolocates at frequencies between 25,000 and 30,000 Hz (MacDonald et al. 1994). Thus, wildlife biologists can identify bat species in the field using relatively low-cost, portable ultrasonic bat detectors that distinguish differences in frequencies and other features of these species-specific signals (e.g., chirp-like in the red bat versus putt-like in the big brown bat) (Hayes 1997). Just as each of our voices has unique characteristics, researchers have noted that echolocation calls can vary among individual bats of the same species. This individual variation in signal characteristics within a species has posed some difficulties in identifying species with the use of ultrasonic detectors in the field. In one study involving ultrasonic detectors, only 70 percent of the calls of sympatric big brown and silver-haired bats were correctly identified to species by field researchers (Betts 1998). However, a combination of ultrasonic detectors and mist-nets has been successfully used to understand population abundance, habitat use, and activity patterns of these very elusive nocturnal mammals (Kuenzi and Morrison 1998).

Echolocation is not unique to bats nor is it solely a mammalian phenomenon. Echolocation is known in at least two bird species—the oilbird of South America and the cave swiftlet of Africa. These bird species produce clicks in the range of 1,000 to 15,000 Hz, but their echolocation system is only about 10 percent as efficient in discriminating objects as that of bats (Gill 1990). There is strong evidence for the existence of echolocation in three very different groups of mammals—terrestrial shrews, aquatic pinnipeds, and toothed whales (Vaughan, Ryan, and Czaplewski 2000).

Echolocation in shrews has been best studied in the northern short-tailed shrew of the mid-eastern states (Tomasi 1979). This species produces ultrasounds in the range of 30,000 to 50,000 Hz, which is beyond the range of human hearing. As we saw in chapter 3, the short-tailed shrew is semifossorial, living in underground burrow systems and foraging in leaf litter on the forest floor. Shrews have small eyes and poor eyesight, so echolocation would facilitate orientation while moving rapidly through dark, underground tunnels. Compared to echolocation in bats, shrew echolocation is only effective for a distance of one meter or less, but it can be used by shrews to distinguish openings as small as 0.6 centimeter in diameter and materials of different texture. Hence, in complete darkness, echolocating shrews can determine tunnel directions and diameters; they also can determine whether or not tunnels or entrances of burrows are plugged and what materials are plugging the burrows. Because short-tailed shrews typically rely on slow-moving insects as food, olfaction is the primary sense used to detect food items. Thus, unlike bats, echolocation in shrews is not believed to function in food acquisition (see essay 2 in chap. 3).

Echolocation is quite sophisticated in pinnipeds and toothed whales, with ultrasounds ranging in frequency from those audible to humans to those well above the hearing range of humans (60,000 Hz). Some pinnipeds forage at night or inhabit turbid waters where light levels are low (Renouf and Davis 1982). The harbor seal, for example, produces two types of low-frequency signals in the range of 7,500 Hz. These signals consist of either a single or double click at rates of about three clicks per second, which is much slower than rates of signals given by bats. Three reasons have been proposed for echolocation in pinnipeds: (1) to locate objects and, hence, orient in the water environment; (2) to discriminate among objects, thereby distinguishing food from other objects in the environment; and (3) to communicate among individuals (Vaughan, Ryan, and Czaplewski 2000).

Like pinnipeds, some species of toothed whales occupy habitats characterized by very poor light conditions. Hence, echolocation in these whales is valuable in orientation, prey detection, and communication. Sperm whales, for instance, give clicks every 0.5 to 1.0 second and presumably use these to detect prey, such as squids, for distances up to 750 meters (Goold and Jones 1995). The elaborate songs of the humpback whale serve as an important means of communication among conspecifics, with each song lasting seven to thirty minutes (Payne and McVay 1971). More recently, a fourth function has been attributed to high-frequency signals in many toothed whales. These aquatic mammals are suspected of using high-intensity pulses to momentarily stun prey and thus facilitate capture of elusive prey. This means of prey immobilization would be adaptive (and is possibly widespread) in toothed whales for two reasons. First, although they are termed "toothed whales," only about 50 percent of these species actually have teeth. Second, prey used by toothed whales is often very fast-moving; sperm whales, for instance, feed on squid capable of swimming 50 kmh. High-intensity pulses work much better in water than in air, traveling five times faster in water and creating sixty times the pressure in air.

In summary, mammals from many taxonomic groups probably exhibit some form of echolocation, but a thorough appreciation of the existence and the role of this phenomenon in mammals will require extensive and well-designed studies. Studies to date have shown that echolocation is best developed in mammals compared to other vertebrate taxa. As visually oriented mammals, we only have begun to realize that echolocation is as important to the way of life of some mammals as vision is to us or as olfaction is to many other mammals (see essay 16 in chap. 8 and essay 28 in chap. 11).

E S S A Y 6

Bat Phobia — Bats in Our Attic

Bats of the mid-eastern states benefit humans by feeding on a variety of hard- and soft-bodied insects, with food type depending on jaw and dental adaptations of each species. The big brown bat, for example, is adapted to feed on hard-bodied insects, like beetles; conversely, the little brown myotis is capable of foraging on soft-bodied insects, such as flies and moths (Whitaker 1972; Whitaker, Maser, and Keller 1977). The quantities of night-flying insects eaten by bats have not been fully determined, but some rough estimates of food consumption give us insight into the potential importance of these mammals as insect predators. The little brown myotis, weighing only seven to nine grams, is capable of eating about one-third its body weight of insects (2.5 g) in a single night (Anthony and Kunz 1977). Brazilian free-tailed bats, which may number about 100 million in the United States, may consume 30 million kilograms of insects annually (Barbour and Davis 1969). Hence, bats confer a tremendous economic value to humans by preying on flying insects and reducing the amount of pesticides needed for insect control in our backyards and on our farms. These services alone justify the need for the development and implementation of sound conservation strategies for bats in the mid-eastern states and elsewhere.

Family Vespertilionidae

39

Bats, like any animal, need food. However, when bats feed on insects in our backyards or on our farm by night and then seek cover in the attics of our homes in the day, their importance as insect predators is occasionally forgotten. Bats roosting in our attics may produce noises, stains, and odors that cause homeowners to regard these intruders as pests (Humphrey 1982). In our area, the big brown bat and the little brown myotis commonly use attics in homes, churches, and other dwellings. These two species have benefited by the arrival of Europeans in North America because tree cavities were probably used by both species prior to European colonization (Whitaker and Hamilton 1998). With the construction of buildings containing attics, populations of big brown bats and little brown myotis are probably much higher today than historically (Barclay, Thomas, and Fenton 1980).

Summer roosts of little brown myotis and big brown bats in attics consist of either females and their young, referred to as maternal colonies, or solitary and small groups of males (Humphrey 1982). But male little brown myotis use caves more often than attics as summer daytime roosts (Whitaker and Hamilton 1998). Males of both species also use other locations as summer roosts, such as within rock crevices or under tree bark (Humphrey 1982).

The use of a given attic as a maternity roost by bats may depend on the characteristics of both the dwelling and the surrounding landscape. For instance, compared to one-story ranch homes with small attics and asphalt shingle roofs, two-story, older wood-frame houses with steel (or tin) roofs and spacious attics are preferred as maternity sites by big brown bats. Buildings with steel (or tin) roofs probably are selected because solar heating increases temperatures within the attic early in spring at a critical time during birth of young. Optimal roost temperatures for maternity colonies of big brown bats and little brown myotis are 33 to 35° C and 37 to 39° C, respectively (Herreid and Schmidt-Nielsen 1966). Because agricultural areas probably provide more flying insect food for bats than forested areas, dwellings with maternity roosts of big brown bats tend to occur in landscapes with more agricultural lands and less forest cover (Williams and Brittingham 1997).

Caves and mines, rather than attics, have traditionally been regarded as important winter hibernacula for bats, such as the little brown myotis and the big brown bat (Humphrey 1982; Merritt 1987). The little brown myotis hibernates as clusters of individuals located in the deep, warmer locations of caves and mines (McManus 1974). The big brown bat, in contrast, occurs in small groups (1–6 individuals) at the entrances and, hence, cooler areas of caves or mines. In Pennsylvania, as many as 1,000 to 6,000 little brown myotis have been counted per cave during winter, but fewer than 100 big brown bats have been observed in these same caves (Dunn and Hall 1989). Thus, from a conservation perspective, caves and mines are important resources for bat populations and require protection from human disturbance and destruction throughout the mid-eastern states. These hibernacula are additionally valuable to other bats, like the northern myotis, the eastern pipistrelle, and the federally endangered Indiana bat. Bats hibernating in caves and mines occasionally may be susceptible to predation by various animals, such as raccoons (Munson and Keith 1984).

Attics in homes, churches, barns, and other structures can also serve as important hibernacula for bats (Whitaker and Gummer 1992). In fact, in a study of sixty-seven buildings used by maternity colonies of big brown bats in summer, nearly 50 percent (32) were used as winter hibernacula. Although big brown bats can tolerate very cold conditions during hibernation (Goehring 1972), each of the thirty-two buildings used in winter by big brown bats was heated and well insulated. Many of the thirty-five unused buildings were either unheated or insufficiently heated, thereby allowing ambient temperatures to drop below freezing (Whitaker and Gummer 1992). On occasion, an individual big brown bat may use the same building during winter and summer.

Bats in dwellings create a catch-22 situation. We want bats in our environment for ecological and aethestic reasons, but sometimes we must draw the line when these mammals become a nuisance. In past decades, bats in dwellings were killed by direct application of pesticides, such as DDT, on the walls and directly on the bats (Kunz, Anthony, and Rumage 1977; Barclay, Thomas, and Fenton 1980). Fortunately, these methods of eradicating bats are now illegal, and less dramatic methods are needed to deter bats from roosting in our dwellings. Moreover, bats are very sensitive to disturbance; a human entering a hibernaculum can arouse bats and thereby negatively affect winter survival (Speakman, Webb, and Racey

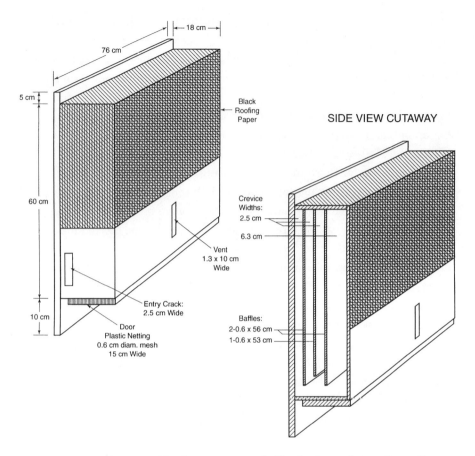

Figure 3. A horizontal bat box recommended by the Pennsylvania Game Commission. *(Modified from Williams-Whitmer 1994.)*

1991; Thomas 1995). A little brown myotis aroused from hibernation can lose 108 mg of body fat, which is the amount of fat required for it to survive over two months (68 days) in winter torpor (Thomas, Fenton, and Barclay 1990).

So how does a homeowner make a dwelling bat-proof without harming or disturbing these valuable mammals? New building designs usually do not allow bats adequate access to attics (Schowalter and Gunson 1979), and older dwellings can be made bat-proof by plugging or caulking cracks or holes in attics (Barclay, Thomas, and Fenton 1980; Humphrey 1982).

Bats

An attic can be made less attractive as a bat maternity site by reducing the temperature in the attic with the use of asphalt shingles on the roof or by placing a fan or vent in the attic (Williams and Brittingham 1997).

One of the most promising ways to lure bats away from attics is to construct bat boxes as alternate maternity sites for bats displaced from attics (Williams and Brittingham 1997). The construction of bat boxes is an excellent way to instill a conservation ethic in youth and homeowners with minimum effort and cost. Bat boxes are especially valuable as maternity sites when they provide high daily temperatures and wide temperature gradients (Williams-Whitmer 1994). An excellent design for a bat house is one that has a ten- to twelve-degree centigrade difference from top to bottom (see fig. 3). The horizontal bat box, which is a design recommended by the Pennsylvania Game Commission, can house 100 to 150 bats. This particular box design ensures high daily temperatures and wide temperature gradients because of the use of vents on the lower side and roofing paper on the roof and upper sides. The box is stained dark brown or black to enhance solar radiation and, thus, high daily temperatures with the box.

The location of a bat box is critical to its use by bats as a substitute "attic" (Williams-Whitmer 1994). Boxes should be oriented in a southeastern or southwestern direction in order to receive at least six to seven hours of morning and afternoon sun. To reduce risks from climbing predators, boxes should be placed at least three and a half meters high on a building or pole rather than on a tree (see fig. 4). If a landowner is using a box for a displaced colony, for example, from an attic, the box should be placed near the location of the original colony and be installed before the colony has been evicted from the dwelling.

BAT BOX PLACEMENT

Figure 4. A bat box should be placed in a location to increase exposure to sunlight but decrease risks to predators.

6

Rabbits and Hares

Family Leporidae

Description of the Family Leporidae

Rabbits and hares are members of the family Leporidae, which is one of two families in the order Lagomorpha. The leporid family consists of fifty-four species, which occur throughout the world with the exception of southern South America, Madagascar, the West Indies, and most islands of Southeast Asia. The other family is Ochotonidae, which comprises twenty-seven species from Eurasia and western North America; two species, the collared pika and the American pika, are found in North America.

Eight species of wild leporids are found in the mid-eastern states, ranging from four species in Virginia to a single species in Delaware (table 1). The most common and widely distributed species in our area is certainly the eastern cottontail, and perhaps the least common is the marsh rabbit, which occurs only in Virginia. Three species of hares have been introduced in two mid-eastern states, New Jersey and New York, including white-tailed and black-tailed jackrabbits (native to the midwestern and western United States, respectively), and European hares (native to northern Europe and parts of Asia). The domestic or European rabbit is not included in our area as a wild form; it is the familiar "Easter bunny" found in many pet stores and on the menu of some restaurants. The European rabbit has been introduced, however, as a wild species into various parts of the world with serious negative consequences. In Australia, for instance, the European rabbit has been blamed for the endangerment or extinction of some native metatherian because it competes with them for food and habitat.

The terms *rabbit* and *hare* often are used incorrectly when referring to common names of several leporids (e.g., jackrabbits are actually hares, not rabbits). Rabbits include several genera worldwide, including four species of the genus *Sylvilagus* in the mid-eastern states (eastern cottontail, marsh rabbit, New England cottontail, and Appalachian cottontail; Table 1). Hares are placed in the single genus *Lepus* and are represented by four species in our area (snowshoe hare, black-tailed jackrabbit, white-tailed jackrabbit, and European hare).

Both rabbits and hares have thick, short pelages. Their ears and legs are long, and tails are short and well furred. All species have twenty-eight teeth. Rabbits can be distinguished from hares morphologically and behaviorally. With the exception of the relatively small snowshoe hare, rabbits tend to be smaller (e.g., 35–43 cm in total length and 0.9–1.8 kg in weight) than hares (43–68 cm and 1.3–4.5 kg). Rabbits have shorter ears and legs than hares and generally rely on cover to escape predators; in contrast, the longer-legged hares use speed to minimize predation risks. For instance, in the extensively farmed areas of southern Minnesota, I recall flushing a white-tailed jackrabbit from the cover of a shelterbelt; the jackrabbit ran several hundred meters across the flat agricultural terrain to the next shelterbelt. Rabbits, on the other hand, exhibit a different strategy when in danger by fleeing a short distance into the nearest brushpile or woodchuck burrow. Many of us have experienced the sudden tail flash of a cottontail as it escapes from our approach.

Another major difference between rabbits and hares is the degree of development at birth. Like songbirds, rabbits have altricial young; they are born helpless, sparsely furred, and with their eyes closed, in a grass- and fur-lined nest. Young cottontails open their eyes within a week of birth and leave the nest within two weeks. On the other hand, like ducks, hares give birth to young in a shallow depression rather than a nest. These young are born fully furred and eyes opened; they are also precocial, that is, capable of moving out of what serves as the nest within twenty-four hours of birth.

Rabbits and hares occur in a variety of disturbed habitats, including early successional forests, brushy areas, and grasslands. Leporids readily use aboveground cover, such as brushpiles or dense low-lying vegetation, as shelter. Cottontails also use burrows constructed by other mammals, like woodchucks, as home sites and refugia. Leporids are nocturnal or crepuscular in activity and feed on a range of herbaceous and woody plant species. Rabbits and hares are solitary, although adult males may form dominance hierarchies while competing for females during the breeding season. Only the European rabbit is territorial.

Family Leporidae

Rabbits and hares have two to five litters per year, and each litter may consist of one to seven young. Gestation is somewhat shorter in rabbits than hares, ranging from about twenty-six to thirty days in the eastern cottontail to thirty-six or thirty-seven days in the snowshoe hare. Young leporids are weaned in about five weeks.

Rabbits and Hares

Conservation of the "Other" Cottontails

Everyone is familiar with the eastern cottontail, which is a very adaptable species found in virtually all habitats from farmland to suburbia (Chapman, Hockman, and Edwards 1982). Although labeled today as the principal "game" species in the United States and found throughout the mid-eastern states, the eastern cottontail historically had its share of conservation problems. Beginning in the mid-1920s fewer eastern cottontails were being harvested compared to the previous decade in parts of the mid-eastern states (Gerstell 1937). This rather rapid decline in cottontail numbers was blamed on intensive farming practices and heavy hunting pressure. From the 1920s to the 1950s wildlife agencies began major release programs to increase cottontail numbers throughout the mid-eastern states (Chapman, Hockman, and Edwards 1982). During these decades, as many as 50,000 eastern cottontails were released annually into Pennsylvania from several states. As a result of these introductions, the "new" eastern cottontail populations were no longer native and became very genetically variable, enabling these cottontails to adapt to changing habitat conditions and perhaps better compete with other cottontail species. Today, eastern cottontail populations are doing quite well in many areas of the mid-eastern states, but large monoculture farms with little natural cover (e.g., woody fencerows) can seriously reduce population numbers and restrict habitat use (Edwards, Havera, Labisky, Ellis, and Warner 1981; Swihart and Yahner 1982; Mankin and Warner 1999).

Two other cottontail species, New England and Appalachian, are reasonably widespread in the northeastern United States, although both are species of concern in the mid-eastern states. Their taxonomic status and subsequent conservation strategies make for an interesting story in wildlife management and conservation. At the turn of the twentieth century, only one cottontail species was believed to inhabit the northeastern United

Family Leporidae

States—the eastern cottontail. Then, in 1895, scientists recognized that the eastern cottontail actually consisted of two species, the eastern cottontail and the New England cottontail (Hall 1981). Nearly a century later, however, the New England cottontail populations were subdivided by taxonomists into two species, the New England cottontail and the Appalachian cottontail (Chapman, Hockman, and Edwards 1982). Both cottontail species have nonoverlapping geographic ranges and apparently exist as isolated populations remaining from repeated north-south shifts in glaciers thousands of years ago in the Northeast (Chapman and Stauffer 1981). The New England cottontail ranges from western New York eastward to eastern Massachusetts and southern Maine, whereas the Appalachian cottontail occurs in disjunct populations at high elevations from Pennsylvania southward to northeastern Alabama (Chapman, Cramer, Dippenaar, and Robinson 1992; Whitaker and Hamilton 1998).

The eastern cottontail and the other two cottontails differ in several ways. Both New England and Appalachian cottontails are physiologically better able to deal with winter conditions and exhibit less overwinter weight loss than the eastern cottontail. This perhaps helps explain why the other two cottontails occur in more northerly latitudes or at higher elevations than the eastern cottontail (Chapman, Harman, and Samuel 1977).

Although the other two cottontails are slightly smaller compared to the eastern cottontail and sometimes exhibit markings more typical of one species than the other (e.g., often a black spot between the ears of the Appalachian cottontail), all three species are virtually identical (Doutt, Heppenstall, and Guilday 1977). Sutures separating bones on the dorsal part of the skull, however, conclusively separate the eastern cottontail from the other two cottontails (Chapman, Cramer, Dippenaar, and Robinson 1992), yet this characteristic has no value when trying to determine the exact species of a live cottontail from a distance with field glasses.

A very important characteristic that separates all three species is the number of chromosomes. In the late 1980s the diploid number of chromosomes in eastern cottontail, New England cottontail, and Appalachian cottontail was determined to be forty-two, fifty-two, and forty-six, respectively (Ruedas, Dowler, and Aita 1989). There is very little evidence that any of these species interbreed (Chapman et al. 1982), resulting in the recognition of three distinct cottontail species, compared to what was thought to be only one near the turn of the twentieth century.

Rabbits and Hares

The three cottontail species pose a conservation dilemma because of similarities in appearance and the fact that the exact geographic distributions of New England and Appalachian cottontails are difficult to distinguish with certainty from that of the eastern cottontail. Furthermore, populations of New England cottontails and Appalachian cottontails have declined markedly over the past few decades (Chapman et al. 1992; Litvaitis 1993), perhaps in response to expanding human population and conversion of early successional forests, like clearcut stands, to older, more mature forest stands (Litvaitis and Villafuerte 1996). Thus, populations of both New England and Appalachian cottontails are of special concern in the mid-eastern states, whereas populations of the eastern cottontail fare quite well in the area (table 1).

As habitat for New England and Appalachian cottontails continues to become less available, a sound conservation strategy needs to be developed in the mid-eastern states. An excellent model for habitat management recently proposed for the long-term conservation of metapopulations of the New England cottontail (Litvaitis and Villafuerte 1996) will likely have applications for the conservation of the Appalachian cottontail in the mid-eastern states. Both cottontail species presumably occur as isolated populations in patches of early successional habitat throughout their range; more individual cottontails are found in larger patches. Suitable early successional habitat of various sizes can be created in mature forest by cutting or burning.

The maintenance of early successional habitat for New England or Appalachian cottontails can be compatible with sustainable forest-management practices (Litvaitis and Villafuerte 1996). Using an even-aged system of forest management with some retention of residual trees (see Boardman and Yahner 1999), a network of early successional habitat patches can be clustered in more contiguous forested landscape rather than scattering them throughout the landscape (see fig. 5). Because dispersal rates of New England (or possibly Appalachian) cottontails decline rapidly when suitable patches are separated by distances greater than one-half to one kilometer, patches should be clustered at distances of one kilometer or less in the landscape to better ensure the long-term survival of these cottontail metapopulations.

Moreover, each patch should be at least fifteen to seventy-five hectares and managed with periodic disturbances on a rotational basis; that is,

Family Leporidae

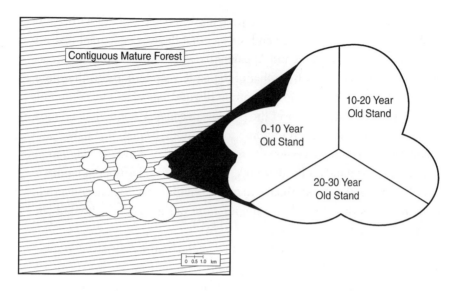

Figure 5. A hypothetical example of forest-habitat management for metapopulations of New England or Appalachian cottontails in a contiguous mature forest. Each early successional habitat (white areas) is between 15 and 75 hectares and clustered at distances of one kilometer or less.

one-third (5–25 ha) of the patch should be cut or burned every ten years to guarantee an adequate amount of suitable habitat in a given patch for cottontails. Larger patches are more likely to be occupied by cottontails than smaller patches. For instance, New England cottontails were found in 90 percent of the early successional patches of at least five hectares in size in New Hampshire, whereas these rabbits occurred in only 70 percent of the patches less than five hectares in size.

In central Pennsylvania, a checkerboard pattern of small one-hectare clearcut stands of various ages in close proximity to each other has been created for the management of ruffed grouse habitat. This series of small even-aged forest stands has benefited a remnant population of Appalachian cottontails over the past couple of decades and simultaneously has provided suitable habitat for eastern cottontails and a variety of early successional bird species (Storm, Shope, and Tzilkowski 1993; Yahner 1997). This area could perhaps be improved for metapopulations of Appalachian cottontails by increasing the patch size to at least five hectares.

In summary, the eastern cottontail, with its relatively high population numbers and adaptability to a variety of land uses, will continue to flourish in the mid-eastern states, provided that early successional habitat is available on farmlands. The other cottontails of special concern, specifically New England and Appalachian, are a different story. The long-term conservation strategy for these cottontails will require a concerted effort to ensure suitable habitat in the face of increasing forest maturation and urbanization.

ESSAY 8

The Ups and Downs of Leporid Populations

In the natural world, two ecological tenets always seem to hold. First, a given ecological phenomenon is a function of a complex set of interacting factors. As an example, consider that the geographic distribution of oaks and other tree species in the eastern deciduous forest is determined by a spectrum of site factors, such as soil moisture, elevation, and solar radiation (Yahner 2000). Second, most, if not all, phenomena in the natural world are dynamic and unpredictable. Populations of plants and animals can vary seasonally and annually, yet an unexpected event can have dramatic consequences on their distribution and abundance. For instance, shrew populations in central Pennsylvania declined markedly in summer 1988 because of a prolonged drought (Yahner 1992).

Population fluctuations, or cycles, are an ecological phenomenon that have intrigued mammalogists for many decades, especially in mammals whose long-term fluctuations are not only dramatic but somewhat predictable (Krebs 1996). Cycles in leporids, voles, common muskrat, and moose (see essays 20 and 21 in chap. 9, and essay 30 in chap. 11) fall into this category of fluctuations and have been reasonably well studied by scientists.

Population cycles in leporids presumably occur in some hare species but not in rabbits. Although a cycle of eight to nine years may have existed at one time in eastern cottontails (Bailey 1968), it has likely been masked by population declines in the early decades of the twentieth century, followed by massive introductions and changing land uses throughout the mid- to late twentieth century (see essay 7 above; Chapman, Hockman, and Edwards 1982). Today, leporid cycles are generally restricted to relatively simple predator-prey systems in northern and western latitudes of North America, like those of snowshoe hares in the North and black-tailed jackrabbits in the West (Clark 1972; Keith and Windberg 1978).

In this essay we will focus on cycles of snowshoe hares in relation to key predators, such as lynx and coyotes. The existence of this cycle has been documented for about 150 years, based on trapping records from the Hudson Bay Company (Vaughan, Ryan, and Czaplewski 2000). In more northerly latitudes, like Alberta and Wisconsin, snowshoe hare undergo a "ten-year cycle," which actually may vary from eight to twelve years. Population abundances of predators dependent on hares as the major food resource typically lag about two years behind those of hares. In some locations, such as Alberta, population densities vary twenty-three-fold over the length of a cycle (Keith and Windberg 1978). During a peak year of this Alberta cycle, population estimates were 2,300 hares/100 hectares, which is about twenty hares in an area equivalent to a football field! During low years of the snowshoe hare cycle, numbers can drop to less than one hare per hectare. Fluctuations of hare populations in northern latitudes are not necessarily synchronous across the geographic range of the species but may vary with differences in weather and predator patterns (Keith 1974).

Cycles in snowshoe hare populations of northern latitudes appear to be linked to winter food shortages (Keith 1974; Vaughan and Keith 1981). In winter, hares feed extensively on browse, which are twigs and shoots of trees and other woody vegetation. As populations of hares increase, the carrying capacity of the habitat is reduced as the supply of browse becomes depleted. Therefore, populations of hares "crash," and predator abundance rather than food supply becomes the most important factor in regulating numbers of hares during decline and low phases of the cycle

Rabbits and Hares

(Keith, Cary, Rongstad, and Brittingham 1984). Another hypothesis is that predation instead of reduced food availability in winter is the key factor causing hare cycles (Krebs 1996).

A shortage of winter food during the snowshoe hare cycle has several immediate consequences to hares. Regardless of age, individuals experience increased overwinter weight loss during years of food scarcity (12–16%) compared to years with abundant food (5%). Adult females produce fewer young, ranging from eighteen young per female per year during the highs of the cycle to eight young per female during the lows of the cycle. The fewer young born during the decline phase of the cycle gain weight slower with food-scarce mothers (9.8 g/day) compared young born during the peak phase with food-abundant mothers (12.1 g/day), presumably because food-scarce mothers have less energy available for milk production for growing young. In addition, lower weight gain in young translates to lower probability of them surviving the following winter.

Precipitous drops in snowshoe hare numbers over the course of the cycle can strongly affect predator populations. For instance, the lynx, which is a well-known predator of snowshoe hares, feeds almost exclusively on hares during the peak years of the hare cycle (Brand, Keith, and Fischer 1976). As hare abundance begins to decline, lynx revert to other food items, for example, carrion and ruffed grouse. This change in food habits in response to a decline in the availability of a preferred prey is known as a functional response.

Predators often exhibit a second response to low prey availability, which is termed a numerical response. For example, lynx numbers in Alberta declined fivefold during years coinciding with low abundance of hares (0.02 lynx/km^2) compared to years with high abundance (0.10 lynx/km^2) (Brand, Keith, and Fischer 1976). Productivity of lynx in this same Alberta study was also markedly influenced by low hare abundance, with no kittens produced on a 130-square-kilometer study area during years with scarce hares compared to two to three lynx litters of one to four kittens each raised in years with abundant hares. In particular, yearling lynx seem to immediately curtail reproduction after hares decline, but adult lynx probably cease reproduction two years after the start of the decline (Mowat, Slough, and Boutin 1996).

In Alberta the coyote, which is another common predator of hares, also exhibits both functional and numerical responses to abundance of snowshoe hares. Hare biomass in the diet of coyotes parallels changes in hare abundance, but during the cyclic low hares comprise no more than 4 percent of the coyote diet. During the cyclic high, hares are as much as 77 percent of the coyote diet. When hare availability is low, coyotes switch diets to larger animals, for example, carrion of livestock, garbage, and cereal grains. Furthermore, coyote numbers are two- to threefold lower in years with low abundance of hares (0.14–0.25 coyotes/km²) than in years with high abundance (0.4 coyotes/km²) (Todd, Keith, and Fischer 1981). Based on placental scars, the number of young coyotes produced during the peak years of the hare cycle range from 5.2 to 6.0, and these decline about 25 percent during the low years to 3.7 to 4.8 scars.

Another predator, the fisher, feeds largely on snowshoe hares during the peak phase of hare cycles in Minnesota (Kuehn 1989). As hares decline, porcupine, squirrel, and deer carrion are among the most frequently used foods. Unlike the previous two examples with lynx and coyotes, however, abundance and reproduction of fishers are not affected by hare declines.

Populations of hares from more southerly locations (e.g., Pennsylvania) do not exhibit dramatic and predictable changes in numbers (Sievert and Keith 1985; Merritt 1987). In these southern limits of the geographic range of hares, reduced cover may increase predation rates. In northern Pennsylvania, for instance, extensive browsing by high populations of white-tailed deer on woody vegetation in clearcut stands negatively affects hare populations by reducing food and cover (Scott and Yahner 1989).

In summary, the snowshoe hare cycle is a good example of how food availability (e.g., browse) can have profound effects on populations of both prey and predators. In some relatively simple predator-prey systems, as with the snowshoe hare and lynx, a lowered prey base can have serious negative ramifications to predator abundances. Yet, as we have seen in the more southerly latitudes of hares and when the predator is less dependent on hares (e.g., the fisher), the ups and downs of leporid populations are either nonexistent or of negligible effect to the predator.

7

Squirrels

Family Sciuridae

Description of the Family Sciuridae

Squirrels are in the family Sciuridae and belong to the largest mammalian order known as Rodentia, which comprises twenty-nine families and 2,052 species (43% of all mammalian species). The squirrel family includes 272 species or 13 percent of the rodents, with a worldwide distribution that excludes only Australia, southern South America, Madagascar, and some desert regions of Arabia and Egypt.

As with leporids, eight species of squirrels occur in the mid-eastern states, with six to eight species per state (see table 1). Five of the species—eastern chipmunk, woodchuck, gray squirrel, red squirrel, and southern flying squirrel—are ubiquitous in the region. The northern flying squirrel is a species of special concern because of declining populations throughout much of the mid-eastern states (see essay 12 below).

Squirrels include a spectrum of "types" referred to generically as ground squirrels, tree squirrels, chipmunks, and marmots. Representative species of these types in the mid-eastern states are the thirteen-lined ground squirrel, gray squirrel, eastern chipmunk, and woodchuck (or groundhog), respectively. A fifth type of squirrel, the prairie dog, is found in western North America.

Squirrels have a thick, short pelage; tails of ground squirrels, chipmunks, and marmots are relatively short, whereas those of tree squirrels are longer. Chipmunks and some species of ground squirrels have dorsal stripes. In the mid-eastern states, the smallest sciurid is the eastern chipmunk (13–15 cm in total length and 65–127 g in weight), and the largest is the woodchuck (40–51 cm and 2.2–4.5 kg). The flying squirrels differ morphologically from other squirrels in having a furred gliding membrane that consists of skin extending from the arms to the legs (see essay 11 below). Squirrels have twenty or twenty-two teeth, depending on the species.

Sciurids are found in many habitats, with eastern chipmunks and tree squirrels (gray, fox, red, and flying squirrels) typical of mature forests and thirteen-lined ground squirrels and woodchucks more characteristic of grassland or other open habitats. Eastern chipmunks, woodchucks, and thirteen-lined ground squirrels use burrows as home sites; tree squirrels use aboveground home sites, such as cavities in trees or leaf nests constructed in trees (or attics, in the case of an occasional gray squirrel).

With the exception of the two species of nocturnal flying squirrels, all squirrel species in our area are diurnal. Hence, squirrels are essentially mammalian counterparts to songbirds in our backyards, woodlots, and farms. Every child, whether from a city or a farm, is familiar with squirrels.

Squirrels are, for the most, part herbivorous; mast (nuts and seeds), herbaceous plant material (grass, forbs), and, on some occasions, animal material, comprise their diet. Chipmunks, thirteen-lined ground squirrels, red squirrels, and marmots are solitary, but gray, fox, and flying squirrels are more social. Eastern chipmunks, red squirrels, and woodchucks are territorial.

Some species of squirrels in the mid-eastern states, such as eastern chipmunks and gray squirrels, occasionally have two litters, whereas others, like woodchucks and southern flying squirrels, have only a single litter. Litter size is usually two to seven young, although the thirteen-lined ground squirrel may have seven to ten young per litter. Gestation for squirrels in our area varies from twenty-eight days in the thirteen-lined ground squirrel to forty-four days in both gray and fox squirrels. The time required to wean young may range from five weeks (eastern chipmunks and woodchucks) to at least two months (gray, fox, and red squirrels).

Family Sciuridae

Food Hoarding in Squirrels and Other Mammals

Winter is the season of low food supplies for most organisms, and mammals are no exception. Mammals essentially survive the rigors of winter using one of three strategies: they migrate to warmer latitudes (as true of some bats, like red bats), hibernate and live off stored body fat reserves (as in woodchuck, see essay 10 below), or hoard a winter supply of food for use throughout the winter. Hoarding in mammals is most conspicuous in squirrels. As children, most of us became familiar with food hoarding (or caching) behavior in mammals by way of the Disney cartoon characters, Chip and Dale, who frantically stored a supply of acorns for winter use. Also, we have already discussed the use of venom by northern short-tailed shrews to immobilize and cache insects as a future food source (see essay 2 in chap. 3).

Food hoarding can be divided into two types: scatter and larder (Smith and Reichman 1984). Scatter hoarding is the storing of one or a few food items in scattered locations. Each of us probably has watched a gray squirrel carefully bury or scatter-hoard an acorn in the leaf litter on the forest floor. Larder hoarding, on the other hand, is the storing of all or most food items in a centralized location. An example of this can be seen in the eastern chipmunk, which busily collects and places acorns into its burrow system in autumn. Larder, rather than scatter hoarding, has generally evolved in solitary, territorial species (Smith 1968; Yahner 1978a). Hoarding most likely occurs when food is in excess supply and just prior to the time it is needed; therefore, hoarding in squirrels is prevalent in autumn when mast, such as acorns, is abundant. This behavior, then, has evolved in some mammals, like squirrels and American beaver (see essay 16 in chap. 8), as a means of avoiding food shortages in winter and early spring.

Hoarding is not limited to mammals but occurs in some birds and invertebrates (e.g., ants and bees); it is not reported in reptiles, amphibians, or fishes. Of the two types, larder hoarding is found more often in mammals, whereas scatter hoarding is more typical of birds (Smith and Reichman 1984; Sherry 1989; Vander Wall 1990). Blue jays, for instance, scatter-hoard large quantities of acorns in the fall. Interestingly, scatter hoarding of acorns by jays is believed to have augmented the historic northward distribution of oaks in the northeastern United States after glaciers receded during the Pleistocene (Johnson and Adkisson 1986). Two common forest birds in the mid-eastern states, white-breasted nuthatches and black-capped chickadees, often take sunflower seeds from backyard birdfeeders and store them in bark crevices of nearby trees. Seeds provide these forest birds with a source of energy prior to beginning each overnight fast (Sherry 1989).

Hoarding of food is reported in fifteen mammalian families, which fall into three major groups on the basis of feeding method: insectivores, herbivores, and carnivores (Smith and Reichman 1984). Insectivores, including shrews and moles, larder-hoard insects and earthworms. Herbivores scatter- or larder-hoard various seeds (e.g., squirrels) or larder-hoard bark and twigs (e.g., beaver). Carnivores, such as brown bear and red fox, larder- and scatter-hoard vertebrate prey, respectively. The scatter hoard of the red fox, for example, might be a small animal that is buried to secure it from other predators, insects, and microbes (MacDonald 1976).

Let's examine hoarding in some detail in gray squirrels and eastern chipmunks. Later, we will discuss hoarding in red squirrels as it relates to the evolution of territoriality (see essay 14 in chap. 7). Gray squirrels cache single or small numbers of food items, like acorns, throughout their home ranges. Because gray squirrels are not territorial (Thompson 1978), other squirrels and seed predators can raid the acorns stored by an individual squirrel. Despite the possibility of theft, however, scatter hoarding is presumably adaptive in gray squirrels because individual caches are abundant, widely scattered, and inconspicuous (Vander Wall 1990).

Squirrels tend to favor acorns produced from tree species in the white oak group (e.g., white and chestnut oaks) rather than those from the black oak group (e.g., northern red and scarlet oaks) because acorns from the white oak group are more palatable (Short 1976). Palatability of acorns is related to a substance known as tannin, which is found in all acorns and may inhibit digestive enzymes at high concentrations (Feeny 1969). Tannin concentrations are lower in acorns from the white oak group (1–2% dry matter) than those from the black oak group (6–9%) (Ofcarcik and Burns 1971). Yet despite the fact that acorns of the white oak group are more palatable to squirrels, acorns of the black oak group are less perishable, and, therefore, are cached more readily by squirrels for winter use (Short 1976; Smallwood 1992). Acorns of the white oak group are important as a food resource to squirrels only for a short time because they germinate soon after falling to the ground (Short 1976). A taproot, which is less digestible to squirrels, rapidly forms in acorns of the white oak group and may be a possible adaptation to escape predation by squirrels and other seed consumers. Hence, in response, squirrels are known to remove (i.e., kill) the embryo of acorns of the white oak group before they are cached to halt taproot germination and slow perishability (Fox 1982).

The value of acorns to squirrels is not only affected by tannin concentrations but also by insect damage. Large quantities (50%) of acorns that fall to the ground can be potentially damaged by infestation of acorn weevil larvae (Andersen and Folk 1993). Squirrels, however, have the ability to make decisions on which acorns to cache or eat based on the presence of weevils (Steele, Hadj-Chikh, and Hazeltine 1996). Acorns with weevils, particularly red oak acorns, are eaten immediately rather than being scatter-hoarded. Noninfested acorns, on the other hand, are hoarded by squirrels. Thus, squirrels can have a major positive effect on the dispersal and subsequent germination of oaks by hoarding only uninfested acorns.

How does a squirrel find an acorn previously scatter-hoarded in leaf litter on the forest floor? Because mammals rely extensively on olfaction, olfactory cues certainly are important (Vander Wall 1990). Visual cues, such as disturbed soil or the location of landmarks (such as a large log), and memory also are important to squirrels in finding stored food items.

The eastern chipmunk uses both scatter and larder hoarding to store food, but the frequency of larder hoarding is about eightfold greater than scatter hoarding during the annual cycle (Yahner 1978a). Furthermore, scatter hoarding in chipmunks predominates in summer, whereas larder hoarding is prevalent in autumn (Yahner 1975; Elliott 1978). The fact that chipmunks shift from scatter hoarding to larder hoarding during the season suggests that scatter hoarding may be some vestigial behavioral pattern common to ancestral chipmunks (Yahner 1975). However, there is no evi-

a. Side View

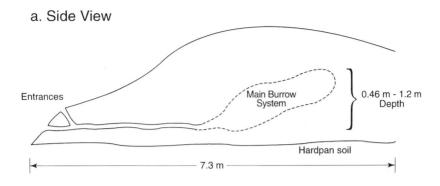

Entrances

Main Burrow System

0.46 m - 1.2 m Depth

Hardpan soil

7.3 m

b. Top View

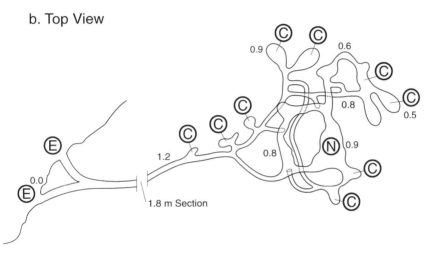

Figure 6. A representative burrow system of an eastern chipmunk, showing entrances (E), nest (N), and storage chambers (C) for food. The numbers are depths (cm) of a particular portion of the burrow system. *(Modified from Elliott 1978.)*

dence that ancestors of chipmunks were scatter hoarders, and the role and evolution of scatter hoarding in the eastern chipmunk remain speculative (Vander Wall 1990).

The evolution of larder hoarding probably is derived from the requirement to find secure feeding and home sites (Vander Wall 1990) and the ability of an animal to defend its territory and cache contained within the territory (Smith 1968). Therefore, because eastern chipmunks are solitary and actively defend individual burrow systems and caches contained

Family Sciuridae

within these systems from conspecifics, larder hoarding is the most efficient means of storing foods (Elliott 1978; Yahner 1978a, 1978b). This cache is vital to chipmunk survival by providing a source of food in both winter and early spring. If necessary, a chipmunk will shift its home range and burrow system in autumn to an area containing high concentrations of food, such as oak acorns, to better ensure access to a cachable source of winter food (Yahner 1978b; Lacher and Mares 1996).

The contents of caches of eastern chipmunks vary because of individual food preferences and regional differences in food availability (Vander Wall 1990). Food caches may contain a variety of nuts, seeds, and bulbs, for example, oak acorns, maple and black cherry seeds, beech and hickory nuts, and lily bulbs (Thomas 1974; Elliott 1978). Quantities of food in a cache can be impressive. For instance, over 1,000 grams of stored food have been found in an excavated burrow system of an eastern chipmunk (see fig. 6). Chambers, which contain the stored food, usually measure ten to thirty-five centimeters in diameter and ten to fifteen centimers in height.

ESSAY 10

Groundhog Day and Social Behavior in Marmots

Every February 2, thousands of people and the media gather in Punxsutawney, Pennsylvania, to watch a sluggish groundhog, alias "Punxsutawney Phil," awaken from a deep "sleep" to give his annual prediction about the weather. Legend has it that winter conditions will last another six weeks if the groundhog sees his shadow. As people and camera lights peer on Punxsutawney Phil and await his prediction, he seems very uninterested in the annual event and appears to be half asleep. In fact, the groundhog, or more appropriately woodchuck, has just been aroused from a lethargic state of hibernation and thus is hardly anxious to be bothered by all these curious people who seemingly have nothing better to do but disturb him.

Hibernation tends to be longer for woodchucks in more northerly latitudes and may not even occur in some individuals occupying southerly latitudes (Nowak 1999). In the mid-eastern states woodchucks tend to hibernate from early November through early February–March (Grizzell 1955; Whitaker and Hamilton 1998). In more northerly latitudes, as in Québec, hibernation may extend from mid-September through late March or early April (Ferron 1996). Once in hibernation, woodchucks may infrequently leave their burrow systems for a short time during winter (Twichell 1939). When woodchucks eventually emerge from hibernation in late winter or early spring, aboveground activity is initially limited to one hour or less (Snyder and Christian 1960). Mating behavior (e.g., a male chasing a female) occurs shortly after emergence, making woodchuck activity more conspicuous to humans (Lee and Funderburg 1982). Thus, the origin of Groundhog Day probably stems from an occasional and often short-term appearance of woodchucks in midwinter or later in the year, followed by aboveground breeding activity.

Hibernation by a woodchuck is a remarkably efficient strategy from an energetic standpoint, saving about seven times as much energy compared to it remaining in an aroused state (Bailey and Davis 1965). A woodchuck may gain over 30 to 40 percent of its body weight by intensive feeding in the autumn and then lose this weight through hibernation; each part of this alternating cycle of weight gain and loss lasts about six months (Grizzell 1955; Snyder, Davis, and Christian 1961; Ferron 1996). During hibernation the heartbeat of woodchucks goes from 100 beats per minute to 15 beats per minute, and body temperatures are reduced from 38 to 8°C (or 96 to 47°F) (Whitaker and Hamilton 1998). To make some sense of this amazing strategy, imagine a 150-pound human gaining about fifty to sixty pounds every autumn and losing this same amount of weight by early spring every year. Also, when in this imaginary state of hibernation, the human also drops breathing rates and body temperatures to around 10 beats per minute and 48°F, respectively, for at least three to four consecutive months!

Family Sciuridae

65

The time spent by woodchucks in hibernation can increase with latitude, suggesting that the length of the hibernation period is a function of environmental harshness, not only within but also among marmot species (Barash 1974). The cold winters experienced by our woodchuck are much less harsh than those faced by two western counterparts, the yellow-bellied and the Olympic marmot. Woodchucks and these two western marmots inhabit grassland areas; those used by woodchucks are at lower elevations compared to grasslands occupied by yellow-bellied and Olympic marmots at intermediate and higher elevations, respectively. Hence, the growing season, which determines the seasonal availability of herbaceous food for marmots, is relatively long for woodchucks (e.g., 150 days/year in Pennsylvania) versus only about one-half (70–100 days/year in Colorado) the length for yellow-bellied marmots and only one-third (40–50 days/year in Washington State) as long for Olympic marmots.

Because young woodchucks are weaned and on their own by late summer in the year of their birth, sufficient time is available during the growing season to acquire adequate body size prior to hibernation. On the other hand, because of a reduced growing season and feeding period, hibernation in the two western marmots is much longer than that of woodchucks. Furthermore, western marmots born in the previous spring are far from adult size by the end of their first summer, and young yellow-bellied and Olympic marmots do not disperse from family groups until the second and third year, respectively.

There is more to this marmot story—it involves an interesting link between environmental conditions and the evolution of social behavior. If young marmots are to be retained within the family group, then aggressive behavior needs to be minimized and amicable behavior enhanced. This is exactly the social situation found in yellow-bellied and Olympic marmots. Both of these species live colonially and are quite social, but especially the Olympic marmot. Play behavior, involving "greeting" between colony members, occurs an average of about ten times per animal per hour for Olympic marmots and one time per animal per hour for yellow-bellied marmots. In contrast, the woodchuck is solitary, aggressive, territorial, and lacks a notable amount of playful, unaggressive behavior. Thus, marmots of North America, including the woodchuck from the mid-eastern states, are excellent models to show how environmental or ecological conditions can affect the evolution of behavior and sociality in mammals.

As an aside, the closely related chipmunk (see also hibernation in black bear, essay 34 in chap. 12) does not truly hibernate but undergoes a state of shallow hibernation, referred to as torpor. Chipmunks usually spend less than one day at a time in torpor, although bouts of torpor may extend several days, depending on the individual (Wang and Hudson 1971; Maclean 1981). In fact, as many as 30 percent of the chipmunks in a population may not even enter torpor (Panuska 1959). Occasionally, chipmunks may be seen above ground in the late winter, particularly during the first breeding season (Yahner and Svendsen 1978).

Chipmunks that enter torpor have lowered body temperatures, heart rates, and breathing rates (Feldhamer, Drickamer, Vessey, and Merritt 1999). When in torpor, chipmunks also rely on small amounts of body fat accumulated in the previous autumn; but when awake in the burrow system, they feed on cached food (see essay 9 in chap. 7). Moreover, those individuals exhibiting torpor store less food than those individuals that do not (Brenner and Lyle 1975). Torpor may be used by chipmunks to conserve cached food, especially when food is limited or lacking, for example, toward the end of winter (Neumann 1967).

ESSAY 11

"Flying" in Flying Squirrels

Two features distinguish southern and northern flying squirrels from other squirrel species in the mid-eastern states: flying squirrels are nocturnal and "fly," whereas other squirrels are diurnal and incapable of "flight." Because flying squirrels are nocturnal, we might speculate that their nighttime activity minimizes competition for food with other squirrels, as suggested with sympatric populations of nocturnal great horned owls and diurnal

Family Sciuridae

red-tailed hawks (Marti and Kochert 1995). The nocturnal way of life of flying squirrels may instead be related to membranes used for "flying," which may make these squirrels more cumbersome and slower moving in trees compared to diurnal tree squirrels, which lack these membranes (Thorington 1984). By evolving nocturnal habits, however, flying squirrels may be less vulnerable to efficient daytime predators, like Cooper's hawks and goshawks. Although extant flying squirrels differ considerably from tree squirrels, flying squirrels probably were derived from the same ancestor as diurnal tree squirrels, such as gray and fox squirrels (Thorington and Heaney 1981).

The genus of flying squirrels, *Glaucomys*, is Greek for "gray mouse," and the specific name for the southern flying squirrel, *volans*, is Latin for "flying" (Dolan and Carter 1977). However, these "flying gray mice" do not truly fly but rather glide; bats are the only true mammalian flyers (see essay 4 in chap. 5). Besides the flying squirrels, three other very different taxonomic groups of mammals have evolved the ability to glide by using elaborate membranes as wing-like or parachute-like structures (Thorington and Heaney 1981; Thorington 1984; Thewissen and Babcock 1992). These include flying lemurs of southeast Asia (see essay 4 in chap. 5), phalangers of Australia, and scaly-tailed squirrels of Africa—thus, gliding in mammals is a perfect example of a phenomenon known as convergent evolution. Gliding membranes in these four mammalian families have developed six different ways of attachment to forelimbs. In our flying squirrels, the hair-covered gliding membrane extends between the wrist of the foreleg and the ankle of the hindleg, with cartilaginous support for the membrane at the wrist. This cartilage at the wrist permits flying squirrels to hold the "wing" tips of the membranes at an upright angle to reduce drag during a glide, which is similar to the function of winglets on modern aircraft (Thorington, Darrow, and Anderson 1998). Because the gliding membrane and skin of flying squirrels are very loose, these squirrels are certainly one of the most difficult small mammals to handle by hand. When grasped, they make every effort to squirm and bite.

Few of us are fortunate enough to see a flying squirrel in the wild. Occasionally, we might catch a glimpse of a flying squirrel feeding on seed in our backyard birdfeeder during a moonlit night. Certainly even fewer of us have seen a flying squirrel actually glide. This means of loco-

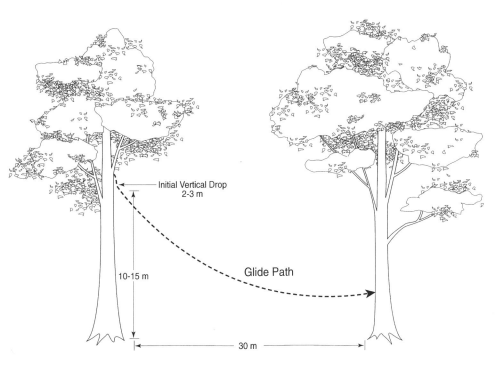

Initial Vertical Drop
2-3 m

Glide Path

10-15 m

30 m

Figure 7. Hypothetical schematic of a glide in a flying squirrel. Maximum distance traversed and velocity are achieved by taking off at a sufficient height and by dropping vertically at the point of takeoff.

motion has its advantages as well as its shortcomings. But when the logistics of gliding in flying squirrels are examined, the advantages of this form of locomotion become clear (Thorington and Heaney 1981). These squirrels are capable of flying distances of nearly fifty meters, or about one-half the length of a football field, in a single glide (see fig. 7). Gliding velocity (30 kmh) is similar to that of some bats, like the little brown myotis and the big brown bat (see essay 4), but is a bit slower than the flight velocity of many familiar songbirds (40–48 kmh).

Flying squirrels are quite maneuverable while gliding because the aspect ratio of the membranes is lower than that of bat wings (see essay 4). Also, while in flight, a squirrel can change the position of the membranes by moving its legs to swerve around obstacles. A good way to describe gliding in flying squirrels is that it closely resembles hang gliding in humans, with both being rather easy to maneuver and requiring little wind turbulence.

The remarkable distance traversed and velocity attained by flying squirrels during a glide are a result of two things: adequate height and an initial drop at takeoff (Thorington and Heaney 1981). The flying squirrel needs to be high enough in a tree to achieve a suitable glide ratio of about one meter above ground for every two to three meters of distance traveled through the forest canopy. Thus, it must climb to a height of ten to fifteen meters at takeoff in order to glide a vertical distance of thirty meters. To achieve maximum velocity, a squirrel initially drops vertically for a meter or so before flattening out its glide. The landing by a squirrel is fast and hard, although the velocity is slowed at the point of impact when the squirrel swoops its body upward toward the end of the glide for a softer landing. In emergency situations, a flying squirrel also can land more softly by using its membranes as a parachute while spiraling downward.

Preferred microhabitat for flying squirrels includes mature forest stands that have large trees with cavities for nesting and escape cover (Bendel and Gates 1987). In addition, these stands need to be relatively open beneath the tree canopy to provide a relatively unobstructed gliding path for movement and predator avoidance. Thus, a shortcoming or disadvantage to gliding in flying squirrels is that movements may be impeded by forest openings, such as those created by clearcutting. Because gliding membranes likely make movement of flying squirrels somewhat cumbersome while they feed on the forest floor, these squirrels favor forests with a relatively dense layer of vegetation near ground level to reduce their conspicuousness to predators.

Northern Flying Squirrel: An Ice-Age Relict in Need of Conservation

The northern flying squirrel is widely distributed in western and northern regions of North America (Hall 1981). It occurs in the mountainous areas of the western United States, in about the southern two-thirds of Canada, and northward into southeastern Alaska. The range of this species continues as well into the northeastern United States, but in this region its distribution is much more discontinuous (Whitaker and Hamilton 1998). In the Northeast populations are relatively contiguous from about central Pennsylvania northward to Maine; however, two separate pockets of northern flying squirrels are found in the southern Appalachian Mountains. The two relict pockets of northern flying squirrels in the southern Appalachians were not discovered until the 1930s–1950s, and both have been designated as federally endangered subspecies under the Endangered Species Act (Matthews 1991). In the mid-eastern states, this squirrel is probably most common in New York and is absent in Delaware, Maryland, and Ohio (see table 1).

Climatic changes in North America several thousands of years ago had a profound influence on the distribution of the northern flying squirrel in the eastern United States (Muul 1968). The historic range of this squirrel in the Appalachian Mountains was considerably greater than it is today because the boreal forest was widespread and found at low elevations prior to the northward movement of glaciers around 10,700 years ago. As the glaciers began to recede northward, the boreal forest was lost from the southern elevations in the Appalachian Mountains, except for isolated areas at high elevations, as in the Smoky Mountains of eastern Tennessee and western North Carolina. Extant populations of northern

Family Sciuridae

flying squirrels in much of the Appalachian Mountains, therefore, represent relict populations left behind at higher elevations during the warm, postglacial period in the eastern United States (Yahner 2000). The most southern relict population consists of Carolina northern flying squirrels, which are found above 1,230 meters in elevation in conifer-hardwood forests along the Tennessee–North Carolina border and into Virginia (Matthews 1991; Whitaker and Hamilton 1998). The more northern relict populations are known as Virginia northern flying squirrels and occur above 1,000 meters in elevation in eastern West Virginia and Virginia.

The loss of suitable habitat, which began centuries ago and continues even today, has negatively affected populations of northern flying squirrels throughout the eastern United States (Matthews 1991). Prior to European colonization, the New England and mid-Atlantic states were covered with old-growth (or virgin) forest containing trees hundreds of years old (Sedjo 1991; MacCleery 1992). Human-induced changes in the landscape, especially those resulting from forest cutting and agricultural practices from the beginning of the seventeenth century and into the early twentieth century, reduced the amount of suitable habitat for this squirrel on a broad scale. Much of the eastern forest was converted to cropland and pasture or cut for its wood products, and old-growth stands were virtually eliminated from the eastern United States (Yahner 2000). Old-growth stands provide important food and cover requirements for the northern flying squirrel, including older trees with cavities as nest sites, lichens and fungi as food resources, and relatively open understory for gliding (Weigl 1978; Whitaker and Hamilton 1998).

In order to minimize further declines in the abundance and distribution of northern flying squirrels in the eastern United States, a crucial conservation strategy is to protect existing old-growth forests (Mahan, Steele, Patrick, and Kirkland 1999). Unfortunately, old-growth forests are virtually nonexistent in the East. Hence, the stewards of large expanses of public and private forestlands in eastern states (i.e., state and federal natural resource agencies and the forest industry) should make a concerted effort to ensure the preservation of large tracts of mature forested lands. However, most stands of mature forest will take at least 100 to 200 years (if ever) to attain characteristics similar to those of old-growth forests in terms of plant and animal species (Lorimer and Frelich 1994). In addition, snags should be retained in the forest for flying squirrels (Gilmore and Gates 1985). These dead or dying trees are a source of natural cavities for flying squirrels. In forested areas, where snags or trees with cavities are scarce or lacking, nest boxes designed specifically for flying squirrels can be placed on live trees to increase the value of stands for these sciurids (Goertz, Dawson, and Mowbray 1975; Gilmore and Gates 1985).

Problems associated with the long-term conservation of northern flying squirrels do not stop with habitat preservation and improvement— three other factors may negatively impact this species. First, if global warming takes place in future decades, suitable habitat for isolated pockets of northern flying squirrels at high elevations in more southerly locations, in particular, could be further diminished (Yahner 2000). Furthermore, both Carolina and Virginia northern flying squirrels may be displaced by their more adaptable and aggressive cousin, the southern flying squirrel (Weigl 1978; Matthews 1991). Third, a parasitic nematode worm may be transferred from southern to northern flying squirrels; this nematode is harmless to the southern flying squirrel but can be fatal to the northern flying squirrel where populations of these two species overlap. Our hope is that enough "flags" have been waved by concerned biologists and conservationists about the potential demise of northern flying squirrels in the eastern states and that enough is known about the basic biology of this species to mitigate its extirpation in our area in the coming decades. State wildlife agencies, such as that in Virginia, have initiated monitoring programs to better understand habitat requirements and population characteristics of northern flying squirrels before it is too late to act (Reynolds, Pagels, and Fies 1998).

ESSAY 13

The Gray Squirrel—An Exotic Species That Backfired

Gray squirrels are a common sight to many of us in our city parks, backyards, and woodlots. They are native to our region, having evolved in the eastern forests of North America (Vaughan, Ryan, and Czaplewski 2000), and their natural range includes the eastern United States and parts of the midwestern United States and southern Canada (Hall 1981). However, the gray squirrel has been introduced into western North America, from California northward into British Columbia, and to other parts of the world, such as Great Britain, South Africa, and Australia (Flyger and Gates 1982). The gray squirrel, therefore, is both a native and an exotic species, depending on its geographic location.

The natural and human-induced distribution of gray squirrels brings us to three important questions facing biologists and conservationists worldwide. First, as an all-encompassing question, what is the definition of naturalness, given natural or human-induced changes in animal and plant distributions and their environments? Second, when is a species considered exotic? Finally, what effects can an exotic species have on native species or their environments?

Let's begin by addressing the first question. A truly natural ecosystem probably does not exist anywhere on the earth today. No part of the biosphere has escaped some degree of disturbance from modern technology; examples are the global distribution of DDT and the stratospheric depletion of the ozone layer (Yahner 2000). Furthermore, the universal flood of exotic species can be found in many disturbed areas of the mid-eastern states, and even in the more pristine national parks of the western United States, such as Glacier National Park, Montana (Tyser and Worley 1992). Hence, what is "naturalness" is debatable and can vary regionally, culturally, or even from one person to the next (Anderson 1991; Götmark

1992; Hunter 1996). One possible measure of naturalness of a given area may be the number of native versus exotic species in that area relative to centuries ago prior to European settlement (Hunter 1996).

This brings us to the second question: what is an exotic species? As we saw earlier, about 20 percent of the mammalian species in the mid-eastern states are exotic (see table 1), but the distinction between native versus exotic designations can be tricky. For instance, even though wildlife agencies in the mid-eastern states consider red foxes and Virginia opossums as native species, both may be loosely considered exotic because neither occurred in the area when Europeans arrived (see essay 1 in chap. 2 and essay 27 in chap. 11). As another example, the feral horse is classified as exotic in North America, yet its ancestors evolved in North America. Thus, as more and more species expand their range intentionally or unintentionally by human intervention in future years, we could be faced with drawing the line between native versus exotic designations for these species.

Red foxes and Virginia opossums have not caused a demonstrable negative impact on native fauna and their environments, but this is probably the exception rather than the rule. Therefore, the introduction of exotic species is considered to be one of the major problems facing natural resource conservationists today (Coblentz 1990). Classic examples of exotic mammalian species gone awry when they enter a new region are Norway and black rats. These two rodents escaped ships and invaded many islands throughout the world over the past few centuries; in doing so, they encountered few or no enemies and often outcompeted and eliminated many native species (see essay 19 in chap. 9) (Goodman 1995).

The gray squirrel does not compete with other squirrel species, such as the fox squirrel, in the eastern deciduous forest. Both gray and fox squirrels can coexist in the same general area, with relatively subtle differences in habitat use; fox squirrels tend to occupy more open forests or areas closer to forest edges than gray squirrels (Armitage and Harris 1982; Derge and Yahner 2000). Gray squirrels in both the eastern and western United States, however, can occasionally become a nuisance to humans by entering attics, gnawing on wires, or feeding on seed intended for backyard songbirds (Flyger and Gates 1982). But a different story can be told about the gray squirrel in Great Britain, where its introduction has unfortunately

Family Sciuridae

backfired, with possible serious consequences to a native squirrel, the Eurasian red squirrel (Kenward and Holm 1989; Usher, Crawford, and Banwell 1992).

Only two species of squirrels occur on the British Isles today, Eurasian red squirrels and gray squirrels. Gray squirrels were initially introduced into country parks and estates of southeast England from the United States in 1876. Thereafter, populations quickly spread northwesterly in England, and by 1930 they were considered pests in the deciduous forests of England. The range of the Eurasian red squirrel then contracted sharply through the 1940s and 1950s, being restricted to some offshore islands and large coniferous tracts of forest in northern England and Scotland. Intensive surveys by the Forestry Commission of Great Britain in the 1970s and 1980s have indicated that red squirrels continued to decline in Scotland and Wales.

Two principal hypotheses have been proposed for the decline of the Eurasian red squirrel in Great Britain in the twentieth century: disease outbreak and interspecific competition. In the 1930s a disease caused a brief die-back of introduced gray squirrel populations in England, but no evidence existed for the disease occurring in Eurasian red squirrel populations (Usher, Crawford, and Banwell 1992). Also, the potential for interspecific competition between gray and Eurasian red squirrels is an attractive hypothesis (see essay 27), but this phenomenon in coexisting gray and Eurasian red squirrel populations is probably nonexistent or, at best, subtle (Kenward and Holm 1989).

The increase in American gray squirrels, coupled with a decline in Eurasian red squirrels in Great Britain, may be best attributed to changing landscapes over the past few decades, with large tracts of deciduous woodlands replacing coniferous woodlands. Deciduous woodlands are preferred by gray squirrels, whereas coniferous woodlands are choice habitat for red squirrels. Therefore, the long-term conservation of Eurasian red squirrels may hinge on the retention of large coniferous forest stands devoid of deciduous trees as refugia for red squirrels, although wildlife authorities in Great Britain believe that the red squirrel is not in danger of extinction in the near future. The preservation of coniferous stands, however, poses a dilemma for conservationists in Great Britain because coniferous forests typically support a much lower biodiversity than deciduous stands. Hence, a value judgment needs to be made by British wildlife biologists between the benefits of ensuring coniferous habitat for the declining Eurasian red squirrel versus providing a greater diversity of species in deciduous forests.

In conclusion, as we sit quietly watching a gray squirrel feeding in a local park or backyard, we may remind ourselves that even this species, when placed in an exotic land, can backfire and become a serious pest. Once an exotic species, such as the gray squirrel in Great Britain, takes a foothold in a new area, it is seldom—if ever—eradicated. This common mid-eastern species stands as a reminder that we will have to deal with challenges posed by many other exotic species for many decades to come (see essays 19 and 23 in chap. 9).

ESSAY 14

Territoriality in Red Squirrels

Many species of vertebrates, especially mammals and birds, defend all or a portion of their home range, which is termed a territory. A territory usually is centered around a home site or foraging area. As a general trend, territoriality is less common in mammals than birds in the mid-eastern states. The familiar American robin of our backyards, for instance, defends a territory surrounding its nest, using a combination of song, chases, and visual displays (Yahner 2000). Similarly, the red fox defends a territory around its den site (Storm, Andrews, Phillips, Bishop, Siniff, and Tester 1976), largely with the use of olfactory signals (see essay 28 in chap. 11). In contrast, eastern cottontails and white-tailed deer are not territorial, although some evidence suggests that female deer will defend limited areas

Family Sciuridae

around fawns, termed a *fawning ground*, for a few weeks after their birth (Ozoga, Verme, and Bienz 1982).

Of the sciurid species in the mid-eastern states, only eastern chipmunks, woodchucks, and red squirrels are territorial (Smith 1968; Yahner 1978a; Lee and Funderberg 1982) (see essays 9 and 10 above). The red squirrel, in particular, is an excellent species to use as a model for an understanding of territoriality in mammals.

Unlike burrowing chipmunks, home sites of red squirrels are typically aboveground leaf nests placed in tree branches or cavities (Layne 1954; Fancy 1980), but red squirrels may occasionally use burrow systems as a home site or refugium (Yahner 1980, 1987; Mahan and Yahner 1992). Red squirrels, like eastern chipmunks, larder-hoard food for winter use (see essay 9); the larder hoard of red squirrels, however, is placed above ground in one or more middens within five to ten meters of its nest site. The nest and midden(s) are the central features of a red squirrel territory (Smith 1968).

A midden is created by an accumulation of cone fragments under a favorite feeding perch, such as a large overhanging branch, as a red squirrel breaks apart cones in search of seeds (Vahle and Patton 1983). The pile of cone fragments can eventually grow to be seven to ten meters in diameter and at least forty centimeters deep (Patton and Vahle 1986). Red squirrels then gather intact cones and fungi and store them within the midden, which provides a cool and moist microenvironment (Shaw 1936). Cones kept in this condition do not open so that cone seeds remain as a viable, long-term food resource for squirrels.

A territory is likely to evolve in red squirrels and other vertebrates if time and energy expended in its defense ensure the territorial holder access to a resource in short supply (Brown 1964). In red squirrels, nest sites usually are not limited because this squirrel is quite adaptable in choice of nest sites. In the boreal forest, cone seeds can be a limited resource, particularly in years of cone failure (Smith 1968). Hence, defense of whole cones stored in a midden from conspecifics better guarantees the territorial holder a winter food supply during years of cone scarcity.

Why is a territory defended by an individual red squirrel rather than jointly by a pair or small group of squirrels? In red squirrels the most efficient way to collect, store, and defend a cache of cones and fungi apparently is for each individual to establish a relatively circular territory and defend the central cache (Smith 1968). The logic behind this is as follows. When food collected near the midden becomes depleted, distance traveled and energy expended to obtain additional food resources increase. As a hypothetical example, consider a territory with a radius of forty meters, which is occupied by an individual red squirrel (see fig. 8). If the territory were jointly defended by two squirrels, the radius of the territory would have to expand to fifty-six meters in order to accommodate a territory with twice the total area. If the territory is twice the area (56m radius) and is defended by two squirrels, each squirrel would have to expend about 1.4 times as much time and energy in its defense, compared to two squirrels each defending separate but smaller territories (each 40m radius) because of the increased distance from a centralized midden to the outer boundary of the larger territory. In biological terms, this translates to a squirrel spending 10 percent versus 14 percent of its time caching food in autumn in the smaller, individually defended territory than in the larger, jointly defended territory, respectively. This 4 percent reduction in time spent collecting food then can be allocated to other important day-to-day activities, such as feeding, resting, or watching for possible predators.

This model for the evolution of an individually defended territory

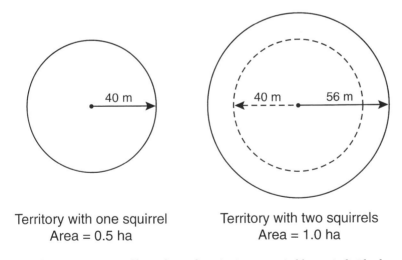

Territory with one squirrel
Area = 0.5 ha

Territory with two squirrels
Area = 1.0 ha

Figure 8. A comparison of hypothetical territories occupied by an individual versus two red squirrels.

with a centralized midden(s) is adaptive for red squirrels in boreal forests in much of North America (Smith 1968). However, defense of territories by solitary red squirrels may not be the norm in red squirrel populations occupying habitats other than boreal coniferous forests. In the eastern and midwestern United States, for instance, red squirrels may occur in deciduous forests or planted linear habitats, known as shelterbelts (Yahner 1980, 1987; Riege 1991). In deciduous stands of northern Minnesota, for example, territoriality in red squirrels is either absent or occurring only in autumn. Similarly, in shelterbelts of southern Minnesota, territoriality was never observed; in some cases, as many as three red squirrels occur in the same tree or group of trees.

In deciduous forests or shelterbelts, red squirrels typically do not rely on seeds of conifers as a major food resource; rather, food resources consist of a diversity of abundant alternative foods (e.g., maple seeds, corn) (Yahner 1980, 1987; Riege 1991). These alternate foods, with the exception of seeds, often cannot be cached as a future food resource because they readily perish (see essay 9). Hence, with a scarcity of conifers in deciduous habitats, middens are not formed, and territorial defense is rare or nonexistent (Yahner 1987; Mahan and Yahner 1992).

Recent studies of red squirrel populations in boreal forests of eastern North America (Ontario and New Brunswick) have revealed another interesting trend in territoriality and midden formation in red squirrels (Hurly and Robertson 1990; Dempsey and Keppie 1993). Even though individual red squirrels in these eastern boreal forests exhibit territoriality and cones are readily available, they do not hoard cones in a midden as true of their western counterparts. Instead, these eastern squirrels scatter-hoard (versus larder-hoard) small numbers of cones in many small caches throughout their territories (see essay 9). Currently, there is no explanation for this dramatic difference in hoarding behavior between eastern and western red squirrel populations occupying boreal forests.

8

Beaver

Family Castoridae

Description of the Family Castoridae

*B*eaver are rodents in the family Castoridae. Unlike the family Sciuridae (discussed in the previous chapter) with 272 species, the family Castoridae contains only two species, American and European beavers. These two beaver species are not to be confused with the mountain beaver in the family Aplodontidae, which is the most primitive extant rodent (Vaughan, Ryan, and Czaplewski 2000). American beaver are found throughout much of North America and in every mid-eastern state, except perhaps Delaware (see table 1). They have been introduced into parts of Europe and Asia, whereas European beaver are native to Europe and Asia (Hill 1982).

Beaver are the largest rodents in North America (63–76 cm in total length and 13–32 kg in weight). They have a stocky, heavily muscled, strong-boned body, and their ears are short and rounded. A dorsally flattened tail, which serves as a sizable paddle (23–32 cm long, 11–18 cm wide) for swimming, is the most conspicuous feature of this mammal. The tail also produces an alarm signal when slapped on the water surface and is a place to store body fat for winter use (see essays 16 and 17 in chap. 8). Beaver are chestnut to dark brown in color in the mid-eastern states, but the pelage may range from black to yellowish brown in some other parts of their geographic range. The dense pelage of beaver has always been a prized resource, and excessive trapping for them led to the near extinction of this species in North America (see essay 15 below).

Beaver move somewhat awkwardly on land because the hind legs are longer than the front legs, but they are quite at home in the water. Beaver are well adapted to an aquatic way of life because of waterproof pelage, webbed hind feet, paddle-like tails, and upper lips and nictitating membranes that prevent water from entering mouths and eyes while swimming underwater. Beaver can remain underwater for periods ranging from a few minutes to over fifteen minutes.

Two other important features of beaver are their teeth and castor glands. Like all rodents, the number of teeth is reduced (20). The orangish incisors, which give them the well-known ability to "chop" (or gnaw) down trees, are prominent and about the same size of human incisors (5 mm in width). As in all rodents, these incisors are evergrowing. The castor (or musk) glands combined with anal glands of beaver produce chemicals that serve as important olfactory signals in the social life of family groups (see essay 16 below).

Beaver use a variety of aquatic habitats, such as large rivers, lakes, impoundments, ponds, and streams with adequate water flow for damming. They prefer relatively flat terrain or valleys, provided that adequate winter foods are present adjacent to these aquatic habitats. Beaver are generalist herbivores and feed on many types of herbaceous and woody plants. Woody material, such as the bark of trees, which comprises 100 percent of their winter diet, is secured in an underwater cache (see essay 17 below). Aspen, maple, and willow are among the tree species selected as winter food, but species used can depend on geographic location (Svendsen 1980a). Over the annual cycle, diets change seasonally: forbs and grasses (50%) and woody material (50%) are primary food types in spring; forbs, grasses, aquatic plants (90%) and woody material (10%) in summer; and forbs, grasses, aquatic plants (50%) and woody material (50%) in autumn.

Dams created by beaver along a stream are a familiar sight in the outdoors (see essay 17). After a dam floods an area, a lodge is constructed near the central portion of the pond (or impoundment) as a home site (see fig. 9). In cases where beaver cannot construct dams, for example, along large rivers or lakes, canals or burrow systems are created in the banks (bank dens) as home sites. Bank dens are placed at the ends of these canals, which may range from 3 meters to over 200 meters in length (Berry 1923; Wilsson 1962). Bank dens may be less likely to occur in habitats with rocky conditions or permafrost (Novak 1987). On occasion, beaver will construct both a lodge and a bank den in older ponds where water depth has gradually increased over time. Beaver usually live in a colony, but sometimes they may occur singly or in pairs; the territory surrounding the home site is defended from conspecifics (see essay 16).

Beaver activity outside lodges or bank dens is crepuscular and nocturnal. Thus, a good way to observe beaver is to arrive at an active beaver dam with field glasses about one hour be-

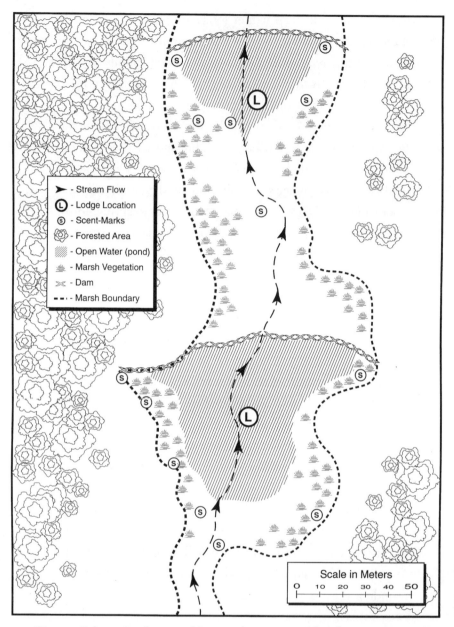

Legend:
- Stream Flow
L - Lodge Location
S - Scent-Marks
- Forested Area
- Open Water (pond)
- Marsh Vegetation
- Dam
- Marsh Boundary

Scale in Meters
0 10 20 30 40 50

Figure 9. Schematic of an actual impoundment created by a beaver colony in Black Moshannon State Forest. *(Modified from photo taken by R. B. Brooks, School of Forest Resources, Penn State University.)*

fore sunset. Because beaver have keen senses of hearing and smell, observers should stay quietly downwind from the colony. Just before dark it may be possible to catch a glimpse of the adult male in the colony, who often emerges from the home site before other colony members as he patrols the area for possible danger.

Beaver are monogamous and breed at the age of two and a half years. One litter of two to four young (but sometimes eight) is born after a gestation of 105–107 days. The young remain in the home site for about one month prior to taking their initial swim or going on land. Beaver may live ten to twenty years, which is an unusually long lifespan for most rodents, except porcupine (see essay 24 in chap. 10).

Family Castoridae

The History of Beaver in North America —

A Conservation Success Story

Picture a seemingly endless expanse of forest in the fifteenth or sixteenth century, with the canopy occasionally broken by natural events, like fires or tornadoes, and by openings created by Native Americans for croplands, villages, or wildlife habitat. In this era forest songbirds, ruffed grouse, gray wolves, and deer are relatively abundant. Nearly every lake, pond, and stream in flat terrain or valleys in this forest is also home to what was to become the currency of the future—beaver. Such was the scene witnessed by Europeans as they initially set foot on the east coast of North America and ventured westward into the mid-eastern states and beyond. Pre-European estimates of beaver populations in North America's forests were between 60 and 400 million individuals!

Prior to and after colonization of North America by Europeans, the American beaver was an important source of protein and fat in the diet of Native Americans (Novak 1987). Beaver pelts were used for clothing and as barter with other tribes and villages in exchange for food such as corn (Cronon 1983). Limited trade in beaver pelts between Native Americans and European cod fishermen began sometime in the sixteenth century (Kimball and Johnson 1978), but trade began in earnest with the French after 1610 and later with the English and other Europeans (Novak 1987; Obbard, Jones, Newman, Booth, Satterthwaite, and Linscombe 1987). Beaver from the New World became a prized commodity at this time because European beaver had already been driven to near extinction because of overexploitation for its fur. Hence, the American beaver became the choice source of fur for hats in Europe until the silk hat became fashionable in the 1840s (Obbard et al. 1987). Beaver pelts from America were especially popular as fur lining for hats, with every "civilized" man in Europe wanting to wear a "beaver" (Lavender 1967; Doutt, Heppenstall, and Guilday 1977).

Native Americans had little incentive to overexploit beaver populations before the fur trade with Europeans became a reality. Typically, Native Americans killed beaver only for clothing and food, personal use, or trade with other tribes and villages. But as trading partnerships began between Native Americans and Europeans, trade in beaver pelts by Native Americans rapidly became very commercialized (Cronon 1983). In return for pelts, Native Americans were rewarded with prized goods, such as brass and copper pots, woven fabrics, and strings of white and purple beads, known as wampum. Wampum was made from shellfish by Europeans in Long Island; this became a form of "money" and a symbol of power and wealth to Native Americans.

The extensive fur trade in beaver pelts in North America probably would not have existed without the cooperation of Native Americans (Cronon 1983). In order to exploit beaver populations efficiently, Europeans needed the expertise of Native Americans, whose hunting and trapping skills were much superior to those of most Europeans arriving in the New World. Thus, a partnership developed, with Native Americans harvesting beaver and processing their pelts for sale to the Europeans. Eventually some Europeans became skilled in hunting and trapping techniques, and these mountain men were the first Europeans to move westward into the Rocky Mountains in pursuit of beaver (Doutt, Heppenstall, and Guilday 1977). Well-known explorers, like Lewis and Clark, followed closely behind these beaver hunters and trappers. Hence, the beaver, more than any other species of wildlife, was responsible for the early settlement of Europeans into the Wild West of North America.

By the end of the eighteenth century, Native Americans began to realize that beaver, once the foundation of their economy, were being destroyed by commercialization. Tribes in New England, for instance, began to establish fixed hunting territories rather than shifting territories; these fixed territories were passed on to the next generation to better ensure a source of beaver and, thus, income for their children. Furthermore, hunting of beaver in some areas was restricted to every third year, and only two-thirds of the beaver in a given hunting territory were killed.

Family Castoridae

In short, Native Americans, who once lived in balance with resources prior to European settlement, now found that harvest restrictions had to be set in order to conserve their most valuable asset—beaver. Hence, we might view some Native American tribes as the first wildlife agencies. Remember that state and federal wildlife agencies, which were instrumental in the careful regulation of wildlife harvest in more recent times, were not in existence until the late nineteenth or early twentieth century.

Beaver harvests began to decline in the early nineteenth century and reached their lowest levels in the first decade of the twentieth century (Obbard et al. 1987). As noted by Henry David Thoreau in 1855, the beaver and other species such as gray wolves were now gone from the New England forests (Cronon 1983). By 1900 the beaver, once perceived as an endless resource, was virtually extirpated in the mid-eastern states (Whitaker and Hamilton 1998). Uncontrolled exploitation of beaver populations by both Native Americans and Europeans was not the only factor causing the historic demise in much of North America. Habitat loss was another prominent factor. Extensive forest cutting and agriculture in the eastern deciduous forest, which began in the seventeenth century and continued into the early twentieth century (see essay 12 in chap. 7), considerably reduced the amount of suitable habitat available to beaver colonies relative to that in the original, pristine eastern forest (Novak 1987).

Many European settlements were established in the nineteenth century in areas that once contained abundant beaver dams and ponds (Cronon 1983). These impoundments left an accumulation of leaves, bark, and silt in sizable areas, which were very productive for agriculture. In fact, today's maps have cities, such as Beaver and Beaver Falls in western Pennsylvania, as evidence of the influence of beaver on the historic geography and culture in the mid-eastern states.

The remarkable comeback of beaver populations in North America is attributed to two factors: forest regeneration and efforts by wildlife agencies. Extensive forest cutting of the eastern forest facilitated the regrowth of important trees, such as aspen, used as food by beaver, in many areas of North America (Novak 1987). Wildlife agencies formulated and enforced strict regulations to conserve the remaining beaver populations by controlling the number harvested and the methods and times of harvests (Hill 1982). In the decades of the 1920s–1950s, wildlife biologists also live-trapped beaver from other areas and restocked them into their former range. As a case in point, a pair of beaver obtained as a gift from Wisconsin was released in Pennsylvania in 1917 (Doutt 1977). From 1919 to 1924 an additional forty-six beaver pairs trapped in New York and Canada were released in Pennsylvania. Soon after, beaver rapidly expanded their distribution into each of the state's sixty-seven counties; over 6,000 beaver were legally harvested in 1934—only seventeen years from the initial release of two beaver. Populations in North America now number between 6 and 12 million, which is at least 10 to 20 percent of the pre-European population estimate (Naiman et al. 1988). Today, annual harvests of beaver in the United States and Canada approach one million, which are higher than harvests ever recorded in history (Novak 1987; Obbard et al. 1987). Incidentally, despite the success of our American beaver, its cousin in Europe has not fared well over the past century. The European beaver is still being reintroduced in countries, such as Sweden, where it was historically abundant but is currently uncommon or absent (Hartman 1994).

The beaver is an incredible mammal, not only from a conservation perspective, but also because of its effects on the environment—both negative and positive. With most of the original forest gone from the beaver's historic range and ever-increasing human populations, beaver problems are inevitable and commonplace today (Hill 1982; Novak 1987). Wildlife biologists now have to deal occasionally with too many beaver in the wrong place. Beaver can become a serious nuisance because of their food habits and ability to modify habitat by creating dams (Payne and Peterson 1986). They cut and girdle trees for food and dam and lodge construction, thereby sometimes damaging timber stands. Beaver dams may cause flooding of roads, railroads, and agricultural fields in low-lying areas. The total estimated loss attributed to American beaver is about $75–100 million annually (Miller 1983).

Ponds created by beaver dams more often have a positive impact on the environment by increasing total water area for aquatic invertebrates, stabilizing stream flow, and creating important habitat for many fish, like brook trout (Novak 1987; Naiman, Johnston, and Kelley 1988). Ponds and adjacent habitat are beneficial to numerous other wildlife, for example, white-tailed deer, common muskrat, mink, cavity-nesting birds, and waterfowl (Rutherford 1955; Cringan 1971). In one study, ninety-two species of songbirds were associated with four beaver ponds in South Carolina (Reese and Hair 1976). Equally important, the beaver has tremendous aesthetic value (Hill 1982). Probably every child is familiar with a beaver and its field signs, such as a dam or a cut tree; these signs can be a fascinating introduction to the wonders of nature and the natural world. The calmness of a pond created by a beaver on a farm or along the city limits can be a symbol of serenity in what often is otherwise a fast-paced and technology-driven world.

Each of us who enjoys the sounds and sights of the outdoors is glad to see that beaver—the currency of Native Americans and Europeans a few centuries ago—are now back in much of the landscape of the mid-eastern states. At the brink of extinction in our recent past, the return represents a classic conservation success story for wildlife agencies throughout North America.

ESSAY 16

Sociality and Communication in Beaver

In the previous chapter, we discussed a variety of mammals whose sociality ranges from solitary, like red squirrels (see essay 14), to very social, like Olympic marmots (see essay 10). Few mammalian species, however, rival the degree of sociality found in the American beaver. A beaver colony often consists as an extended family occurring in the same lodge or bank den (see essay 17 below). Three to four generations may live in the lodge during winter, including an adult pair, and one or more 2.5-year-olds, yearlings (1.5 years old), and kits from the previous spring (Hill 1982). Colony members share in the construction of the lodge and dam. The average colony size varies geographically, with five or six beaver per colony in southerly latitudes of the United States versus three to four beaver per colony in the more northerly latitudes of Canada. But not all beaver live in colonies. In fact, an extensive study of beaver colonies in Newfoundland found that 15 percent of the "colonies" consisted of a single beaver, and 24 percent were a pair of beavers (Payne 1982). New colonies form by dispersal of 2.5-year-olds, which generally occurs from April through September (Hodgdon 1978; Svendsen 1980b). Young beaver apparently disperse from the colony voluntarily (as with other mammals) rather than being evicted by adult occupants of the colony (Leege 1968).

The density of beaver colonies (expressed as number/km of stream or survey route) may range from about one to twenty lodges per ten kilometers (Hill 1982; Broschart, Johnston, and Naiman 1989). The boundaries between lodges are maintained by territorial behavior (Hill 1982). Unlike some species of territorial vertebrates, like diurnal songbirds or red squirrels, beaver are nocturnal or crepuscular. Thus, song and visual displays are not effective means of communicating to other beavers that a territory is occupied. Instead, olfactory signals (see essay 28 in chap. 11) are more useful in advertising territorial occupancy (Aleksuik 1968).

Beaver create mounds of mud and vegetation that vary in size from relatively small "mud pies" to piles approaching one meter in height (see fig. 10). Olfactory signals are then placed on these mounds by beaver (Aleksuik 1968; Hill 1982). Usually two to eight mounds are associated with each colony (see fig. 9 above), and these mounds are located along the water edge near the territory boundary or lodge. All members of the colony visit the scent mounds, although the females visit less often than the males.

Beaver mark scent mounds using chemicals produced by castor and anal glands (Svendsen 1978). Both types of glands are found on the underside of the base of the tail. Castor glands produce a yellowish substance that turns brown when exposed to air and sunlight; this substance is mixed with urine to form castoreum, which is expelled via the cloaca and deposited without the beaver touching the scent mound. Scent-marking with castor glands acts to delineate the boundaries of a beaver colony territory (Aleksuik 1968; Schulte 1998). In addition, the scent from castor glands of individuals from the same colony seems to elicit a sense of confidence in colony members (Svendsen 1980b). Beaver can distinguish mounds scented with castoreum from unscented mounds and can dis-

Figure 10. A beaver scent-mark or mound. *(Photo taken by R. B. Brooks, School of Forest Resources, Penn State University.)*

criminate mounds scented by family members from those scented by nonfamily members (Schulte 1998). Scent from castor glands of intruding beavers elicits aggressive behavior, such as hissing and tail slapping (Müller-Schwarze, Heckman, and Stagge 1983). Anal glands produce a drop of pungent, straw- to brown-colored substance, which is deposited by rubbing the gland on the scent mound. The primary functions of scent produced by anal glands appear to be identifying individuals and water-proofing the pelage (Walro and Svendsen 1982).

Because scent marks aid in maintaining territorial rights in beaver society, population densities and intraspecific strife are reduced before the lack of food becomes a limiting factor in an otherwise overpopulated environment (Aleksuik 1968). As 2.5-year-old beaver disperse from their natal lodge in spring and summer, they become a "floater" segment of the population and may follow watercourses for distances as far as twenty-one kilometers from their birth site (Beer 1955; Aleksuik 1968). Scent mounds located along water edges communicate with beaver in adjacent colonies and with floaters that a given area is already occupied.

Beaver also communicate with conspecifics using three primary vocalizations. These include whines, given while begging for food or when initiating play or grooming, and growls and hisses, used during aggressive interactions (Hodgdon and Larson 1973). But perhaps the most famous sound produced by beaver is the tail slap. Tail slaps are given by young as early as thirteen to twenty days old, although adults are more likely to tail-slap than other age classes (Brady and Svendsen 1981; Lancia and Hodgdon 1983). Adult females, in particular, typically tail-slap at times of the year when young are resident in the lodge (Hodgdon 1978). Tail-slapping behavior does not seem to have a territorial function but acts to warn colony members of danger (Brady and Svendsen 1981) and to startle or frighten enemies (Leighton 1932; Hodgdon and Lancia 1983).

We have seen that the sociality in beaver is quite sophisticated and complex relative to other mammals in the mid-eastern states. Communication, especially olfaction, is the binding force that mediates or "binds" together the way of life of beaver and most other mammals (Eisenberg and Kleiman 1972). The role of olfaction versus audition in sociality and territoriality of gray wolves and coyotes will be explored later (see essay 28 in chap. 11).

ESSAY 17

Winter Adaptations in Beaver

Winters in the mid-eastern states can be harsh. Mammals in this region have evolved some very ingenious ways to cope with winter conditions. For instance, eastern chipmunks larder-hoard food for winter use while remaining active or semiactive in underground burrow systems, while woodchucks survive winter by living on stored body fat during hiberna-

Family Castoridae

93

tion within their burrow systems (see essays 9 and 10 in chap. 7). A few species of larger bats, for example, red bats, migrate to more southerly latitudes during winter (see chapter 5). American beaver, on the other hand, have evolved four interesting strategies to deal with the rigors of winter. These include creating a stable microclimate by constructing a dam and lodge, larder hoarding a food cache, reducing the metabolism, and storing body fat.

In northerly latitudes, beaver can be confined for up to nine months under ice in a lodge or bank den. This period of "confinement" declines in more southerly locations because ponds and lakes remain ice-free for greater lengths of time during the year (Novak 1987). In autumn, however, older beaver (at least one year old) are especially "busy as a beaver" as they construct dams, lodges, and caches prior to the onset of winter (Hall 1981; Patenaude 1984). Dams are often built along sections of streams characterized by high densities of woody vegetation on both shorelines (Barnes and Mallik 1997). This woody vegetation is a source of food and construction materials; peeled logs and sticks are carried to the location of the future dam and placed parallel to the water current (Wilsson 1962). Then mud and stones are put on the upstream side of the logs and sticks to seal the water flow. Beaver continue to add sealants to the dam until the sound of flowing water is reduced or minimized (Wilsson 1971).

Dams are about thirty to sixty meters long (Buckley 1950). On average, each beaver colony creates at least two dams within its territory (Pullen 1975). A dam causes water levels to rise to form a pond, thereby flooding and killing standing trees and shrubs in the immediate area. The resultant pond is usually less than four hectares but can be as large as thirty hectares (Knudsen 1962).

Lodges, like dams, are built with piles of peeled logs and sticks, which are then covered and sealed with mud (Wilsson 1971). Because of these similarities in dam and lodge construction, dam-construction behavior in beaver may have evolved from lodge-construction behavior (Richard 1964). Lodges are usually built in the center of the pond created by the dam; if water flow is deep and fast, they may be placed along the shore edge. The beaver colony does not pack the top of the lodge with mud but leaves a vent hole for gas exchange. Also, one or two exits are created in the center of the lodge to allow colony members access to the surrounding water. The living quarters in the lodge may be about two meters wide and 0.6 meter high (Buckley 1950).

The lodge is more than a secure home site, protecting beaver from gray wolves, feral dogs, and other predators. It also provides occupants with a relatively warm microclimate to survive the rigors of winter (Dyck and MacArthur 1993). Mean monthly temperatures within the living quarters of lodges are always higher in winter than mean monthly air or water temperatures. For example, the mean temperature within beaver lodges in Manitoba, Canada, in February was about 11°C, while water and air temperatures were around 2°C and -18°C, respectively. Furthermore, temperatures within the lodge may only vary a degree over the course of the entire winter (Stephenson 1969). The comfort of the lodge's microclimate can be witnessed by observing plumes of warm air coming from the vent on the top of lodges occupied by a beaver colony in winter. Thus, the lodge buffers a beaver colony from the winter cold, which ultimately reduces energy loss and food requirements.

A second winter adaptation in beaver is food caching (Hill 1982). Like eastern chipmunks and red squirrels (see essays 9 and 14 in chap. 7), beaver larder-hoard food for winter use. Caches are usually established north of the 38-degree latitude and less often south of this latitude (Hill 1982), corresponding to about southern Ohio and Maryland in the mid-eastern states. The cache is formed from August through October, being established later (rather than earlier) during autumn in more southerly latitudes (Aleksuik 1970a; Svendsen 1980a). The cache is actually a "raft" consisting of two types of woody material: low preference or nonfood items and preferred food items (Roberts 1937; Slough 1978). Low preference or nonfood items might be alder, peeled aspen logs, or spruce logs; depending on geographic location, examples of preferred food items include sugar maple, aspen, and tulip poplar (Slough 1978; Svendsen 1980a). Low preference or nonfood items are placed in the upper layers of the raft, and preferred food items are put in the lower layers. Then as the raft sinks, it becomes waterlogged (Slough 1978), so that even when the upper layers of the cache are frozen in the ice, the lower layers with food remain ice-free and are usable by beaver throughout winter. In lower latitudes, the cache may not be completely depleted during winter.

A third means by which beaver circumvent the rigors of winter is by depressing their metabolic rates (Aleksuik and Cowan 1969a). As the amount of daylight diminishes in autumn, thyroid activity is lowered, thereby reducing metabolic rates during autumn and into winter. In northerly latitudes a lower metabolism may decrease food intake by as much as 40 percent in winter compared to summer. Hence, metabolic rates in beaver vary seasonally, providing these mammals with an excellent way of matching energy expenditure with the food availability in the environment.

A final winter adaptation in beaver is their ability to store up to 30 to 40 percent of their body weight in fat during autumn (Aleksuik and Cowan 1969b). Fat is stored throughout the body in a manner similar to that of the woodchuck (see essay 10 in chap. 7). Beaver also store fat in the tail, which can swell to about twice its thickness to accommodate increased fat (Aleksuik 1970b). However, unlike woodchuck, beaver tend to rely on body fat in early spring more so than in winter. Adults with young in the colonies lose more body fat (-12%) and tail fat (-6%) compared to adults without young (Smith and Jenkins 1997).

In summary, American beaver have evolved a very interesting and intricate way of life to cope with seasonal changes in food and climate. Their ability to construct a well-protected home site, store food for winter use, reduce metabolism, and use stored body fat during early spring as an energy source have played a major role in adapting these interesting mammals to a wide range of aquatic habitats stretching from Alaska to northern Mexico.

9

Mice, Rats, and Voles

Family Muridae

Description of the Family Muridae

The family Muridae is the largest mammalian family in the order Rodentia, containing 1,336 species of mice, rats, and voles. At one time, this family was divided into two families, Muridae and Cricetidae, which separated Old World from New World species, respectively. Today most authorities, however, agree that there are enough similarities between these two subgroups to warrant a single family status. The murids are found worldwide, except for Antarctica, certain Arctic and oceanic islands, New Zealand, and parts of the West Indies.

Eighteen, or about one in every five mammalian species found in the mid-eastern states, are murids (see table 1). The number of species varies from seventeen species in Virginia to eight in Delaware. White-footed mice, Norway rats, house mice, meadow voles, woodland voles, and common muskrats occur in all eight states, whereas certain species, like cotton mice and hispid cotton rats, have a limited distribution. Three species of murids, that is, Norway rats, black rats, and house mice, are exotic, having been introduced from Eurasia into the mid-eastern states and much of North America. These three Old World species are sometimes referred to as commensals because of their close association with humans and dwellings (see essay 19 below). Mice and rats are quite similar in morphology, with large ears and eyes and a relatively long, naked tail. Rats in the mid-eastern states tend to be considerably larger (231–457 mm and 40–456 g in total length and weight, respectively) than mice (112–209 mm and 9–51 g). Some mice, termed *voles*, have inconspicuous ears and eyes, a short tail, and are more mole-like than mouse-like in appearance. Most voles are small (88–193 mm and 14–70 g), whereas the common muskrat is considerably larger (45–64 cm and 908–1,816 g). Most murids have only sixteen teeth.

Murids typically are found in a variety of terrestrial habitats; however, muskrats are well adapted to aquatic habitats, and woodland voles are very subterranean in their way of life. Home sites used by murids include burrow systems, cavities in trees or logs, refugia under logs, or lodges (such as for muskrats).

Murids may be nocturnal, crepuscular, or diurnal, depending on the species. Food habits vary from being herbivorous, insectivorous, or omnivorous. Most species are solitary, but some, like house mice, are communal. Territoriality is exhibited in certain species, such as common muskrats.

Murids in the mid-eastern states are very prolific. Most species have two to four litters per year, although the number of litters may range from only one in the eastern harvest mouse to as many as twelve per year in the Norway rat. Similarly, murids often have two to six young per litter, but litter size can be as high as twenty-two young in Norway rats. Gestation is shortest in the southern red-backed vole (17–19 days) and longest in the Appalachian woodrat (30–37 days). All murids are born helpless, blind, and naked and are weaned within about three weeks. Many of our murid species can breed as early as two to three months after birth.

Family Muridae

ESSAY 18

What's Happening to the Appalachian Woodrat?

"What is happening to the Appalachian woodrat in the mid-eastern states?" is an important question for wildlife biologists. This question becomes even more intriguing when we consider the fact that, like the Appalachian cottontail (see essay 7 in chap. 6), this woodrat has been recognized as a distinct species only since the mid-1990s (Jones et al. 1997). At one time, the Appalachian woodrat was classified as a subspecies of the eastern woodrat. However, despite a similar phylogeny (Planz, Zimmerman, Spradling, and Akins 1996), these two woodrat species are sufficiently distinct in cranial characteristics and genetics to warrant separate taxonomic status (Hayes and Harrison 1992; Hayes and Richmond 1993).

A century ago, the range of the Appalachian woodrat extended from western New Jersey (perhaps also western Connecticut) and southern New York southwestward to western Tennessee, northern Alabama, and northwestern Georgia (Hall 1981). The range of its cousin, the eastern woodrat, stretched from the southeastern states (except southern Florida) westward to eastern Colorado and eastern Texas.

Appalachian woodrats apparently were abundant as recently as the 1930s and 1940s in many of the mid-eastern states, such as Pennsylvania (Hall 1985). However, since the mid-twentieth century, wildlife biologists have become concerned about declining Appalachian woodrat populations in the mid-eastern states. In the 1960s populations of Appalachian woodrats were extirpated (or nearly so) from New Jersey and New York and declined dramatically in eastern Pennsylvania (Balcom and Yahner 1996; Whitaker and Hamilton 1998). Today all populations of Appalachian woodrats in the mid-eastern states are in trouble, except possibly those in Virginia (see table 1). Yet even in Virginia, wildlife biologists are uncertain whether or not woodrat populations are declining (Mengak 1998).

Populations of Appalachian woodrats have also exhibited declines just west of the mid-eastern states; in Indiana, for instance, Appalachian wood-rats are currently found only in a limited number of sites in the south-central part of the state; at these sites, numbers of woodrats have dropped from the 1980s and into the 1990s (Johnson and Madej 1993; Johnson, Berkley, and Fisher 1997). Therefore, the contemporary dilemma facing wildlife biologists is that now we have a "new" mammalian species whose regional populations are disappearing or decreasing at a rapid rate with no solid evidence to explain these population changes (Hicks 1989; Balcom and Yahner 1996). Conservation efforts for this new species are further complicated because much of our understanding of the natural history of Appalachian woodrats has been extrapolated from studies of eastern wood-rats in more westerly locations (e.g., Rainey 1956).

At least four possible reasons have been given to explain the recent demise of Appalachian woodrat populations. First, acorns are a major win-ter food source for woodrats. Thus, some biologists have speculated that oak defoliation and its concomitant reduction on acorn production in the mid-eastern states of New Jersey, New York, and Pennsylvania may be a factor causing woodrat declines (Hall 1988). However, the major epidemics of gypsy moth populations have spread through these states a few decades after documented declines in woodrat populations (Yahner 2000).

Raccoon populations have been implicated as a second potential rea-son woodrat population declined (Kazacos 1982). Because raccoons prefer agricultural areas (Sonenshine and Winslow 1972), sites used by woodrats near agricultural areas may overlap home ranges of individual raccoons. Raccoons can carry a parasitic roundworm, which is harmless to them but fatal to woodrats (Kazacos 1982). The Appalachian woodrat, like the eastern woodrat and its "packrat" cousins in the West, larder-hoard food for winter use (Post, Reichman, and Wooster 1993). Hence, woodrats may pick up and transport raccoon feces back to caches; consumption of these roundworm-infected feces then kill woodrats (McGowan 1993). This par-asite is suspected of being a major culprit in the decline of woodrats from New Jersey and New York, but evidence for contamination of woodrat caches with raccoon roundworm is lacking in Pennsylvania (McGowan 1993; Balcom and Yahner 1996).

A third possible reason given for woodrat declines may be forest fragmentation. At least in Pennsylvania, fragmentation is probably not directly involved with the demise of the Appalachian woodrat because sites historically occupied (in the 1950s) versus those used more recently (1980s) did not differ in the amount of forest and urban cover in the surrounding landscape (Balcom and Yahner 1996). Rather, the extent of forest is actually increasing in Pennsylvania about 1 percent every ten years due to farmland conversion and forest maturation (Powell and Considine 1982).

A fourth factor proposed for the decline in populations of Appalachian woodrats is a change in tree species composition via natural plant succession (Balcom and Yahner 1996). Forests once dominated by oak are now converting to later-successional, shade-tolerant tree species like red maple, black cherry, and eastern hemlock (Abrams and Nowacki 1992; Widmann 1994). These late-successional tree species do not provide preferred food (e.g., acorns) for woodrats. Trees found on sites used by woodrats historically in Pennsylvania, for example, are now characterized mainly by red maple (Balcom and Yahner 1996), and sites used historically in the highlands of New York now contain a considerable amount of eastern hemlock in the surrounding forest (Charney 1980). Also, tree species composition in much of the eastern forest changed by the 1940s because the American chestnut, which probably provided a major food resource for the Appalachian woodrat (Newcombe 1930; Poole 1940), was nearly eradicated by a disease called the chestnut blight (Yahner 2000).

An understanding of causal factor(s) to explain "what is happening to the Appalachian woodrat in the mid-eastern states?" will need further research. A single factor is probably not solely responsible for these population declines. Furthermore, we know that the forest of the mid-eastern states is dynamic and considerably different from what it was decades ago. Hence, the future outlook for Appalachian woodrat populations may depend in part on their ability to adapt to changing forest conditions in the mid-eastern states and on continued efforts by state wildlife agencies to develop conservation strategies (Balcom and Yahner 1996).

E S S A Y   1 9

Commensal Mice in the New World

Mammals have been admired and harvested or domesticated for food, clothing, and other resources since early times in human history. Yet, as we survey the different kinds of mammals, three groups of mammals seem to be unduly feared or despised by humans: bats, large predators, and rodents. Bats have been given bad press because of unfounded fears associated with folklores or myths, like "they fly in your hair." Large predators were historically hated and persecuted to near extinction because of our fear of the big bad wolf (see essay 29 in chap. 11) or because they prey occasionally on livestock or other domesticated animals. Rodents also felt the wrath of humans with sayings like "your apartment looks like a rat's nest" or "you dirty rat." However, our fear and dislike for rodents are largely unfounded and unwarranted; instead, we can pretty much blame our negativism toward rodents on just three commensal species of rodents: house mice, black rats, and Norway rats (Delaney 1984).

The term *commensal* refers to sharing the table with humans and relates to the close association that these species have with humans since the earliest of times. Fear and dislike of these commensal rodents began many centuries ago in the Old World. Mouse outbreaks were a common and dreaded phenomenon in Asia and Europe (see essay 20 below) (Doutt, Heppenstall, and Guilday 1977; Jackson 1982). Population irruptions of house mice in Europe in historic times, for instance, resulted in large numbers of mice wandering the countryside eating most anything edible, in a manner reminiscent of locust outbreaks that we occasionally hear about today in the media. Outbreaks of rat populations struck fear in humans because these rodents were hosts to fleas and lice, which carried infectious, fatal diseases that caused massive loss of human life in much of Europe

Family Muridae

and Asia. From about 3,500 years ago to about the year 1720, 195 plagues were recorded in Europe and Asia; these plagues, although poorly understood at the time, were later attributed to disease transmitted by high populations of black and Norway rats. In fact, one-third of the human population in Europe died from these plagues during the Middle Ages.

Two of the diseases collectively called "the plague" were bubonic plague and typhus (Jackson 1982). Bubonic plague was last recorded in the United States (Los Angeles) in 1924. It is caused by a bacterium transmitted by flea bites or fecal contamination associated with rats; it is fatal to humans in 30 to 75 percent of all cases (Dickey 1986). One form of typhus, known as New World typhus, was reported during the early 1940s in Lavaca County, Texas (Whitaker and Hamilton 1998). New World typhus is also attributed to a bacterium transmitted via the bites of rat fleas; this disease can cause death in humans, but the likelihood of fatality is much lower compared to bubonic plague.

In short, the three commensal murids seem to be troublemakers everywhere they go, which today is virtually worldwide (Anderson 1964). In the mid-eastern states house mice are common in granaries, corncribs, and croplands associated with farms, and even occasionally occur as noncommensals in managed forest stands (Kirkland 1977; Petras and Topping 1981; Jackson 1982; Yahner 1988). Likewise, Norway and black rats are found in a variety of situations in close association with humans or in more natural habitats as noncommensals (Robitaille and Bovet 1976; Jackson 1982; Stroud 1982).

Who invited these commensals to the New World and our mid-eastern states? House mice and black rats arrived in the New World on ships with early colonists and explorers in the seventeenth and early eighteenth century (Doutt, Heppenstall, and Guilday 1977; Jackson 1982). Norway rats made their way a little later on ships to the New World, sometime around the American Revolution (about 1775). Once the aggressive Norway rats became established, they easily displaced black rats from most of the northern states, including the mid-eastern states.

We can raise two interesting questions about these very successful and adaptable newcomers. First, besides being the vectors of human diseases historically and to some extent today, what other problems are attributed to these murids? Second, what measures can be taken to mitigate the problems caused by these murids? To address the first question, we can divide the problems caused by murids into three categories: problems directly affecting humans, indirectly affecting humans, and directly affecting other wildlife. In addition to having a direct effect on humans as vectors of diseases, Norway and black rats inflict bites at an estimated rate of one in every 100,000 humans (Jackson 1982). Rat bites usually afflict young children and infirmed adults, causing physical and emotional harm; on rare occasions, rat bites can be fatal.

These commensals can have indirect effects on people by damaging property and food. Economic losses attributed to the two rat species (Norway and black combined) is at least $10 per year per rat (1970 U.S. dollars), or about $0.5–1.0 billion per year in the United States alone (Jackson 1982; Whitaker and Hamilton 1998). Commensal rats and mice gnaw on insulation in human dwellings, causing about 25 percent of the fires of undetermined origin in homes and buildings. Gnawing on wire also can result in power outages and communication interruptions. These commensal rodents feed on crops and stored grain intended for consumption by humans or farm animals; moreover, feces, urine, and hair in grain reduce the quality of these foodstuffs. On the other hand, one positive indirect effect of commensal murids has been their tremendous value for use as lab animals in medical and behavioral research over recent decades. Studies conducted on the white mouse and white rat, which are domesticated versions of house mice and Norway rats, respectively, have provided beneficial information for an understanding and treatment of many physical and mental diseases in humans, for example, alcoholism, obesity, and stress.

From a conservation perspective, commensal murids have been an ecological disaster from the time they set foot in any new land. This has been particularly true on islands, where endemic fauna, for example, ground-nesting birds, are very vulnerable to predation by introduced populations of black and Norway rats (Diamond 1985). Birds and other fauna on islands typically evolved in the absence of predators and are thereby defenseless against aggressive predators, like the Old World rats. Because of their burrowing habits and larger body size, Norway rats appear to be much more detrimental than black rats to island bird populations, such as seabird colonies (Hobson, Drever, and Kaiser 1999).

Conservationists must be concerned about the potential impact of exotic species in general on native fauna and their habitats. However, winning the war against certain exotics, like commensal rats, will be an uphill battle because of misconceptions about the nature and magnitude of the problems, fear of negative public reactions to eradication programs, and the labor-intensive nature of these programs (Temple 1990). Furthermore, eradication campaigns directed at rats are costly and potentially risky to native fauna and their habitats (Hobson et al. 1999). One reason for the high cost of rat-eradication efforts is that rats learn to avoid traps (Lefebvre, Holler, and Decker 1985). Hence, the eradication of commensal rodents will not be feasible in the mid-eastern states or most other places. A more reasonable approach to dealing with commensal rodent populations is to create a "clean" environment by enforcing garbage storage regulations and properly storing foodstuffs in homes, and using traps and poisons carefully (Jackson 1982; Bomford and O'Brien 1995; Whitaker and Hamilton 1998).

I must emphasize that not all exotic species have a negative impact on other biota or their environments, and some actually play positive ecological roles (Lugo 1990). A case in point is the high importance of exotic flowering plants as energy (nectar) sources for native butterfly populations. These exotic plants, located along field edges and logging roads, are used by a sizable number of native butterfly species in agricultural and forested landscapes of the mid-eastern states (Yahner 1998).

"Mouse Outbreaks" or

Why Do Vole Populations Cycle?

Humans have historically been well aware of "mouse outbreaks." Through-out the Old World, irruptions of mouse or rat populations were feared be-cause they seemed to be linked with devastating plagues that killed large numbers of humans (see essay 19 above). Beginning in the early twentieth century, biologists in Norway began to take a serious look at the ecology of "mouse outbreaks" by examining dramatic population fluctuations in a group of vole-like mammals, known as lemmings. Over the past few dec-ades, periodic fluctuations in populations, or cycles, have been given con-siderable attention by ecologists; however, no consensus has been reached regarding the cause(s) of these cycles (Krebs 1996). As a result, vole pop-ulation cycles have been described as the best-known "unsolved mystery" in mammalian ecology (Lidicker 1988).

The vole population cycle, which is sometimes termed the "micro-tine cycle," is typically three to four years in duration. This cycle is quite short compared to the longer cycles in leporids (see essay 8 in chap. 6) and common muskrats (see essay 21 below). The vole cycle consists of low, increase, peak, and decline phases (see fig. 11); vole densities generally range twentyfold from the start of the increase phase to the peak phase (Krebs, Gaines, Keller, Myers, and Tamarin 1973). In a Maryland study, densities of meadow voles increased even more dramatically, ranging from less than three voles per hectare to nearly 400 voles per hectare (133-fold difference) over a four-year period (Jett and Nichols 1987). A study of a western species of vole (montane vole) reported that populations increased about seventy-five-fold, from less than three voles per hectare to nearly 225 voles per hectare within only a five-month period (Negus, Berger, and Forsland 1977). This rapid increase in population numbers within only a few years is possible because voles have exceptional reproductive capabilities, ranking them among the world's most prolific mammals (Johnson and Johnson 1982). For example, in some vole species, breeding can occur at three weeks of age, gestation is twenty to twenty-three days, and litters are produced year-round in more southerly latitudes.

At least two facts have emerged from studies of vole cycles. First, at the increase phase, smaller individuals in the population tend to disperse, whereas larger individuals often remain through peak and decline phases (Boonstra and Krebs 1979). The tendency for large individual voles to remain at peak and decline phases appears to be related to behavior and mating habits of a given species. For instance, the meadow vole in the northernmost latitudes (e.g., Canada) of their range is not only more docile but produces more and larger litters compared to the more aggressive prairie vole, which has fewer and smaller litters. Hence, relative to each other, the meadow vole is more of an r-strategist, and the prairie vole tends to be a K-strategist. The larger body size in the northerly meadow vole is adaptive by better ensuring that individuals can divert more energy to breeding. Conversely, large body size in the prairie vole allows these individuals to better compete with smaller conspecifics for space and important resources.

A second fact regarding vole cycles is that they occur in a variety of habitats from lemmings of the frozen tundra to meadow voles of temperate regions. There have been at least three studies, however, which show possible exceptions to a cyclic trend in vole populations. These include noncyclic populations of beach voles on islands (Tamarin 1977), prairie voles in manipulated shortgrass prairies where immigration is not feasible (Abramsky and Tracy 1979), and woodland voles occupying orchards, which represent unnatural habitats for this species (Anthony, Simpson, and Kelly 1986).

Vole population cycles may be caused by two general set of factors: extrinsic and intrinsic (Lidicker 1988; Krebs 1996). Examples of extrinsic, or environmental, factors are food availability, predation pressures, and weather. Intrinsic factors, which are characteristic of individuals comprising the population, may involve stress, spacing behavior related to resource availability (e.g., territoriality), or spacing behavior that is genetically linked (often termed the *Chitty hypothesis*).

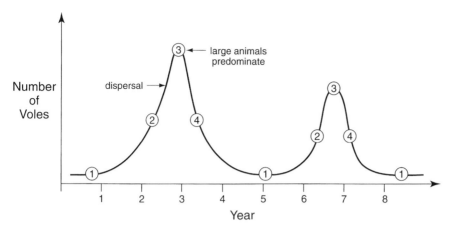

Figure 11. The population cycle in voles, showing the low (1), increase (2), peak (3), and decline (4) phases.

The debate over the role of various extrinsic and/or intrinsic factors in causing vole cycles continues today, and most mammalogists concur that a single factor does not seem to offer an explanation for this phenomenon. One prominent hypothesis recently published contends that vole cycles are a product of an interaction between extrinsic factors, for example, food and predation, and intrinsic factors involving spacing behavior (Krebs 1996). A second notable hypothesis has proposed that vole cycles are a function of a complex interacting set of four extrinsic and four intrinsic factors (Lidicker 1988). Some of these representative factors are food and water resources, predation pressure, reproduction characteristics (e.g., litter size), and stress. Assuming that vole cycles are a product of several factors, the next challenge is to understand how these factors affect individual animals at different phases of the cycle (Gaines, Stenseth, Johnson, Ims, and Bondrup-Nielsen 1991).

In summary, I think it is fair to state that scientists actively involved with seeking explanations for vole cycles believe that some progress is being made to provide answers to the whys and hows of these cycles. However, a complete insight into this mammalian enigma will require additional comparative and long-term experimental studies of various vole populations and species.

Family Muridae

Muskrat Cycles and Waterfowl Management

From an economic perspective, the common muskrat is one of the most valuable furbearers because of its luxuriant, waterproof underfur (Perry 1982). Muskrats are common in much of North America, but they are being replaced in some southern states by nutria, which are introduced rodents from South America. Nutria also are valuable furbearers, especially in some states, such as Louisiana (Whitaker and Hamilton 1998).

Although closely related to voles, the common muskrat is more beaver-like in its way of life (Perry 1982). Muskrats are excellent swimmers, and their hind feet are webbed with stiff hairs along the sides of toes and feet. These webbed feet serve as paddles, and their laterally flattened tails act as rudders. As true of beaver, muskrats den in banks or build lodges (Brooks and Dodge 1986; Kurta 1995). Bank dens are placed along edges of lakes, rivers, or streams, particularly if the immediate shoreline is elevated. Lodges are built in shallow (<0.6 m deep) marshes and ponds; they are about 2 meters in diameter and 1.2 meters in height, with an underwater entrance (Kurta 1995; Whitaker and Hamilton 1998). Lodges usually are found when water levels in marshes or ponds are relatively constant; lodge densities usually range from one to seven per hectare in good habitat. Also, like beaver, muskrat are territorial; but unlike beaver, muskrat are not colonial (see essay 16 in chap. 8).

Muskrats feed on lush aquatic vegetation, such as cattail and bulrush (Perry 1982). The relationship between the abundance of muskrats and the availability of emergent vegetation is the key factor driving population cycles in this rodent. Compared to relatively predictable cycles in leporids and voles (e.g., 8–12 years and 3–4 years, respectively; see essay 8 in chap. 6 and essay 20 above), the duration of muskrat population cycles

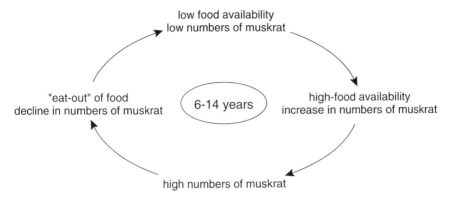

Figure 12. The population cycle in common muskrats.

seems to be more unpredictable (6–14 years), with cycles being longer rather than shorter in less favorable habitats.

The muskrat population cycle can be divided into four phases (Perry 1982) (see fig. 12). We can arbitrarily begin the cycle at a phase characterized by reduced muskrat numbers and low food availability. During the second phase, food availability increases, which in turn results in a rise in muskrat numbers in response to the greater amounts of food. The third phase occurs when muskrat populations reach carrying capacity in relation to the food supply. In this phase, populations can reach densities of about eighty individuals per hectare, which can be visualized as about forty individuals (or lodges) in a marsh about the size of a football field! The fourth phase of the muskrat cycle begins when high numbers of muskrats deplete food resources, causing an "eat-out." In this latter phase, many muskrats starve; populations then decline, and the cycle is restarted.

Other aspects of the population biology of muskrats, besides densities, are tied to food availability. For instance, body size and reproductive potential of individual muskrats can also vary among different phases of the cycle (Dozier, Markley, and Llewellyn 1948; Neal 1968). Muskrats weigh more, produce more and larger litters, and have a longer breeding season in the second (increasing) phase compared to the fourth (decreasing) phase. Furthermore, from an ecological perspective, marshes, ponds,

Family Muridae

and similar habitats occupied by muskrats can be damaged during the fourth phase of the cycle (Perry 1982). If populations of muskrats are left unchecked by wildlife managers, the "eat-out" can cause devastating extended losses of both food and cover and occasionally force muskrats to dig into the bottom of marshes and ponds for plant roots (Lowery 1974).

Wildlife managers agree that optimal muskrat habitat in marshes and ponds must include a combination of adequate food resources and relatively constant but shallow water levels (15–60 cm deep) (Bellrose and Brown 1941; Gashwiler 1948; Glass 1952; Perry 1982). However, marshes are very dynamic and may naturally alternate from being dominated by emergent vegetation to being nearly free of vegetation (Weller 1978). Prolonged flooding of a marsh can kill important food for muskrat, such as cattails (Errington 1948), thereby forcing wildlife managers to intervene by lowering water levels, thereby simulating the growth of emergent vegetation (Phillips 1979). Because muskrat populations are relatively low in marshes predominated by either dense emergent vegetation or open water, a challenge for wildlife managers interested in managing both waterfowl and muskrat populations is to maintain a "hemi-marsh" of about 50 percent emergent vegetation and 50 percent open water; a hemi-marsh condition is valuable habitat for an impressive number of waterfowl species (Weller and Spatcher 1965; Weller 1978).

We can view the common muskrat of the mideastern states as sharing many characteristics of the way of life of a much larger aquatic rodent, the American beaver. Like the beaver, the muskrat can modify the environment for a diversity of wildlife and has been intensively exploited as a furbearer (Boutin and Birkenholz 1987). But at least in one ecological respect, the muskrat is more similar to its vole cousins by exhibiting dramatic population fluctuations.

Lyme Disease and the Mouse-Deer-Acorn Connection

Lyme disease has become a serious concern for many of us who spend time in the outdoors, particularly if we are from certain parts of the United States, such as the East Coast or upper Midwest (Booth 1991). Lyme disease initially was diagnosed in 1975 near Lyme, Connecticut (Ostfeld 1997), hence the origin of its name. But there are hints in the literature that this disease existed during the turn of the twentieth century in Massachusetts, New York, and Europe (Ginsberg 1994). Since the early 1990s the number of reported Lyme disease cases in humans has risen rapidly (Ginsberg 1994; Fraser et al. 1997). Today, the disease is reported in all of the lower forty-eight states (Ostfeld 1997); interestingly, nearly 77 percent of the 9,677 cases recorded in the United States in 1992 were from three mid-eastern states (New Jersey, New York, and Pennsylvania), plus three others in the Northeast (Connecticut, Massachusetts, and Rhode Island) (Stafford 1993).

One factor contributing to reported increases in the incidences of this disease has been a better familiarity with its symptoms. These symptoms may initially include a circular rash that develops at the site of the tick bite (Ostfeld 1997). Later symptoms include flu-like fever and muscle aches, which are often followed by arthritis and damage to the nervous system and heart (Barbour and Fish 1993; Gage, Ostfeld, and Olson 1995). Therefore, we can see how this disease was, and still can be, confused with other ailments, diseases, and illnesses such as influenza and arthritis. Lyme disease also can cause fever, arthritis, and lameness in dogs, cats, and domestic animals, but it presumably has minimal or no effect on most wildlife species (Ginsberg 1994).

A second factor responsible for greater incidences of Lyme disease since the early 1990s is the increased density and the expanding geographic distribution of a major vector, the deer tick (Spielman 1988). Reasons for higher numbers and the rapid spread of deer tick populations are speculative but include higher deer populations associated with humans in suburban and rural areas, increased outdoor recreational activities by humans, and landscape changes that create favorable habitat for ticks (Ginsberg 1994). As an aside, the deer tick should not be confused with the larger wood (dog) tick, which is common in much of the mid-eastern states; the wood tick does not transmit Lyme disease.

White-tailed deer, white-footed mice, and deer ticks are linked together in a somewhat complicated two-year cycle (see fig. 13). Deer ticks have four life stages: eggs, larvae, nymphs, and adults; egg and larval stages occur in the first year of the cycle, and nymphal and adult stages are found in the second year. Eggs hatch into larvae in midsummer, and they actively seek hosts from midsummer to early autumn (Ginsberg 1994). Because the Lyme disease bacterium (or spirochete) is seldom transmitted in ticks from mother to young, eggs and larvae are rarely infected with the bacterium (Gage, Ostfeld, and Olson 1995). Instead, larval ticks acquire the bacterium by feeding on infected competent hosts; these hosts probably become infected earlier in the summer when they are fed upon by nymphs in the second year of their life cycle (a competent host is one that can harbor the spirochete in its bloodstream). Over thirty mammalian and fifty avian host species have already been reported for larvae and nymphs (Stafford 1993), and these hosts are typically small vertebrates, for example, birds and small mammals (Van Buskirk and Ostfeld 1995). Of these smaller hosts, the white-footed mouse stands out as being the most competent (Fish and Daniels 1990). In contrast, adult ticks prefer to feed on larger hosts such as deer and humans (Van Buskirk and Ostfeld 1995). Interestingly, most cases of Lyme disease transmission to humans are caused by nymphs because this life stage is smaller than adult ticks and, therefore, is harder to detect on the human body. Furthermore, nymphs actively seek hosts in summer when humans are often enjoying the outdoors. Adult ticks, on the other hand, are most active in spring and autumn (Stafford 1993; Gage, Ostfeld, and Olson 1995).

Two questions can be asked about Lyme disease. First, can wildlife and land managers implement management strategies to mitigate greater incidences or spread of this disease? Second, how can we protect our-

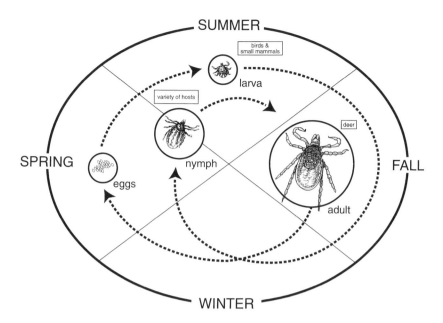

Figure 13. The two-year cycle of the deer tick.

selves from Lyme disease? A plausible strategy that has been proposed to reduce the spread of deer ticks and Lyme disease is a deer-reduction program; the white-tailed deer is a major host of deer ticks and suspected of contributing to the range expansion of the deer tick (Ginsberg 1994). Yet in areas reporting Lyme disease, a lowering of deer populations has not reduced tick populations or incidences of Lyme disease (Wilson and Deblinger 1993). Other methods of control, including mowing and burning of habitat used by ticks, have temporarily reduced tick populations, but they rebound in a year or less (Wilson 1986).

Perhaps an alternative and ecologically interesting way to reduce the spread of Lyme disease is provide a diversity of habitat types at both local and regional scales, which would in effect ensure habitat conditions for a variety of small mammal species (Anthony, Niles, and Spring 1981; Yahner 1988). If several small mammal species can coexist in an area containing deer ticks, the chances of deer ticks selecting the most competent host, for example, the white-footed mouse, would be reduced if incompetent hosts, such as shrew and other species of mice, were abundant in the area (Van Buskirk and Ostfeld 1995). Thus, a high diversity of both habitat conditions and small mammal species could dilute the transmission of Lyme disease in wild animals and humans.

The linkages among deer, mice, and ticks become even more intriguing when we introduce acorns into the Lyme disease picture. Deer feed extensively on acorns in the autumn, and they may shift their home ranges to areas with high concentrations of acorns on the forest floor (McShea and Schwede 1993). Some of the deer moving to these acorn sources could conceivably have infected deer ticks attached to them; the larval ticks produced by these adult ticks in the following spring could then become infected with the spirochete by feeding on resident white-footed mice containing the bacterium (Ostfeld, Miller, and Hazler 1996; Ostfeld 1997). These infected larvae would mature the next year (year 2); thus, given a two-year tick cycle, incidences of Lyme disease in humans using these forested areas while camping, hiking, and so on, could peak two summers following the abundant autumn crop.

As many as 25–35 percent of the nymphs and 50–70 percent of adult ticks can be infected by the bacterium in areas with Lyme disease epidemics (Ostfeld 1997). Hence, if we spend time in the outdoors in areas heavily infested with deer ticks, we need to be cautious and use common sense. Exposed areas, such as arms and legs, should be covered with long-sleeved shirts and pants that are tucked into socks. Light-colored clothing should be worn to better detect ticks, and insect repellent containing DEET should be applied. After returning from the outdoors, immediately inspect your clothing and body for ticks. Remember that larval deer ticks are about the size of a printed period, and nymphs are not much larger, making them very difficult to detect on humans and pets. Since January 1999 a vaccine has become available for humans to reduce the chance of contracting Lyme disease. If the disease is contracted, it can be treated with antibiotics (Ostfeld 1997).

Gypsy Moths and the Mouse-Acorn Connection

White-footed mice are not only linked in an intricate way with incidences of Lyme disease (see essay 22 above), but this common small mammal of the mid-eastern states has also played an important ecological role in keeping populations of gypsy moths at innocuous levels (Smith 1985). The gypsy moth is the major exotic insect pest in the eastern deciduous forest (Cutter, Renwick, and Renwick 1991). It arrived in Massachusetts, back in 1869, when a French scientist, Leopold Trouvelot, brought the moth from Europe to start a silk industry. Eventually some moths escaped in the wild, and by 1910 they had spread to Connecticut, eastern Massachusetts, and Vermont. Visible defoliation of forests was evident in New York by 1934 and in Pennsylvania by 1968. Currently, gypsy moths are found in at least seventeen northeastern states (Skelly, Davis, Merrill, and Cameron 1989; Sharov, Mayo, and Leonard 1998), and they are spreading about twenty kilometers per year (Liebhold, Halverson, and Elmes 1992).

My initial exposure to the devastating impact of gypsy moth defoliation occurred when I took an airline flight from Minneapolis to State College in midsummer 1981 when the moth "front" initially moved westward into the State College area. As I looked down from the jet, a brown (defoliated) landscape was to the east and a green (foliated) landscape was to the west, going almost through the center of the State College borough. The gypsy moth front had been stopped a few weeks earlier via aerial pesticide spray and left in its wake an impressive visual picture of the effects of extensive gypsy moth defoliation on forests east versus west of the borough. When I later moved to State College in autumn 1981, our new neighbors told us there were so many gypsy moths in the early summer that they didn't want to sit outside and barbecue; also, if they listened

Family Muridae

carefully, they claimed that they could even hear the larvae "chewing" on the leaves in the canopy above!

Besides the negative aesthetic effects of gypsy moth defoliation, this forest pest can damage trees by reducing growth rates and even causing the death of poor-condition trees (Powell and Barnard 1982). Defoliation by gypsy moths also may reduce foods for wildlife by lowering acorn production of oak trees in heavily defoliated stands. Some wildlife, for example, black bears, will shift to alternate food resources when acorns become scarce (Kasbohm, Vaughan, and Kraus 1995). In addition, areas heavily defoliated by gypsy moths can indirectly cause higher rates of predation on forest bird nests by eliminating foliage around nests that otherwise would conceal the nests from predators (Thurber, McClain, and Whitmore 1994; Yahner and Mahan 1996).

Native predator species in the mid-eastern states have not effectively controlled gypsy moth populations for a few reasons (Smith 1985). First, because the gypsy moth is an exotic species, predator-prey relationships have not had ample time to evolve in the United States as compared to Eurasia. Second, gypsy moths have an interesting behavior, whereby older larvae descend and hide in bark crevices near the base of trees or even in leaf litter on the forest floor during the day; they then ascend into the foliage of trees to feed at night. By doing so, they tend to avoid predation by diurnal, canopy-foraging birds and nocturnal, forest-floor small mammals over the twenty-four-hour cycle (Campbell and Sloan 1976). Third, gypsy moth larvae are covered with abundant hairs, making them difficult to eat by predators (Smith 1985). Two predators undeterred by abundant hairs on larval gypsy moths, however, are black-billed and yellow-billed cuckoos.

The pupae, which is the next stage in the life cycle of the gypsy moth, is especially vulnerable to predation by white-footed mice and shrews in summer (Campbell and Sloan 1976; Smith 1985). For example, nearly two-thirds of the pupae in one study were preyed upon in leaf litter by small mammals (H. Smith 1989). Thus, the annual survivorship of gypsy moth pupae can decline with higher abundances of small mammals in mideastern forests. Let's now add a complicating factor, the availability of acorns in autumn. Densities of white-footed mice decrease dramatically in eastern deciduous forests following an autumn with poor acorn production because acorns are very important as a winter food resource for this mammal (Elkinton et al. 1996). As a result, mouse densities drop when acorn crops are poor, thereby resulting in lower predation on gypsy moth pupae in summer and a subsequent increase in gypsy moth densities.

In the long term, the major enemies of gypsy moths will continue to be introduced invertebrate predators, viral diseases, fungi, parasites, and insecticides (Leonard 1981; Smith 1985; Reardon 1995; Elkinton et al. 1996). However, white-footed mice are a vertebrate species that can potentially control innocuous levels of this insect pest. Habitat can be managed specifically for white-footed mice and other small mammals, such as shrews, by leaving stumps, logs, and tree cavities in the forest; these features provide home and resting sites for small mammals (Yahner and Smith 1991).

10

Porcupine

Family Erethizontidae

Description of the Family Erethizontidae

*T*he common porcupine is one of twelve species in the family
Erethizontidae and order Rodentia. This family is referred to
as New World porcupines because its range extends from the
Arctic in the north to northern Argentina in the south (Nowak
1999; Vaughan, Ryan, and Czaplewski 2000). A second family
of porcupines, known as the Old World porcupines, consists
of eleven species in the family Hystricidae of southern Europe,
southern Asia, Africa, and some East Indies islands. Both New
World and Old World porcupines have conspicuous quills
that evolved from modified guard hairs. Compared to New
World porcupines, those in the Old World tend to be less arboreal and more aggressive when provoked.

The common porcupine is the only member of its family

represented in North America. It occurs from Newfoundland and northern Alaska in the north to the mountainous regions of Maryland and northern Mexico in the south (Whitaker and Hamilton 1998; Nowak 1999). The common porcupine is found in five of the mid-eastern states (see table 1).

Porcupines are the second largest rodent in North America (64–79 cm in total length and 4–13 kg in weight), with the American beaver being the largest (see chap. 8). Porcupines have stocky bodies, small heads and ears, and short tails and legs; they are dark brown to blackish. The feet are naked and heavily soled with long claws for climbing in trees; the forefeet are very dexterous and capable of grasping objects between the claws and foot pads. The skull is massive from a rodent perspective, and like that of the American beaver, it contains twenty teeth.

Without question, the most unique feature of porcupines is their quills. Each animal is covered with about 30,000 quills on its dorsal surface (e.g., head, back, sides, and tail); dense fur covers its ventral surface. Quills on the neck (nape) and upper rump area are white-tipped, whereas others are whitish at the base and black-tipped. This dorsal grouping of white-tipped versus black-tipped quills gives porcupines somewhat of a black-and-white warning pattern for potential attackers, which is reminiscent of the conspicuous black-and-white pattern of skunks (see essay 39 in chap. 15). Quills are usually large, being approximately two millimeters in diameter and seventy-five millimeters in length. Because of color patterns and size, these quills were used often by Native Americans for decorative purposes.

Despite being a slow-moving animal, the porcupine is well protected by its quills from most predators. When initially provoked, a porcupine exhibits a show of force by erecting

Family Erethizontidae

quills via muscles on its back. If further provoked, it may make noises by rattling its teeth or emitting a pungent odor. Finally, if these defensive strategies fail, the porcupine relies on its quills for protection against predators.

Quills are excellent weapons. They are pointed tips with shingle-lapped barbules at the tip; the interiors are spongy to reduce breakage. Strong muscles in the porcupine's tail can drive quills two centimeters or more into the tissue of an attacker. Quills in the tail region are thinner than those elsewhere and, thus, are able to penetrate more easily into an attacker. Contrary to popular belief, a porcupine cannot throw quills at an attacker.

Once a quill is embedded in an attacker's tissue, the barbules at the tip expand. In addition, "grease" on a quill allows it to penetrate at a rate of about one millimeter per hour into the muscular tissue of the attacker as the muscle contracts. An attacker may die when a mouth full of quills leads to starvation or when a quill impales a vital organ. Interestingly, by using its incisors and dexterous forefeet, a porcupine can remove quills received during hostile encounters with a conspecific.

Common porcupines prefer forested habitats, although they may be found living in desert, tundra, and rangeland. They are strictly herbivorous, feeding at night on the forest floor or in trees in spring, summer, and autumn on a variety of food items, for example, twigs, buds, leaves, flowers, stems, roots, seeds, and nuts. In winter, porcupines rely on tree bark and conifer needles, often remaining high in a tree (see fig. 14). Unlike tree squirrels (see chap. 7), porcupines climb trees slowly and deliberately.

Porcupines do not hibernate and are typically solitary. Tree cavities, caves, rock crevices, or hollow logs are favorite den sites used during the day. Occasionally, porcupines den com-

Figure 14. Bark girdled from the base of a pine tree by a feeding porcupine. *(Photo by author; original figure appeared in the book* Eastern Deciduous Forest: Ecology and Wildlife Conservation, *copyrighted 1995 by the Regents of the University of Minnesota.)*

Family Erethizontidae

munally in winter; use of the same den site by more than one individual tends to occur when the number of sites is limited.

The porcupine is certainly not an average rodent. Besides being unique for its quills, it restricts the breeding season to late summer and early fall (September–November), and only a single pup or "porcupette" is born (without quills!) in spring (April–May). This is in marked contrast to some very prolific rodents, such as the murids (see essays 19 and 20 in chap. 9). Furthermore, gestation is between 205 and 215 days, which is more like that of a deer than a rodent. Porcupines also are relatively long-lived, with a lifespan of ten to twelve years compared to other rodents that usually live only one to three years.

Porcupine

The Role of Porcupines in Our Northern Forests

Porcupines may come into potential conflict with humans because they are fond of salt, some synthetic materials, and the inner bark of trees (Dodge 1982; Whitaker and Hamilton 1998). These rodents can find natural sources of salt in the outer bark of trees, bones and antlers found on the forest floor, and some species of aquatic plants. However, when porcupines chew on canoe paddles or axes because of the salty residue left by human perspiration, they can be viewed as pests. They also seek salt used along roadways during winter to treat ice and snow conditions.

Porcupines are known to gnaw on plywood signs and other building materials because of synthetic glues used in these materials. Other synthetic items, including tires, fuel and hydraulic lines on vehicles, seat covers, and electrical cables, may be nibbled by porcupines, causing potential problems ranging from loss of vehicular brakes to localized power outages.

A favorite food of porcupines during winter is the inner bark of certain tree species, such as maple, pine, and spruce. As a result of this feeding, bark is often girdled in the upper branches of preferred trees, which serves as a good indication that porcupines are in the vicinity. Thus, from a timber-industry perspective, porcupines may sometimes be regarded as a pest, especially in forest stands with high-quality, commercial timber but not necessarily so in stands where timber is not a major product (Dodge 1982). In some white pine stands, 40 to 70 percent of the individual trees have been damaged by the feeding activity of porcupines in winter (Tenneson and Oring 1985). This bark removal can reduce the vigor of individual trees for up to seven to ten years (Storm and Halvorson 1967), or it may result in tree mortality (Gill and Cordes 1972). Porcupine also feed on needles and branches of conifers, such as eastern hemlocks, during winter (Dodge 1982; Whitaker and Hamilton 1998). This type of feed-ing activity can actually be a positive because branches and twigs that drop to the ground may be an important source of browse for other wildlife, for example, snowshoe hares (Ferguson and Merriam 1978).

Wildlife agencies have historically imposed bounties on porcupines in states with a major timber industry, and the last bounty system on por-cupines was discontinued in New Hampshire in 1979 (Dodge 1982). There are other plausible ways of reducing the number of porcupines if they have a detrimental effect on localized timber stands. First, porcupine numbers may decline naturally as forest stands mature because this rodent has difficulty climbing large (>25 cm diameter at breast height) individual trees (Harder 1979). Selective removal of preferred tree species, such as eastern hemlock, may help to control porcupine numbers. In some areas of the Northeast, an exotic insect pest, the hemlock woolly adelgid, is causing widespread mortality of eastern hemlocks (Yahner 2000). Hence, any future loss of hemlocks by adelgid infestation could negatively affect porcupine populations (Griesemer, DeGraaf, and Fuller 1994).

An ecologically sound means of controlling porcupines is by manag-ing for populations of natural predators, such as bobcats, wolverines, and fishers. Of these three species, the fisher, which is one of the largest mem-bers of the weasel family (see chap. 14), is the most efficient predator. A fisher kills a porcupine by flipping it on its back, thereby exposing the prey's vulnerable underside (Banfield 1974; Powell 1981). Adult males probably hunt porcupines more often than do adult females because only 0.3 percent of adult female versus 5 percent of adult male fishers were ob-served with embedded porcupine quills (Arthur, Krohn, and Gilbert 1989; Kuehn 1989).

In Michigan, populations of porcupine declined 76 percent over a thirteen-year period once fishers were reintroduced into the state (Powell and Brander 1977). Conversely, when fisher numbers are low, porcupine populations may increase (Gill and Cordes 1972). Fisher populations have been reintroduced successfully into many states in recent years, includ-ing two mid-eastern states—New York and Pennsylvania (see essay 36 in chap. 14).

In summary, the well-armed, slow-moving porcupine is hated by some because of its negative impact on certain tree species, but wildlife biologists and foresters generally agree that damage by porcupines to forests is usually negligible and, if present, can be tolerated. This unique rodent clearly has a place in the north woods of the mid-eastern states. It serves as a key prey for one of our most aesthetic mammals, the fisher. Also, because of its sloppy feeding habits, the porcupine can provide a source of browse for other wildlife. Thus, the next time you walk in the north woods during winter, look in the tree canopy—if you're lucky, you might catch a glimpse of a porcupine rolled in a ball waiting for nightfall to feed.

Family Erethizontidae

11

Dogs, Foxes, Wolves, and Allies

Family Canidae

Description of the Family Canidae

The family Canidae is in the order Carnivora and comprises thirty-six species of dogs, foxes, wolves, coyotes, and jackals. In general, carnivores are meat-eaters and usually have shearing teeth that act as guillotines to cut through flesh of prey. These shearing teeth are called carnassials and consist of the fourth premolar on the upper jaw and the third molar on the lower jaw. Of the six families of carnivores in the mid-eastern states (see table 1), carnassials are best developed in Canidae, Mustelidae, and Felidae, and least developed or absent in Ursidae, Procyonidae, and Mephitidae.

Canids have a natural distribution that encompasses all land areas, except Antarctica, Australia, Madagascar, New Guinea, New Zealand, Taiwan, and a few other islands. Wild

populations of the dog, known as the dingo, have been introduced by humans into Australia and New Zealand. Four canid
species occur throughout each of the eight mid-eastern
states: feral dogs, coyotes, and both foxes (red and gray). The
feral dog is considered an exotic species.

Most canid species have long, slender legs and deep-
chested, muscular bodies. They have long muzzles, large, erect
ears, and bushy tails (except some domestic dog breeds; see
essay 25 below). Canids range considerably in size (0.5–2.0 m
in total length and 1–80 kg in weight). The fennec, which is a
fox of Egypt and Morocco, is the smallest canid; the gray wolf of
North America and Eurasia is the largest. In the mid-eastern
states, red and gray foxes are the smallest native canids and coyotes are the largest. All wild species of canids in our area have
forty-two teeth, which include well-developed carnassials and
large canines.

Canids can be found in a wide range of habitats; for example, arctic foxes occupy tundra in the far North, and kit
foxes occur in the deserts of the Southwest. Home sites of
canids include burrows, hollow trees, rock crevices, and caves.
Most canids are well adapted to a cursorial way of life, being
quite capable of traveling considerable distances in their day-
to-day activities. The gray fox is very adept at climbing trees.

Canids are active year-round, and their day-to-day activity
is typically nocturnal or crepuscular. Olfaction, vision, and
hearing are well developed. Canid food habits can be best
described as omnivorous, with some species relying more on
vegetation than others. One species, the bat-eared fox of Africa,
feeds almost exclusively on invertebrates. Larger species of
canids, like the gray wolf, are quite social and live in packs,
whereas smaller species, such as the red fox, are solitary or
live as pairs. Pack-forming canids generally use chases rather

Family Canidae

129

than stalking to capture large prey (e.g., deer); in contrast, solitary species hunt by stalking and pouncing on smaller prey (e.g., mice).

Canids typically produce one litter of two to thirteen pups per year. Gestation averages about sixty-three days. Both parents care for the young; other pack members may help raise young in more social canids. Canids are sexually mature at one or two years, and their life span is generally at least ten years.

Dogs, Foxes, Wolves, and Allies

Ancestry, Domestication, and Ecology of Dogs

Over the years, my family has owned a number of dogs of various breeds. One of these was the miniature dachshund, which, when compared to breeds like the Siberian husky, is a far cry in appearance from its wolf-like ancestors. All 400 or so breeds of dogs (American Kennel Club 1973), however, share a common ancestry with gray (or timber) wolves (Clutton-Brock 1977; Nowak 1999).

Domestication is defined as the exploitation of a group of animals (e.g., ancestral wolves) by a more dominant group (humans), which maintains complete mastery over breeding, food supply, and territory of the subordinant group (Clutton-Brock 1977). Domestic dogs presumably became a separate species only after being kept as tamed animals by humans in isolation from wild wolves for a sufficient time period. Some scientists have speculated that the ancestor to domestic dogs was likely a small subspecies of the gray wolf from Eurasia (Nowak 1979), whereas others view their ancestor as being a gray wolf subspecies from either China (Olsen and Olsen 1977) or India (Clutton-Brock, Corbet, and Hills 1976).

For many years, the oldest remains of domestic dogs were thought to be those found in Idaho and Iraq, which were estimated to be 11,000 and 12,000 years old, respectively. This gives dogs the distinction of being the first mammalian species domesticated by humans (Nowak 1999). Fossil remains of dogs, dating around 10,000 years ago, also have been found in many parts of the world, including England, Iran, Israel, Japan, and western Asia. However, new light has recently been shed on the issue of wolf-dog ancestry based on the use of a technique called mitochondrial DNA sequencing (Vilà et al. 1997). This study confirmed that dogs originated from gray wolves, not 10,000 to 12,000 years ago, but instead about 135,000 years ago! Furthermore, because both wolves and humans coexisted in

Europe and Asia 150,000 years ago, wolves were conceivably domesticated in different places and times in history.

Once these dogs became domesticated, they rapidly spread throughout the world in close association with nomadic human family groups (Clutton-Brock 1977; Paradiso and Nowak 1982). Yet despite a long history of domestication, wolf-like dogs probably only became morphologically different from wolf relatives as "dog breeds" around 10,000 to 15,000 years ago as humans reverted from a nomadic, hunter-gatherer to a more sedentary, agrarian way of life (Vilà et al. 1997). After being domesticated, dogs still possibly mated with stray wolves on occasion, thereby increasing the genetic diversity of dogs and providing raw material for artificial selection of many contemporary breeds. In fact, some dog breeders sometimes breed dogs with wolves to improve the vigor of domesticated dogs (Schwartz 1997). Today, most dog breeds are selected for specific traits (Allman 1998), for example, as toy breeds with small jaws (chihuahuas, Pekingese, and Yorkshire terriers), sporting companions (Labrador retrievers, cocker spaniels, and English springer spaniels), or guard dogs (German shepherds, Great Danes, or rottweilers).

Why were gray wolves rather than some other wild canid species the "best" ancestor of domestic dogs? This is a particularly intriguing question from two perspectives. First, gray wolves are genetically similar not only to domestic dogs but also to six other canid species: red wolves, coyotes, and four species of jackals (Clutton-Brock 1977). Each of these eight species is a member of the same genus (*Canis*), can presumably interbreed (see essay 26 below), and has seventy-eight chromosomes. Thus, why didn't any of these other six species act as the dog ancestor?

Second, gray wolves were not the only canid found in close contact with humans in prehistoric times (Clutton-Brock 1977). Ephemeral, loose associations between humans and other canids were likely widespread in various parts of the world. For instance, human groups lived in close association with coyotes in North America, jackals in Africa and Asia, and Falkland Island wolves in South America. The Falkland Island wolf, in particular, was a very tame canid that probably was taken to the island from South America by prehistoric Native Americans. Although Charles Darwin encountered this wolf species in his journeys, it was killed to extinction by 1876 (Nowak 1999). Hence, other canids besides gray wolves could have been candidates for domestication by possessing some degree of tolerance for humans.

Third, gray wolves stand out among other *Canis* species as the most likely candidate for the dog ancestor because of several important aspects of their way of life (Clutton-Brock 1977; Allman 1998). Wild gray wolves hunt cooperatively, which closely resembled the social way of life of prehistoric human social groups. Domestic dogs accompanied early humans during hunts and assisted them in finding and capturing prey. While they were hunting, vision in humans complemented the excellent senses of hearing and smell in dogs.

Both early humans and wolves also lived in small groups, consisting of related individuals from more than one generation (Allmann 1998). Early human groups existed as dominance hierarchies, with men and women caring for and providing necessities for the young children. Wolves easily adapted to this hierarchy in human groups because its structure was similar to that of a wolf pack. Domestication of dogs from gray wolves was assured when humans raised wolf pups within the human family group. These young "dogs" imprinted on a human(s) as the group leader into their adult life. Humans determined the amount of food given to these submissive adult animals and their young, which is thought to have led to the evolution of two litters per year in dogs (compared to one litter in wild gray wolves).

Domestic dogs provided two additional advantages to early human groups. Like the modern-day relationship between some aborigines and dingoes in Australia (Macintosh 1975), dogs in early human societies could help provide warmth and protection from the cold while sleeping together. Moreover, although wolves howl (see essay 28 below), they also bark; thus, humans living in small, cohesive groups presumably selected individual "watchdogs" as companions, especially those that barked frequently in response to possible danger.

An interesting sidebar to the domestication of dogs is that their long-term association with humans may have caused a reduction in the brain size of dogs (Allman 1998). In dogs and gray wolves of equivalent body size, the brains of the dogs are only about two-thirds of those of wolves! An explanation for this phenomenon is that humans provided dogs with food, shelter, and other necessities over many generations and, hence, natural selection no longer favored the evolution of large brain size. A smaller brain size in domesticated dogs would then be a benefit because energy otherwise diverted into the maintenance of a larger brain could be used instead in growth or rearing of young (Armstrong 1983).

Domestic dogs gone wild, termed *feral dogs*, are commonplace throughout the world today. The most famous feral dog is the dingo of Australia, which was brought to the continent by humans about 8,000 to 9,000 years ago where it quickly became established as wild populations (Nowak 1999). Dingoes are generally solitary but may live in loose packs (Corbett and Newsome 1975). Their diet usually consists of small mammals, particularly the introduced European rabbit, rather than large prey (see chap. 6). Another feral or semidomesticated dog, closely related to the dingo, is the pariah of southeast Asia, northern Africa, and the Balkans (Nowak 1999). Pariahs live in small packs near human villages, where they often scavenge for food or hunt live prey (Fox 1978).

Some domestic dogs in North America may exist as either free-ranging or feral populations in urban or rural areas (Daniels and Bekoff 1989; Nowak 1999). Based on a Baltimore study, nearly 50 percent of the 80,000 to 100,000 dogs in the city were classified as free-ranging, with the rest considered as house pets (Beck 1973, 1975). Free-ranging dogs are mainly active at dawn and dusk, live in vacant buildings or beneath various structures, and feed on garbage or hunt small mammals and birds. They are usually solitary but occasionally occur in pairs and rarely in groups of three or more (Beck 1975; Daniels 1983a). However, in the presence of an estrous female, five or six free-ranging males may aggregate with the female, forming a dominance hierarchy prior to mating, which helps to minimize aggression between rival males (Daniels 1983b). Compared to free-ranging dogs, feral dogs are common in countrysides away from humans (Nowak 1999). Feral dogs often form packs, which may be advantageous by increasing vigilance against humans and when hunting cooperatively for larger prey (Daniels and Bekoff 1989).

Mortality rates in both free-ranging and feral dog populations are quite high, with nearly 50 percent dying in the first year. Fewer than 2 percent are considered old dogs (e.g., >10 years old) (Beck 1973; Daniels and Bekoff 1989). Population densities of free-ranging and feral dogs range from 150 to 936 dogs per square kilometer (Beck 1973, 1975; Daniels 1983a;

Daniels and Bekoff 1989). These dog densities are much higher than those of gray wolves; for instance, wolf population densities in the upper Midwest range from 0.04 to 0.08 individuals per square kilometer (Mech 1970; Peterson 1977).

Domestic dogs are without question one of the most valued mammals in the world. An estimated 52 million dogs occur in the United States alone. This mammal provides us with countless services, but it can become a problem as a vector of rabies (see essay 29 below). Dogs also account for an estimated one million attacks per year on humans worldwide (Nowak 1999). Furthermore, feral dogs may sometimes become a serious nuisance by preying on livestock, although they usually have a negligible effect on wildlife, for example, on white-tailed deer (Gipson and Sealander 1977).

In summary, the domestic dog has become our "best friend" because of its ancestral ability to coexist and adapt to human society. Yet, the next time we see two very different breeds, such as a miniature dachshund and a Siberian husky, remember that both share a common ancestor that was associated with the human family for many thousands of years. The value of dogs to humans—as companions, guardians, and helpers—is unsurpassed in the animal world.

ESSAY 26

The Return of the Eastern Coyote

Childhood memories of Wile E. Coyote chasing the Roadrunner in cartoons or the howls of the coyote at night in a classic western movie leave us with the impression that this canid is a creature of deserts, chaparral,

Family Canidae

and prairies in the western and southwestern United States. However, this view of the coyote's current (or historic) place in North America's landscape is not accurate. Instead, today's coyote is a product of an ancestral coyote, whose distribution was once widespread throughout North America during the Pleistocene a couple of million years ago (Bekoff 1982). Coyotes actually were found in much of eastern North America until about 1,000 years ago, which was well before the arrival of Europeans in North America (McGinnis and George 1980). Reasons for the disappearance of eastern coyotes in pre-European times are unclear (Voigt and Berg 1987).

In the early nineteenth century, however, the coyote began to gradually return to eastern North America as midwestern prairies were converted to agriculture. Coyotes readily adapted to agricultural landscapes. Around 1890 a few sightings of coyotes were reported from Illinois, Indiana, Ohio, and western Ontario (McGinnis and George 1980). By the middle of the twentieth century, populations of coyotes or coyote-like canids were once again established in New York, Pennsylvania, New England, and southeastern Canada. Today, the coyote can be found throughout the eastern United States and Canada (Voigt and Berg 1987), having increased its geographic range sevenfold within only the last hundred years (Wayne, Lehman, Allard, and Honcycutt 1992).

Another major factor for the rapid expansion of the coyote's range into eastern North America was the regional extirpation of gray wolves. Wolves were eliminated from much of the eastern forest because humans relentlessly persecuted them as feared and hated predators (see essay 30 below) and because extensive tracts of forests were logged for timber products and agriculture (Mech 1970; Nowak 1978; Yahner 2000). In addition, some coyotes entered the southeastern states as escapees from captivity or when released by hunters for chase with hounds (Hill, Sumner, and Wooding 1987).

As coyote populations rapidly moved from west to east, an interesting phenomenon occurred, which is still a subject of an ongoing debate — that is, eastern coyotes became larger than their western counterparts. Today, the average weights of adult male and female coyotes in the East are greater (e.g., 17 and 15 kg, respectively) than those in the West (14 and

11 kg) (McGinnis and George 1980; Thurber and Peterson 1991). Three hypotheses have been given for these regional differences in coyote body sizes. First, coyotes are larger in the East because they interbreed with other large canids. As coyotes dispersed eastward from the Great Plains, some probably mated with gray wolves from the upper Midwest or southeastern Canada (Voigt and Berg 1987; Lehman, Eisenhawer, Hansen, Mech, Peterson, and Wayne 1991; Wayne et al. 1992) or large domestic and feral dogs (Gipson, Gipson, and Sealander 1975; Vilà and Wayne 1999). All members of the genus *Canis* are closely related (Wayne et al. 1992), and hybrid young are fertile (Kolenosky 1971; Gipson, Gipson, and Sealander 1975).

A second hypothesis proposed for regional differences in coyote body sizes is greater food availability in the East versus the West (Schmitz and Lavigne 1987; Thurber and Peterson 1991). Mid-eastern and northeastern states typically have diverse and abundant food resources, such as high deer populations, a variety of smaller forest and farmland prey, and food associated with humans (e.g., farm animals, garbage) compared to the drier, less productive areas of midwestern or western states. Diverse and abundant food types in the East enhanced nutritional opportunities for coyotes, resulting in an eventual gradual increase in body size of eastern coyotes over successive generations.

Third, larger body size in eastern coyotes may be explained in part by differences in regional prey size (Schmitz and Lavigne 1987; Larivière and Crête 1993). Western coyotes rely on principally rabbits, hares, and other small mammals as food (Hilton 1978). In contrast, as coyotes moved eastward, they encountered an abundance of larger prey, such as white-tailed deer. Thus, a larger body size in eastern coyotes may be a possible evolutionary adaptation to more efficiently exploit larger prey. For example, a three-kilogram increase in average body weight (from 14 kg to 17 kg in adult male coyotes) theoretically would allow individual coyotes to kill prey that is 33 percent larger (Vézina 1985). As an interesting reverse trend, gray wolves in southeastern Ontario have become smaller over time in possible response to the extirpation of their preferred larger prey, moose and caribou; these Ontario wolves now rely primarily on the smaller white-tailed deer as prey (Schmitz and Lavigne 1987).

The return of the eastern coyote to landscapes of the mid-eastern states raises several issues, such as the effects of this predator on native and domestic species. As mentioned, although coyotes tend to hunt principally rabbits and hares (Hilton 1978), they also prey on deer, especially fawns or adults in poor health or with abnormalities (Korschgen 1957; Stout 1982; Messier and Barrette 1985). In states with high deer density (e.g., Pennsylvania), coyotes may feed heavily on road- or hunter-killed deer (Witmer, Pipas, and Hayden 1995). Coyotes usually do not have a major impact on certain livestock, such as pigs and cows (Jones and Woolf 1983), but can have a major effect on sheep (Voigt and Berg 1987).

Some studies have provided evidence that increases in coyote numbers can affect the abundance and distribution of red fox populations (e.g., Harrison, Bissonette, and Sherburne 1989) (see essay 27 below). Coyotes are often intolerant of red foxes and may occasionally kill and eat them (Voigt and Earle 1983; Gese, Stotts, and Grothe 1996). Finally, individual coyotes occasionally have lost their fear of humans, and food-stressed coyotes lacking a fear of humans have attacked infants or small children, which has created a serious social problem in some national parks and urban areas (Carbyn 1989). In contrast to coyotes, gray wolves are neither aggressive nor dangerous to humans (Munthe and Hutchinson 1978).

In summary, within a span of only about 100 years or so, the coyote has once again found a home in the forests of the mid-eastern states. They also have been able to survive in close association with humans in agricultural and urban areas (Person and Hirth 1991). Hence, the highly adaptable coyote is one of only a handful of large mammal species that has successfully expanded its range and abundance in the face of changing and human-modified landscapes. With the return of the eastern coyote, wildlife biologists will have much to learn about the ecology of this newcomer and its effects, both positive and negative, on other wildlife.

Conservation and Ecological Issues

Related to Canid Interactions

The landscape in the mid-eastern states has changed considerably since Europeans settled the area about 300 years ago. The original deciduous forest was extensively logged and has been replaced with secondary forests, agriculture, urban sprawl, and other human-dominated features (Yahner 2000). As a result of these landscape changes, the abundance and the distribution of our native canid species have been altered dramatically. Red wolves once occurred as far north as central Ohio, southern Pennsylvania, and southern New Jersey, but now have been extirpated from the region. Similarly, gray wolves have been eliminated, with opportunistic coyotes taking their place in the landscape (see essay 26 above). Red foxes were probably scarce or absent when Europeans first arrived in the mid-eastern states (Samuel and Nelson 1982; Whitaker and Hamilton 1998). However, introductions of red foxes by British hunters in southeastern states, dispersal of red foxes from more northerly latitudes, and conversion of forests to farmland eventually paved the way for this canid to become well established in our area. Gray foxes, on the other hand, are native and seem to be most resilient to historic changes in the mid-eastern landscape.

Besides the impacts of changing landscapes on canid population trends in the mid-eastern states, behavioral interactions between coexisting species can have potential impacts on their abundance and distribution. Interactions between canid species present some interesting conservation and ecological implications for the closely related red and gray foxes. Although the red fox is slightly larger (3–7 kg) than its close relation, the gray fox (4–5 kg), gray foxes may be more aggressive than red foxes (Samuel and Nelson 1982; Rue 1969).

Family Canidae

139

Competition between the similar-sized red and gray foxes, however, is minimized in two ways. First, red foxes tend to prefer farmlands, open areas, and suburbia, whereas gray foxes are more likely associated with deciduous woodlands (Samuel and Nelson 1982; Whitaker and Hamilton 1998). In some areas of the mid-eastern states, both species occur more often in agricultural habitats than in forested habitats (Carey, Giles, and McLean 1978). Second, although both species are opportunistic predators, red foxes primarily feed on small mammals (mice and rabbits) and insects; in contrast, gray foxes, although preying on small mammals and insects, rely extensively on plant materials (e.g., wild grape, corn) (Hockman and Chapman 1983). Hence, negative interactions and competition between red and gray foxes are probably minimal in the wild, and neither species has negatively affected the abundance or distribution of the other in the mid-eastern states.

Negative interspecific interactions between red foxes and coyotes are well documented. As coyotes moved eastward in the nineteenth century (see essay 26 above), their geographic ranges began to overlap those of established red fox populations. Like red foxes, coyotes tend to prefer farmlands and other open areas, thereby increasing the chance of interspecific encounters (Whitaker and Hamilton 1998). During an interspecific encounter, red foxes are at a disadvantage because they are about three times lower in body weight than coyotes (Bekoff 1982; Samuel and Nelson 1982). Coyotes are known to attack and occasionally kill and eat red foxes, especially pups or adult foxes caught in traps (Voigt and Earle 1983; Sargeant and Allen 1989).

Red foxes may minimize negative interspecific encounters with coyotes by placing their territories in areas devoid of coyote territories or along boundaries of adjacent coyote territories (see fig. 15). In addition, red foxes avoid using the core areas of coyote territories as a means of reducing chance encounters with coyotes (Voigt and Earle 1983; Major and Sherburne 1987; Sargeant, Allen, and Hastings 1987; Harrison, Bissonette, and Sherburne 1989). Because of this avoidance of coyotes by red foxes, the habitat available for red foxes has probably been reduced with the coyote invasion into eastern North America.

The extent to which red foxes will be affected by range expansion of coyotes into the mid-eastern landscape will likely depend on the avail-

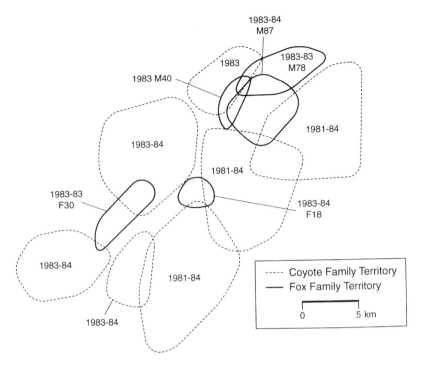

Figure 15. The placement of red fox territories in relation to the location of coyote territories. *(Modified from Harrison, Bissonette, and Sherburne 1989.)*

ability of refugia habitat for placement of their territories. For example, riparian habitats can delineate the boundaries between adjacent coyote territories, thereby serving as refugia habitat for red fox territories (Voigt and Earle 1983; Harrison, Bissonette, and Sherburne 1989). Red fox populations can persist in refugia habitat because their territories are only about one-third the size of coyotes' (Harrison, Bissonette, and Sherburne 1989). Furthermore, red foxes have ecological advantages over coyotes by having higher fecundity and lower food-intake requirements (Voigt and Earle 1983).

A positive spin on population declines of red fox populations, at least from a waterfowl-conservation perspective, has been observed by wildlife biologists in the Prairie Pothole Region of midwestern North America. Rates of nest predation by red foxes in areas devoid of coyotes (28%) on nesting ducks and duck clutches were sevenfold higher than rates in areas occupied by both red foxes and coyotes (4%). Hence, the nesting success of upland-nesting ducks (e.g., mallards and blue-winged teal) has been enhanced where coyotes have reduced the numbers of red foxes (Sovada, Sargeant, and Grier 1995). An expanding coyote population in the Prairie Pothole Region may contribute to future increases in waterfowl populations in the Midwest.

Coyotes are probably not displacing other carnivores in the mideastern states, such as gray foxes or bobcats. Although gray fox and coyote territories can overlap, limited evidence indicates that the two species simply avoid each other in the wild with no apparent aggression (Wooding 1984; Edwards 1996). Similarly, in Maine, bobcat territories overlapped those of coyotes with no discernible impact on bobcat abundance or distribution (Major and Sherburne 1987).

Aggressive interactions between coyotes and gray wolves often resemble those observed between coyotes and red foxes—but in reverse. Gray wolves will kill coyotes on occasion, especially if food resources are low (Paquet 1992). When wolves are feeding on large carcasses, such as deer, they tend to ignore coyotes in the immediate vicinity. Coyotes stay nearby to scavenge from the carcasses once they are abandoned by the satiated wolves. As with red foxes and coyote territories, coyotes may establish territories between boundaries of adjacent wolf packs (Fuller and Keith 1981). Coyotes apparently place their territories entirely within those of wolves only when food is sufficiently abundant for both species (Carbyn 1982).

Gray wolves can be aggressive toward domestic dogs (Mech 1970). In some instances, wolves may deliberately hunt dogs, particularly small- or medium-sized breeds that are excitable or vocal (Fritts and Paul 1989). Thus, when wolves are known to be in the area, dog owners are advised to keep their pets inside.

Hybridization is a very interesting interspecific interaction within the "*Canis* complex" of North America—coyotes, domestic dogs, gray wolves, and red wolves. These four species are closely related phylogenetically (Wayne et al. 1992), and fertile young are produced when these canids interbreed (Kolenosky 1971; Gipson, Gipson, and Sealander 1975) (see essay 26 above). Hybrid pups resulting from coyote and dog crosses are referred to as "coy-dogs." The average number of coy-dogs produced per litter (3.5 pups) is somewhat lower than those produced between dog-dog or coyote-coyote crosses (usually >4.5 pups).

Matings between female dogs and either male coyotes or wolves (which result in pups termed "coy-wolves") may not always occur because the timing of estrous cycles in one species may not coincide with the timing of sperm production in the other (Moore and Millar 1984; Vilà and Wayne 1999). Furthermore, once dogs are crossed with either coyotes or gray wolves, the timing of reproductive cycles in the hybrid offspring shifts, which minimizes the likelihood of these hybrids mating again with pure coyotes or gray wolves (Schmitz and Kolenosky 1985). Litter survival of coy-dog or coy-wolf crosses may be reduced compared to that of pure litters because adult male dogs, unlike adult male coyotes or wolves, provide limited parental care. Historically, coy-wolf hybridizations have been much more prevalent in North America than wolf-dog hybridizations (Wayne et al. 1992) (see essay 25 above).

The endangered red wolf, which is smaller than the gray wolf but larger than the coyote, is virtually gone as a pure, wild species (Paradiso and Nowak 1982). Red wolves have likely hybridized with coyotes and gray wolves since the 1700s (Roy, Geffen, Smith, and Wayne 1996); thus, all individuals remaining today probably are hybrid progeny of matings with either gray wolves and coyotes (Wayne and Jenks 1991; Brownlow 1996). Others biologists contend, however, that some red wolves may exist as a distinct species despite a history of interbreeding with other canids (Nowak 1992). Since the 1950s, additional factors besides hybridization have taken a toll on populations of this small, aesthetic wolf (Gipson and Sealander 1976). These include dramatic declines in feral pigs in the Southeast (which served as the major food of red wolves), restricted feeding habits (e.g., specializing on live prey rather than scavenging like the coyote), and habitat loss (forests replaced with agricultural lands).

Wildlife biologists have attempted to reestablish red wolf populations in the southeastern states (Parker and Phillips 1991). These efforts have carefully considered the problems with coyote hybridization. Areas targeted for reintroduction had to be free of coyotes before red wolves were released. In 1986, a few pair of "pure" red wolves raised in captivity were released at the Alligator River National Wildlife Refuge in coastal North

Carolina once it was established that coyotes were not on the refuge. By the late 1990s, red wolves have been reintroduced into several other locations, giving a total of about seventy to eighty individuals in the wild (Gilbreath 1998). As a result of these introductions, a slim margin of optimism still remains for the future success of this small endangered wolf in North America.

E S S A Y   2 8

Why Do Wolves and Coyotes Scent-Mark and Howl?

Communication mediates all aspects of the interactions among members of species (Crook, Ellis, and Goss-Custard 1976). Olfactory, auditory, visual, and tactile communication are commonplace in vertebrates, but olfactory and auditory senses are particularly keen in many mammalian species (Vaughan, Ryan, and Czaplewski 2000). Intriguing types of communication signals exist in gray wolves and coyotes—scent-marking and howling.

Before discussing these communication signals, let's explore why olfactory and auditory signals are important as well as the advantages and disadvantages of each. Remember that many mammals are nocturnal and wide-ranging, and signals that either persist for a long time or are transmitted over a distance have special adaptive value to mammals. Olfactory signals are advantageous because they are long term and site-specific by remaining in the environment in the absence of the sender. But a disadvantage of a single olfactory signal (the scent-mark) is that it lacks directionality. So, as we shall see, if scent-marks are used to delineate the boundary of a territory, the sender(s) must use a gradient of signals. In contrast, auditory signals, such as howls, can be transmitted over long distances. A disadvantage of an auditory signal, however, is that it is short term and does not persist in the absence of the sender.

Olfactory communication involves a chemical signal, often called a pheromone, which is sent by one organism to another of the same species to elicit a behavioral or physiological response (Eisenberg and Kleiman 1972). Chemical signals can be contained within urine and feces or be produced by scent (or musk) glands, as by the castor glands of American beaver (see essay 16 in chap. 8). Depending on the species, well-developed scent glands can occur at various locations on the body, such as along the flank or near the mouth, eyes, and sex organs (Vaughan, Ryan, and Czaplewski 2000).

Scent-marking in domestic dogs is familiar to all of us. A mature male dog frequently exhibits leg-raised urination, which leaves a chemical signal on conspicuous objects, such as a fire hydrant or telephone pole. This means of scent-marking is characteristic of other canids, such as male gray wolves and coyotes (Peters and Mech 1975; Bowen and Cowan 1980). In addition, canids create other species-specific scent-marks by defecating and scratching (Rothman and Mech 1979). Scent-marking by canids possibly originated as a means of providing security or reassurance by sending the message that "I've been here before" and "this is a familiar area" (Kleiman 1966). These types of scent-marks later evolved into more sophisticated messages, which provided "To Whom It May Concern" information about individual identity, sex, age, reproductive status, and perhaps dominance status of the sender (Eisenberg and Kleiman 1972).

A universal trend in mammals is that dominant individuals scent-mark more often than subordinate individuals (Rothman and Mech 1979; Ough 1982). For instance, lone wolves seldom mark, presumably to keep a low profile and reduce the likelihood of being detected by members of a nearby pack (Rothman and Mech 1979). Lone individuals are often young animals that have recently left their natal pack in search of a mate and place to settle. Once a lone wolf finds another wolf of the opposite sex, scent-marking occurs at rates higher than those of established packs, suggesting that these signals help ensure successful courtship in newly formed pairs of wolves.

As alluded to earlier, a single scent-mark provides limited information because it is not directional. For instance, imagine a lone wolf (or coyote) encountering a scent-mark deposited by an established pack. If the lone wolf opts to move in the wrong direction and heads into the interior of a neighboring wolf pack's territory, it may be attacked and perhaps killed by the pack (Peters and Mech 1975; Okoniewski 1982). So, given this nondirectionality of a single scent-mark, how does scent-marking serve to delineate territorial boundaries and thereby minimize strife in wolf (and coyote) societies?

Members of a wolf pack often travel along logging roads, trails, or other established routes within their territory at about 8 kmh (Mech 1970). While en route and depending on their location within the territory, wolves vary the rate of scent-marking (and hence the distance between scent-marks). For example, if the pack is along the edge of its territory, scent-marks are deposited on average every 110 meters; however, if the pack is traveling within the center of its territory, scent-marks may be given every 180 meters (Peters and Mech 1975; see also Bowen and Cowan 1980). Furthermore, when members of a neighboring pack encounter scent-marks deposited by the resident pack, the neighbors leave their scent-marks on the marks of the resident pack. As a result, more scent-marks (those of resident and neighboring packs combined) accumulate along territorial edges of packs, which produces an "olfactory bowl" (see fig. 16), with about twice the number of scent-marks along the edges versus the interior of a territory.

In nature, the territory of a wolf pack may be ten to twenty kilometers wide (Zimen 1984), with the outer one kilometer being shared real estate with neighboring packs. Hence, the high-to-low gradient of scent-marks from a territory's edge (area shared by packs) relative to its interior functions as an impregnable barrier to neighboring packs or to a lone wolf in the absence of the resident pack members. These areas of interpack overlap are visited less frequently than areas of non-overlap, probably as a means of reducing interpack encounters. In turn, the lower concentration of scent-marks in the interior of a pack's territory helps members orient themselves within their territory.

Howling is another major means of communication in gray wolves and coyotes (Harrington and Mech 1979; Lehner 1982). The sound of a wolf or coyote howl ranks as one of the most aesthetic outdoor experi-

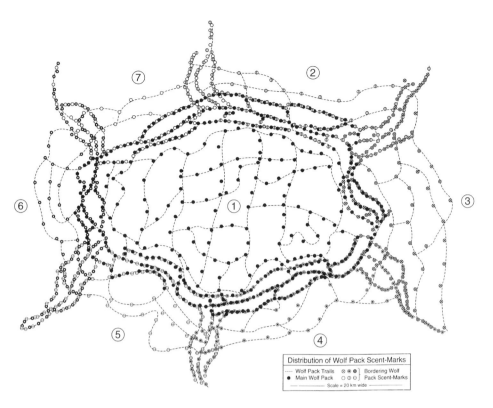

Figure 16. An olfactory bowl created by scent-marks of a resident pack and those of neighboring packs. *(Modified from Peters and Mech 1975.)*

ences. I once heard a wolf pack howling in Minnesota, but unfortunately for me (and them), it was given by a captive pack in response to the sound of a siren. In the wild, these howls can be heard for an average distance of two kilometers (Fuller and Sampson 1988) and can serve both intrapack and interpack functions (Harrington and Mech 1979). All pack members may howl, but when alone only the dominant (termed *alpha*) male will howl. In contrast, a subordinate, lone wolf will seldom howl because it might attract a strange pack and may result in death. A dominant male may howl to reunite other members of his pack separated after a hunt.

Interpack howling by gray wolves may be given in two general contexts. First, all or most pack members may howl when approaching an area used jointly by a neighboring pack, such as along the boundaries

Family Canidae

separating two territories. In this context, howling advertises the presence of the pack in case the rival pack is in the immediate area. Second, several members of a pack may howl when returning to a portion of their territory not visited in some time, which suggests that older scent-marks had lost their effectiveness as possible deterrents to other packs. Because wolves howl in response to howls produced by conspecifics, wildlife biologists have used human howls to successfully survey the locations of packs in the wild (Fuller and Sampson 1988).

Coyotes produce two major types of long-distance vocalizations: the group howl and the group yip-howl (Lehner 1982). The group howl in coyotes is similar in context to the howls of an alpha gray wolf by reuniting the pack. Conversely, the group yip-howl in coyotes signals to a nearby pack that a given territory is occupied; this vocalization functions similarly to the group howl in wolves.

E S S A Y   2 9

The Natural History and Ecology of "Madness"

(Rabies) in Canids

Rabies is one of the most dreaded infectious diseases known to humans and animals. The rabies virus is Greek derived and means "madness"; the word *rabies* is Latin derived and is translated as "to do violence" (Krebs et al. 1995a). The rabies virus is usually transmitted in contaminated saliva of an infected animal to a susceptible host through cuts, scratches, and wounds caused by bites; the virus can also enter the host's body through mucous membranes lining the mouth and eyes (Krebs,

Wilson, and Childs 1995; http://www.vpeds.com.rabies). Once the virus enters the body, it travels to the central nervous system (brain and spinal cord) and spreads via nerves to other parts of the body; the disease eventually causes altered behavior, paralysis, and death.

There are several geographic strains (or variants) of the rabies virus throughout the world, and all mammals, including humans, are susceptible to these strains. In humans, the incubation period (i.e., time from exposure to onset of symptoms) can vary from five days to over one year (http://www.vpeds.com.rabies). At the beginning of the twentieth century, about 100 human deaths in the United States per year were attributed to rabies, but this number is now about one to two per year (http://www.cdc.gov/ncidod/dvrd/rabies). Today, nearly 50,000 humans worldwide die each year from rabies (Kuwert, Merieux, Koprowski, and Bokel 1985).

The oldest record of rabies in canids was recorded in Europe and Asia about 2,500 years ago. In the literature, aggressive dogs were described as having a madness, which is characterized by irritability and biting of other animals. Epidemics of rabies in gray wolves were initially noted by the French in 1271 (ntri.tamuk.edu/class). In the 1200s these aggressive attacks by wolves on humans were documented as being prevalent, perhaps giving rise to the "Big Bad Wolf" fairy tale that we hear as a child (Sikes 1970). Most historic attacks by wolves on humans probably involved rabid wolves that lived at high densities near human population centers in the Mediterranean region. Although rabies was first noted in Mexico in 1709 this disease occurred in the New World as early as the sixteenth century, based on reports of madness in Spanish soldiers bitten by rabid vampire bats (ntri.tamuk.edu). Rabies transmitted to humans by rabid dogs or wolves during the eighteenth century in Europe may have inspired the vampire legend made famous in many horror movies over the past few decades (http://www.rabies.com).

The fear of the Big Bad Wolf in the Old World unfortunately carried over to the New World with the arrival of Europeans. As a consequence, the gray wolf, which was once widespread in North America, was hunted and trapped relentlessly by Europeans settlers to near extinction (see essay 26 above). Paradoxically, the wolf was revered and respected by Native Americans in the New World well before the arrival of Europeans (Storm 1972). The reality is that wild wolves in North America have never been

Family Canidae

149

aggressive or dangerous to humans, and the occurrence of rabies in wild wolves in North America is extremely rare (Chapman 1978). Wolves in North America simply are not good vectors of rabies because they are relatively scarce, live in packs, and inhabit remote areas away from human population centers. Furthermore, once a pack member is infected, the pack is quickly decimated by the disease, which stops its transmission to other packs or wildlife species.

In historic times and even today in developing countries, the domestic dog was (is) the principal rabies vector and source of rabies transmission to humans. The dog was the major rabies vector in the United States until the mid-twentieth century when dog owners were mandated to vaccinate their pets (J. Smith 1989; Krebs, Wilson, and Childs 1995). With a subsequent decline in rabies in dogs in the United States, wild mammals then became the major rabies vectors (Rosatte 1987; J. Smith 1989, Krebs, Wilson, and Childs 1995; http://www.vpeds.com/rabies). In the 1950s, red and gray foxes were the most commonly reported rabid species of wildlife. From the early 1960s through 1989, the numbers of rabid cases in skunks exceeded those of other species. Since the early 1990s, however, the raccoon has become the major wild vector of rabies in the United States (see essay 35 in chap. 13). With the exception of woodchucks, many small mammals, such as chipmunks, squirrels, mice, and rabbits, generally do not carry rabies. In the United States about 94 percent of the 10,000 or so cases of rabies per year are reported in wild animals versus only 6 percent in domestic animals. Domestic cats are more likely to get rabies than dogs or other domestic animals in the United States, perhaps because of the lack of legislation requiring the vaccination of domestic cats in some states.

There are two manifestations of rabies: dumb and furious forms (Webster 1942; Jennings, Schneider, Lewis, and Scatterday 1960; Johnston and Beauregard 1969). About 50–60 percent of rabid canids and skunks display the dumb form, whereby the animals are not aggressive but instead are visibly weak, docile, and lack control of jaw musculature. The remaining 40–50 percent of rabid animals exhibit the furious mad dog form, which is characterized by aggressive attacks and biting. Because of this aggressive behavior, combined with restlessness and wandering, almost all cases of rabies are transmitted by animals showing the furious form

(Preston 1973). During the symptomatic period of one to eighteen days (average seven days), a red fox with the furious form of rabies can potentially travel thirty to fifty kilometers per day. Thus, if the size of a fox territory in good quality habitat is about six square kilometers (Storm 1965), a rabid fox with furious rabies is capable of traversing several (e.g., 6–8) fox territories and possibly infecting a number of foxes or other mammals in a single day.

The occurrence of rabies transmission may be dependent on a number of interrelated and poorly understood factors, such as season, habitat quality, and proportion of immune animals in the population (Carey 1982). Incidences of rabies in foxes seem to follow an annual cycle, being lowest in summer, increasing from late summer through autumn, and highest in late winter (Jennings et al. 1960; Preston 1973). The increase in rabid animals in late summer through winter may be related to increased movements by foxes and, hence, higher probabilities of chance encounters between rabid and nonrabid animals. Juvenile males usually disperse from family groups in late summer and autumn, and adult males move considerable distances in search of estrous females during the breeding season in late winter. In Virginia, for example, 83 percent of forty-four rabies outbreaks occurred in autumn and winter (Carey 1982).

Rabies may reach epidemic levels on a regular basis in foxes, depending on habitat quality. The cycle can occur regularly every three years in good fox habitat and every four to five years in poor fox habitat (Johnston and Beauregard 1969). Moreover, the percentage of animals in a given population exposed yet immune to the disease may vary from 29 to 65 percent (Schoening 1956; Preston 1973; Carey 1982). Thus, like common cold viruses in humans, rabies viruses can be retained in wild populations. Rabies viruses in fox populations, for example, persist at low levels from southern New York to northern Georgia (McLean 1970).

Much is yet to be learned about the ecology of rabies transmission and effective ways to reduce its transmission in wild populations, domestic animals, and humans. Rabies has been eradicated or controlled in wild animals to some degree in North America and Europe by delivering vaccines in edible food over relatively large areas via some ingenious methods, for example, dropping chicken heads containing a vaccine from aircraft

Family Canidae

(Rosatte 1987; Krebs, Wilson, and Childs 1995)! In metropolitan Toronto, 52 to 72 percent of the wild skunks were successfully vaccinated by placing vaccines in edible baits along ravines (Rosatte, Power, and MacInnes 1992). To date, vaccination programs have not convincingly shown a decrease in the incidences of rabies followed by an increase in population numbers. Future studies may show that the timing of a vaccination program for wild populations is critical for its success. For instance, the placement of bait in summer prior to the onset of dispersal by juveniles rather than in autumn may better ensure that more animals would be immunized against the disease (Schubert, Rosatte, MacInnes, and Nudds 1998).

In summary, rabies is a frightening disease—once the symptoms develop, the disease is 100 percent fatal! We need to take a few common-sense steps to prevent this dreaded disease. Pet dogs and cats should be kept up-to-date with rabies vaccinations and be confined to homes or yards (http://www.rabies.com). Care must be taken when disposing of a dead animal, such as a road-killed animal, which may have been rabid and was hit by a vehicle because of its altered behavior. When disposing of a carcass, waterproof gloves and a shovel should be used to prevent possible transmission of the virus into cuts or scratches on your hands. We should never approach a seemingly docile wild animal—a friendly raccoon or skunk may actually be exhibiting the docile form of rabies. If bitten by a wild carnivore, bat, or woodchuck, we should assume that it is rabid, immediately wash the wound, and contact the appropriate officials (e.g., animal control officer, family health care provider). Fortunately, rabies can be treated in humans and domestic animals, provided that we seek the proper treatment as soon as possible after a potential exposure to its infection (Krebs, Wilson, and Childs 1995).

Wolf Reintroductions in the Northeast?

Gray wolves and mountain lions (see essay 42 in chap. 16) are large, charismatic carnivores, which are occasionally mentioned as candidates for reintroduction into their former range. The gray wolf was once widely distributed throughout the northern hemisphere, including North America, Asia, and Europe, but now is found in scattered populations throughout a fraction of its original range (Wayne et al. 1992; Mech 1995). This canid was gone from the mid-eastern states by the turn of the nineteenth century because it was hunted relentlessly by settlers as a feared and hated predator (Doutt, Heppenstall, and Guilday 1977). For instance, during the 1800s, Pennsylvanians were paid a $25 bounty for a wolf head. Since the 1920s the wolf has also been eliminated from some of the most remote areas in North America, such as Yellowstone National Park. Finally in 1974, the gray wolf was given complete protection in the lower forty-eight states with the passage of the second U.S. Endangered Species Act of 1973 (Mech 1995). As a result of this protection, a remarkable conservation story has unfolded—populations of this aesthetic carnivore have increased and expanded in some areas of North America where they were once scarce or absent. In addition, wildlife biologists and the general public have expressed an interest in restoring the gray wolf to its former haunts. As we shall see, the recent restoration efforts for gray wolves have been successful in the Yellowstone area.

In the lower forty-eight states, populations of gray wolves have their strongest foothold in Minnesota, even prior to the Endangered Species Act (Mech 1995; Mladenoff and Sickley 1998). Today, the status of midwestern timber wolves is continuing to improve, with about 2,000 wolves present in Minnesota by the late 1990s. A few hundred or so have spread from Minnesota eastward into Michigan and Wisconsin and westward into North and South Dakota.

Populations of gray wolves have also become established in some of the northern Rocky Mountain states in recent years with the protection afforded by the Endangered Species Act (Fritts, Bangs, Fontaine, Brewster, and Gore 1995). These wolves arrived in the northern Rockies from Canada by natural dispersal, and now about seventy wolves live in parts of Montana, for example, Glacier National Park; in addition, Canadian wolves have moved into Washington and Idaho over the past few decades. The ability of wolves to disperse extensive distances in the western United States is encouraging because it not only restores this canid to its former range but helps ensure adequate genetic variation, which is vital to the successful recovery and long-term survival of wolf populations in the northern Rockies (Forbes and Boyd 1996, 1997). Evidence for the importance of dispersal comes from studies of gray wolves in Isle Royale National Park in Lake Superior, where limited dispersal by wolves to the park has reduced the overall genetic variation and long-term survival of this small, isolated wolf population (Wayne et al. 1991).

Recovery plans for gray wolf populations in the United States began in 1985 when the National Park Service (NPS) proposed the reintroduction of gray wolves into America's first national park, Yellowstone National Park (Northern Rocky Mountain Wolf Recovery Team 1985). This was an important landmark in the history of predator conservation because it was the first effort by the NPS to restore populations of one of America's most controversial predators. Furthermore, this effort is a milestone in the philosophy of wildlife conservation, in that a predator, once hunted, feared, and hated, was now being viewed as a vital component of a healthy ecosystem.

Ten years later (in 1995), the gray wolf was reintroduced into the Greater Yellowstone Area (GYA) ecosystem in Montana and Wyoming. As with the midwestern wolves, the population in the GYA ecosystem has rapidly increased and expanded its range. Eleven packs composed of 111 animals make their home in the GYA ecosystem as of February 1999 (http://www.yellowstone-nat-park.com/wolfnews.htm); nine packs occur within Yellowstone National Park and Grand Teton National Park, and two packs are on the border of Yellowstone National Park. Fortunately, the wolf reintroduction into the GYA ecosystem has generally received broad-based public support. At the very onset of the proposed recovery effort, visitors to Yellowstone have expressed a strong sentiment for the reintroduction of this aesthetic canid (McNaught 1987). Based on a questionnaire given to park visitors, for instance, the prowolf sentiment outweighed the antiwolf sentiment by a ratio of nine to one, and 74 percent of the respondents felt that the presence of wolves would enhance the aesthetic value of their visit to Yellowstone.

The success of wolf recovery in the Midwest and northern Rockies has stirred interest in restoring gray wolves into the Northeast (Mladenoff and Sickley 1998). Imagine having an opportunity to hear the howls of a wolf pack in the mid-eastern states, such as New York! However, before a population of wolves can be successfully introduced into the Northeast, an area of at least 3,000 square kilometers is required, which should be large enough to sustain at least 100 wolves (Fritts and Carbyn 1995). Such an area does not necessarily have to be free of human disturbance, provided that adequate prey is available and wolves are not indiscriminately killed (Mech 1995).

An area that has recently been given special attention as a location for the possible introduction of gray wolves in the Northeast is about twenty-five-fold greater than the required area (3,000 km²). It consists of 77,000 square kilometers of suitable contiguous habitat, extending from upstate New York to northern Maine (see fig. 17). This area is projected to be large enough to sustain a population of about 1,300 wolves (Mladenoff and Sickley 1998). A portion of this area from northeastern Maine to northern Maine, in particular, is a contiguous tract of 53,500 square kilometers capable of supporting over 1,000 wolves.

Densities of wolves in the northeastern United States will depend on the availability of two important prey species, white-tailed deer and moose. Given the known densities of these ungulates, wolf densities may potentially range from just under one wolf per 100 square kilometers to at least two to three wolves per 100 square kilometers in upstate New York and Maine, respectively. Habitat in upstate New York is less suitable for wolves because of relatively low deer populations, whereas habitat for wolves in Maine is more optimal because of relatively high moose populations.

Family Canidae

155

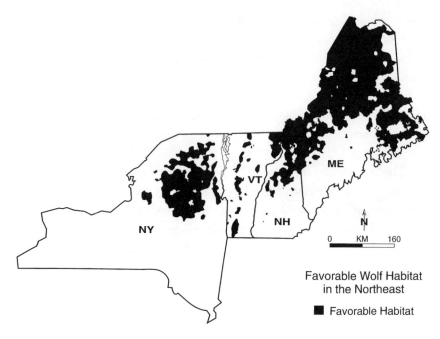

Figure 17. Potential suitable habitat for the introduction of gray wolves into the northeastern United States. *(Modified from Mladenoff and Sickley 1998.)*

A wolf reintroduction program may be more likely to succeed in Maine (and northern New Hampshire) compared to elsewhere in the 77,000-square-kilometer area for some additional reasons (Harrison and Chapin 1998). For instance, human populations (<4 people/km^2) and road densities (<0.70 km roads/km^2) are low in Maine. Whether or not gray wolves are intentionally introduced into the Northeast, gray wolves from southeastern Canada will eventually colonize (if they haven't already) this area (Harrison and Chapin 1998; Mladenoff and Sickley 1998). Wolves have been observed traveling considerable distances (>600 km) across rather inhospitable agricultural landscapes in the upper Midwest (Mech, Fritts, and Wagner 1995).

Wildlife biologists must give additional biological and social considerations when reintroducing gray wolves into the Northeast or elsewhere. As mentioned, an important consideration in the large-scale restoration of wolves into the Northeast is the need for high populations of prey, for example, white-tailed deer. High deer populations, however, can have a negative long-term impact on forest biodiversity (see essay 46 in chap. 19). A second consideration is that gray wolves that colonize the Northeast may possibly hybridize with resident coyotes, thereby genetically diluting the gray wolf population (see essay 26 above). A third consideration is that wolves are wide-ranging and do not recognize boundaries between public and private lands. Hence, protection of stray wolves needs to extend beyond any designated nature reserve and include a buffer zone between the reserve and adjacent land uses (Forbes and Theberge 1996). Furthermore, interagency cooperation, such as among state and federal wildlife agencies, is indispensable for the long-term success of a wolf reintroduction and management program (Mladenoff, Sickley, Haight, and Wydeven 1995).

One of the best ways to get a buy-in for wolf recovery will be to educate the public about issues and controversies that may arise (Mech 1995). For example, public and private landowners must be prepared to deal with conflicts if and when reintroduced wolves move out of a reserve and kill livestock or pets (Fritts and Paul 1989; Mech 1995). Farmers and pet owners should be compensated for damage caused by wolves, therefore minimizing public resentment toward wolves and enhancing the success of the recovery program.

In conclusion, we have seen a remarkable and rapid turnaround regarding the philosophy of gray wolf conservation in North America. In the foreseeable future, we may soon hear gray wolves howling within easy driving distance of our homes. The return of this magnificent predator would be a welcome addition to our forests; its return would bring us closer to the pristine conditions once found in our region before European settlement.

Family Canidae

12

Bears

Family Ursidae

Description of the Family Ursidae

$\mathcal{E}$ight species of bears are the family Ursidae (order Carnivora). These include small bears (spectacled bear of South America and Asian black, sloth, sun bears of Eurasia) and large bears (black bears of North America, brown [or grizzly] bears of North America and Eurasia, polar bears of the circumpolar arctic region, and giant pandas of China). Black bears are the only ursid in the mid-eastern states but are absent in Delaware (see table 1).

Bears are heavily built mammals, with large heads, short powerful limbs, short tails, relatively long muzzles, and small ears. They vary in size from the small sun bears (1.1–1.4 m and 27–65 kg in body length and weight, respectively) to the large polar bears (2.0–2.5 m and 150–800 kg), which are the largest terrestrial carnivores in the world. Bear claws are long and curved and are used to climb trees, dig in soil, and tear apart logs for food. Compared to canids, ursids are not well adapted to a cursorial way of life but, instead, move with a shuffling gait. This gait is in part because of plantigrade feet, which means their heels touch the ground as humans do when walking. Most species of bears have forty-two teeth, elongated canines, and lack carnassials (see chap. 11).

Bears are found in a wide range of habitats from tundra to tropical forests. Hollow trees and logs, caves, excavated dens, or dense vegetation are used as dens. In northerly latitudes, most bears reduce winter activity by entering hibernation (see essay 34 below); at other times of the year, activity is crepuscular or nocturnal. Bears are omnivorous; however, polar bears are strict meateaters (e.g., feeding on seals), and giant pandas rely almost exclusively on bamboo. Olfactory and auditory senses are acute in bears, whereas vision is less developed.

Ursids are solitary, except during courtship or when the female is raising her young. Depending on the species, gestation varies from six to nine months and follows a period of delayed implantation of the fertilized egg (see chap. 14); one to four young per litter are produced at one- to four-year intervals. Young bears are very tiny at birth, which often occurs during hibernation (see essay 34). Only the female cares for the young, and the young remain with the mother for one to four years. Sexual maturity is reached at two and a half to six years, and bears in the wild can live fifteen to thirty years.

Family Ursidae

ESSAY 31

Why Are Grizzly Bears More Aggressive

than Black Bears?

As Europeans ventured west of the Mississippi River, they encountered a magnificent, powerful bear called the grizzly bear. The bear's name is derived from its "silver hair'd" or "frosted" hair (Craighead and Mitchell 1982). Grizzly bears are actually the same species as the brown bear of Eurasia. In North America two subspecies are recognized: one occupying mainland North America and another on the islands off Alaska (e.g., Kodiak Island). Grizzly bears, which once roamed throughout much of western North America, are now confined to an area extending from Alaska to the remote areas of the northern Rocky Mountains.

Grizzly bears have always carried a certain mystique. Native Americans respected and revered these powerful ursids (Storm 1972). Because of the grizzly's aggressiveness, most European settlers feared and hunted them relentlessly as the "manly" thing to do (Herrero 1985). An early taxonomist gave it the scientific name of *Ursus horribilis*, which means "horrible bear" (Craighead and Mitchell 1982).

While walking in the eastern deciduous forest, some of us have been fortunate to catch a brief glimpse of the grizzly's cousin, the smaller black bear. In western North America we are more likely to encounter black bears than grizzly bears because the former are much more common. An encounter with a black bear does not usually evoke the same level of fear (if any) in us compared to an encounter with the grizzly bear, in part because the black bear is generally a much more docile animal. Furthermore, most attacks by black bears on humans result in minor or no injury; often these attacks occur when people attempt to feed black bears by hand (Herrero 1970; Pelton, Scott, and Burchardt 1976). Hand-fed bears can lose their fear of humans, thereby increasing the likelihood of close encounters with humans. In recent years, feeding of bears has been prohibited in national parks, such as in the Great Smoky Mountains National Park (Wright 1992). In western parks (e.g., Yellowstone National Park) the National Park Service closed garbage dumps in 1970 so that black and grizzly bears would not become conditioned to humans and their foods.

Compared to black bear attacks, grizzly attacks are less frequent but are often more serious and likely to be fatal; in general, about 50 percent of the grizzly attacks on humans have required at least twenty-four hours of hospitalization (Smith 1998). In Yellowstone National Park from 1930 to 1978, for instance, 2,002 injuries to humans were caused by bears (Schullery 1980; McCullough 1982). Only seventy-five (3.7%) of these attacks were caused by grizzlies, whereas 1,927 (96.3%) were attributed to black bears, even though black bears outnumbered grizzlies only by two to one in the park. Two of the seventy-five grizzly bear attacks (2.6%) and one of 1,927 black bear attacks (0.05%) resulted in human fatalities. In Glacier National Park from 1939 to 1980, the likelihood of human fatalities caused by grizzly attacks on humans was even higher, with six (20%) of thirty grizzly attacks on humans ending in death.

About 70 percent of the grizzly bears' attacks on humans are related to defense of young by the adult female, and 30 percent are attributed to bears associating humans with food (Craighead and Mitchell 1982; McCullough 1982; Herrero 1985). Grizzly bear–human confrontations may range from instances in which a bear enters a campground to obtain food even if people are present to those in which a bear approaches, charges, or follows a person (Albert and Bowyer 1991). A disturbing trend with the establishment of national parks and increased recreational activities since the 1950s is that some unwary grizzly bears have now became potential predators of humans for the first time in the history of North America (Herrero 1989). As we will see below, they will actually stalk humans as prey.

Every encounter between a grizzly bear and an unsuspecting human does not result in an attack, but the mere presence of humans seems to be enough to alter the overall behavior of adult grizzly bears (White, Kendall, and Picton 1999). For instance, when grizzlies were disturbed by mountain climbers in Glacier National Park, the bears spent 23 percent more time acting aggressively toward conspecifics, 52 percent more time moving, and 53 percent less time foraging for food compared to times when climbers were not in the vicinity. Thus, in the very least, grizzly bears become agitated when humans are in the vicinity.

Why is the grizzly so much more aggressive and, hence, dangerous to humans compared to the black bear? In order to get some answers to this question, we need to go back in evolutionary time. Both grizzly (or brown) and black bears evolved in Asia from an extinct, relatively small bear called the Etruscan bear sometime in the Pleistocene (about two million years ago). The Etruscan bear and its ancestors were small, forest-dwelling animals capable of climbing trees to escape danger. Incidentally, the third species of bear in North America, the polar bear, evolved from coastal grizzly (brown) bears; it remains today as an arctic specialist adapted to the icy, treeless conditions in the far north (Herrero 1970).

Grizzly and black bears then entered North America by crossing a land bridge connecting Asia with Alaska (Herrero 1970; Craighead and Mitchell 1982). Black bears remained associated with forests and retained the tree-climbing ability of the Etruscan bear. Grizzlies, on the other hand, became adapted to more open areas left treeless by glaciers, thereby foregoing their need to climb trees. Even today, the geographic ranges of black and grizzly bears overlap in western North America (see essay 32 below). But in this area of overlap, black and grizzly bears are principally confined to forested and open habitats, respectively.

Black bears are better adapted to tree climbing compared to grizzly bears because of body size and morphological differences between the two species. Black bears weigh two to three times less than grizzlies (Craighead and Mitchell 1982; Pelton 1982), making tree climbing less cumbersome for black bears. The short, curved front claws of black bears are useful for climbing; conversely, the long front claws and powerful shoulder and back muscles (and hence, the hump seen on the back of a grizzly) of grizzly bears are specialized for digging up roots, small mammals, and other food items. As a result, black bears are expert tree climbers throughout their lifetime, but grizzly bears are unable to climb trees once they reach subadult size (Herrero 1970, 1978). When faced with danger from an attack by dogs, wolves, or a grizzly bear, a female black bear with young responds by climbing a nearby tree (Herrero 1970, 1985). On the other hand, a female grizzly bear with young shows a very different response when confronted with danger by standing her ground and aggressively warding off attackers.

A secondary factor contributing to differential aggressiveness between black and grizzly bears is related to their reproductive potential (Herrero 1970, 1978). A female black bear might raise twelve to thirteen young in her lifetime, and the young remain with her for only one and a half years. In contrast, a female grizzly produces only six to eight young in a lifetime, and the young remain with her for about two and a half years (Herrero 1970; Bunnell 1984a, 1984b). Hence, black bear young are, in a sense, more "expendable" than grizzly bear young. Increased aggressiveness in a female grizzly bear probably better ensures survival of her young to reproductive age and thereby protects her "investment" in each offspring.

When in grizzly bear country, humans may minimize encounters and better ensure coexistence with these bears in a few ways. Educational programs can be used to inform hikers and campers about areas occupied by adult females with young and even limit (or restrict) access to these areas (McCullough 1982; Herrero 1985; Peek, Pelton, Picton, Schoen, and Zager 1987; Albert and Bowyer 1991). When camping, people should cook their food at least 100 meters from sleeping areas and also store their garbage in bearproof containers at least 100 meters from sleeping areas (Herrero 1985). When hiking, people should go in groups, follow heavily used trails, and wear loud bear-bells or make loud noises (Herrero 1985; Jobe 1985). Incidences of injuries to hikers by grizzly bears in Glacier National Park, for example, were about six times lower when hikers wore bells versus no bells (4% and 25%, respectively). Bells, unlike whistling or yelling, presumably provide bears with unambiguous information that hikers are present, which reduces the chances of bears being startled or threatened. Also, hikers should be aware of wind direction because bears have an excellent sense of smell and can easily detect humans located upwind and avoid them well before short-range visual contact is made.

Humans can protect themselves from most bear attacks by using commercial products referred to as red-pepper sprays (Smith 1998). These sprays contain oleoresin capsicum, an irritant that usually stops aggressive behavior in grizzly and black bears (Herrero 1985; Herrero and Higgins 1998). When attacked by a bear, a person should disperse the red-pepper spray toward the bear as a cloud rather than a narrow stream; also, the liquid should not be sprayed into the wind because it might blow back into the face of the user. Ironically, residues from red-pepper spray evoke scent-marking and rolling behavior in bears (Smith 1998)! Thus, red-pepper should not be sprayed around campsites as a means of discouraging bears from entering the campground, and used canisters should be cleaned of residues if stored near sleeping areas.

Grizzly bears often give a hop charge when startled by oncoming hikers, whereas they usually use a full charge when a human is apparently perceived as a threat to cubs (Jobe 1985). When a grizzly bear directs a full charge, all possible means of defense should be used to fight back—pepper spray, rocks, sticks, firearms, clapping hands, and shouting (Herrero 1985; Herrero and Higgins 1995). If possible, a person should climb a tree. However, for someone who does not have pepper spray, a firearm, or access to a tree, the bear is extremely close, and the attack is imminent, the best strategy to minimize severe injury is to use passive resistance, that is, to play dead and cover the head and neck area (Herrero 1985).

On rare occasions, a grizzly bear (or even an adult male black bear) may deliberately follow a person, presumably viewing that human as potential prey (Herrero 1985). In this type of attack, passive resistance is not advisable. Instead, the person should confront this type of attack with aggression by throwing rocks or sticks at the bear, clapping hands, and shouting to ward off its approach. A slow retreat is good, but not a run. If the bear is a grizzly, climbing the nearest tree is best.

In conclusion, bears are powerful mammals that sometimes exhibit unpredictable and dangerous behavior. In order to promote a mutual coexistence of humans and bears, respect and caution must be exercised in bear country (McCullough 1982). We must make every effort to minimize negative encounters with bears, thereby allowing us to live in harmony with these magnificent carnivores in the wilds of North America for many generations to come.

Bear Coloration: Why Are Black Bears Brown?

Grizzly bears and gray wolves are capable of killing black bears, and some-times black bears kill other black bears (Herrero 1978; Tietje, Pelchat, and Ruff 1986; Mattson, Knight, and Blanchard 1992; Wielgus and Bunnell 1995). Thus, in areas where the geographic range of black bears overlaps that of either grizzlies or wolves, it would be "strategic" for black bears to resemble a grizzly bear in coloration. In fact, this is one of the hypothe-ses given for the evolution of nonblack coloration in black bears (Rogers 1980). A brown-phased black bear would better mimic the larger and more powerful grizzly bear, especially from a distance, compared to a black-phased black bear. Hence, if a black bear were nonblack in coloration, the probability of a potential fatal interaction with either a grizzly bear or a pack of gray wolves could be reduced.

Support for this mimicry hypothesis makes some sense when we examine the historic distribution of grizzly and black bears. When Euro-peans colonized North America, grizzlies occupied much of the continent west of the Mississippi River, whereas black bears ranged widely through-out the continent (Craighead and Mitchell 1982; Pelton 1982). If black bear populations evolved color patterns to mimic coexisting grizzly bear populations, we would expect a greater percentage of black bears west of the Mississippi to be nonblack versus those east of the Mississippi. Indeed, this is exactly what occurs when the percentage of black and nonblack individuals is compared between eastern and western black bear popula-tions (see fig. 18). For instance, brown or blonde coloration is found in about 63 percent of the black bears in Idaho and the northern Rockies, 58 percent of the black bears in eastern Washington state, and 46 percent of the black bears in Arizona (Cowan 1938; Waddell and Brown 1984). In marked contrast, adult black bears in the midwestern and eastern states

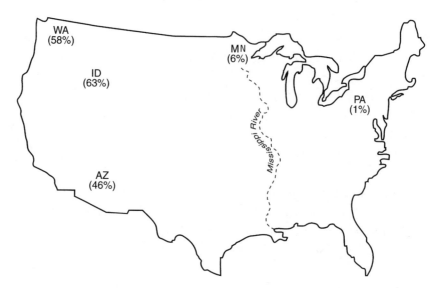

Figure 18. The percentage of individuals in black bear populations with non-black coloration in various regions of the United States.

are virtually always black-phased (Rogers 1980). Only about 6 percent of the black bears in Minnesota and 1 percent or less in mid-eastern states, for example, New York, Pennsylvania, and West Virginia, are of nonblack coloration. Most black bears born with nonblack pelage east of the Mississippi River eventually molt into a black phase by the age of two years.

Three additional hypotheses have been proposed to explain why there is a disproportionate percentage of black-phased black bears in eastern versus western states (Rogers 1980). First, early successional (brushy) habitats in the eastern deciduous forest are typically characterized by dense vegetation, which are frequently used by black bears while searching for food, for example, blackberries. Some of us have probably encountered a black bear while berry picking in brushy thickets during summer. Based on studies of bird feathers containing the black pigmentation (melanin), the pelage of black-phased bears probably wears better in brushy habitats than brown or blonde pigmentation.

Second, bear habitats in western areas tend to be more "open" (lower tree density and less canopy cover) than those in the eastern United States

(Rogers 1980). Most western black bears observed feeding during the midday in open habitats in the West are brown or blonde in coloration rather than black. This suggests that when the amount of solar radiation is highest (in midday), black-phased bears minimize heat stress by avoiding alpine meadows and open habitats.

Finally, the percentage of nonblack bears in the population may serve a camouflage purpose (Rogers 1980). In Arizona, black-phased black bears generally occur on the cooler and wetter (i.e., darker) sides of mountains, whereas black bears with nonblack coloration tend to be found on warmer and drier (i.e., lighter) sides of mountains (Waddell and Brown 1984). This relationship between pelage color and degree of aridity may enable these bears to better blend with the coloration of the local environment.

ESSAY 33

Conservation of Black Bears in the East

The black bear is the widest ranging ursid in North America and historically occurred in forested areas throughout much of North America (Pelton 1982; Whitaker and Hamilton 1998). Today, the black bear is found in at least thirty-nine states. In the eastern United States, its range is contiguous in much of the northeastern United States but becomes increasingly fragmented in the southeastern states (Pelton and Van Manen 1994). In some southern Appalachian states, for example, Georgia, North Carolina, and Tennessee, black bear populations are relatively low but stable in numbers (Clark and Pelton 1999). In six of the eight mid-eastern states, including Maryland, New Jersey, New York, Pennsylvania, Virginia, and

West Virginia, populations of black bear have either stabilized or increased over the past couple of decades (e.g., from 1984 to 1993). Conversely, urbanization and agriculture land uses have eliminated black bear populations in two mid-eastern states, Delaware and Ohio.

The successful conservation of black bears in states with remnant populations is contingent on several factors. Black bear populations are reliant on large areas containing a diversity of habitats (Landers, Hamilton, Johnson, and Marchinton 1979). Extensive forested tracts, such as those in northcentral and northeastern Pennsylvania, are beneficial to black bears because they contain a variety of abundant food resources. Under these conditions, black bears are not only very abundant, but litter sizes are higher, females breed at an earlier age, and adult body sizes are larger than elsewhere in North America (Alt 1980, 1982; Kordek and Lindzey 1980).

Historically, mast produced by the American chestnut was an extremely important food source for bears and other wildlife, but with the accidental introduction of the chestnut blight from Asia in 1904 this tree species was virtually eradicated from New England by the early 1920s and from the southern Appalachians by the 1940s (Yahner 2000). Today acorn crops serve as a critical source of hard mast as food for bears and other wildlife. If acorn crops fail in a given autumn and alternative foods are scarce, the nutritional condition of adult female bears may be lowered, thereby reducing cub survival (Eiler, Wathen, and Pelton 1989). After a poor acorn crop, female bears also may not breed in the following summer. In the Great Smoky Mountains National Park, however, bears compensated for a scarcity of acorns (resulting from extensive gypsy moth defoliation) by feeding on other food resources, for example, wild grape, pokeweed, and spicebush, in the autumn, with no discernible effects on survival or reproduction (Kasbohm, Vaughan, and Kraus 1996).

Large tracts of habitat can support higher populations of black bears than smaller tracts, thereby enhancing genetic diversity and long-term survival of bear populations (Wathen, McCracken, and Pelton 1985; Pelton 1990). These tracts are especially valuable to remnant or low bear populations if they are relatively inaccessible to humans (Landers et al. 1979). For instance, dramatic declines in bear populations in the southern Appalachians, which began in the 1960s, were partially attributed to hunters who had ready access to bear habitat on national forests, combined with their improved hunting efficiency and use of high-tech equipment, such as CB radios and radio-collared hunting dogs (Clark and Pelton 1999).

Wildlife agencies in the southern Appalachian states have taken three measures over the recent decades to help offset the precipitous declines in bear populations: hunting restrictions, bear introductions, and establishment of sanctuaries (Clark and Pelton 1999). Bear hunting was closed in Tennessee from 1970 to 1973, and bears were reintroduced into some areas of Tennessee and Virginia. North Carolina set aside a network of sanctuaries, such as the 200-square-kilometer Pisgah Bear Sanctuary in western North Carolina, specifically for the conservation of remnant bear populations (Powell, Zimmermann, Seaman, and Gilliam 1996). Because bear habitat in the southeastern United States has been reduced to about 5 to 10 percent of its former extent, the future survival of black bears in the Southeast largely hinges on the availability of large tracts of federal lands as bear habitat (Pelton 1986; Wooding, Cox, and Pelton 1994).

Construction of major highways or other developments (e.g., residential areas) should be avoided in large tracts of bear habitat (Clark and Pelton 1999). Wide-ranging male bears and translocated nuisance bears are particularly vulnerable to vehicular collisions along major highways; vehicular collisions have taken an increasing toll on bear populations in some states, such as Tennessee, North Carolina, and Florida (Harris and Gallagher 1989; Clark and Pelton 1999). Individual black bears are known to shift their home ranges away from interstate highways as a means of reducing human contact (Brody and Pelton 1989).

Large, relatively road-free tracts of bear habitat can also make it more difficult for poachers to gain access to suitable bear populations; this will help to curtail the illegal killing of bears for sale of their body parts (gallbladders, claws, and teeth) (Pelton and Van Manen 1987). Gallbladders and paws of bears are highly prized in some Asian markets (Geist 1988; McCracken, Rose, and Johnson 1995; Feldhamer, Drickamer, Vessey, and Merritt 1999). The tennis-ball-size gallbladder of a black bear in 1995, for instance, sold for as much as $200 in the United States and for thousands of dollars in some Asian markets (McCracken, Rose, and Johnson 1995).

Some Asian cultures believe that gallbladders and bile relieve stomach ailments and fever, prevent liver cancer, and serve as an aphrodisiac (Mills 1994; McCracken, Rose, and Johnson 1995).

Although the extent of bear poaching in North America is unknown, it continues to occur with potentially serious impacts on local bear populations (Rose 1994; Clark and Pelton 1999). For instance, a well-publicized investigation in the late 1980s, called Operation Smoky, was conducted by personnel from the U.S. Fish and Wildlife Service, the National Park Service, and wildlife agencies in Tennessee, North Carolina, and Georgia in an effort to curb black bear poaching in the Great Smoky Mountains National Park and vicinity (McCracken, Rose, and Johnson 1995; Yahner 2000). During a three-year period ending in 1988, Operation Smoky resulted in the arrest and conviction of fifty-two poachers; over $100,000 was levied in fines for the illegal killing of 368 black bears. Obviously, poaching of this magnitude can have substantial negative effects on remnant populations of black bears in some of the southeastern states. In a case closer to home, two people were charged in 1999 with illegally buying gallbladders in Pennsylvania; fines for these offenses ranged from $4,000 to $8,000 (Two charged in illegal bear gallbladder trading 1999).

In summary, the conservation of black bears will require the cooperation of public and private landowners to provide large tracts of roadless (or relatively roadless), "secure" habitat. Furthermore, trade in bear parts will be an ongoing problem for wildlife agencies as long as a market is available for these items, and strict law enforcement will help mitigate poaching of bears (Mills 1994; Pelton and Van Manen 1997; Clark and Pelton 1999). State, national, and international trade in bear parts must be effectively monitored and regulated to ensure the future survival of American black bears and other bear species worldwide (Berchielli 1994; McCracken, Rose, and Johnson 1995).

"Hibernation" in Black Bears —

A Metabolic and Ecological Wonder

We have seen earlier that certain rodents, for example, eastern chipmunks, become inactive in winter by entering a "shallow" state of hibernation, referred to as *torpor* (see essay 10 in chap. 7). Other small mammals, like woodchucks, exhibit true or deep hibernation in winter, where their body temperatures and other physiological functions decline dramatically for several weeks. Mammals larger than woodchucks, however, do not undergo true hibernation, perhaps because too much fat would have to be stored in the body as an energy source for winter survival (Morrison 1960; Feldhamer et al. 1999). Thus, large black bears enter an amazing state of semi-inactivity, which is better termed *winter lethargy*.

Black bears begin entering their dens for winter lethargy when adequate body fat reserves are accumulated and food supplies become scarce in autumn (Schooley, McLaughlin, Matula, and Krohn 1994). Depending on the latitude, winter lethargy begins between October and early January and ends from mid-March to early May (Pelton 1982). Typically, adult females den earlier and emerge later than subadults or adult males (Lindzey and Meslow 1976; Johnson and Pelton 1980). Entrance into and out of winter lethargy is not instantaneous (like entering and leaving a house); instead, bears must gradually adapt physiologically and behaviorally to this extended period of inactivity by fasting and reducing day-to-day activity away from the den over an approximate one-month period (Johnson and Pelton 1979, 1980; Nelson, Steiger, and Beck 1983).

Like woodchucks, "hibernating" black bears depend exclusively on fat reserves as an energy source over winter. But winter weight gain and loss

Family Ursidae

in black bears are somewhat lower (20–27%) than in woodchucks (30–40%) (Hock 1960; Ferron 1996). While in winter lethargy, body temperatures of black bears drop from a normal 40°C to 33°C, heart rate goes from forty to fifty beats per minute to eight to ten beats per minute, and oxygen consumption is about 50 to 60 percent that of the normal metabolic rate. This winter lethargic state is maintained without eating, drinking, defecating, or urinating; the highly toxic urea is recycled into nontoxic amino acids (Pelton 1982; Nelson, Steiger, and Beck 1983; Hellgren, Vaughan, Kirkpatrick, and Scanlon 1990). In adult females, these remarkable physiological adaptations are occurring while also giving birth and lactating the young over winter!

Two factors have been given to explain the evolution of winter lethargy in black bears: a seasonal scarcity of food and a need to care for newborn young. Food shortages, especially plant material in northern latitudes, has long been thought to be the principal reason why bears enter winter dormancy (Bunnell 1984b). Both sexes hibernate during winter in northern latitudes. However, food is available throughout the year in southern latitudes, yet female black bears "hibernate" while males remain active. Thus, the evolution of winter lethargy apparently has some relation to the need to care for young.

Cubs born during winter lethargy are very small at birth, weighing less than 1 percent of the body weight of the female (compared to 5–10% in humans). Because of this very small body size in newborn cubs, they have a high surface area to volume ratio and thereby experience considerable loss of body heat. Hence, the body heat produced by the dormant, lactating mother is vital in ensuring survival of her young over winter.

The survival of "hibernating" black bears is often contingent on den-site selection; dens provide protection from predators and inclement weather. Black bears in more southerly latitudes tend to use aboveground rather than ground-level dens (Johnson and Pelton 1981). In the Great Smoky Mountains National Park, Tennessee, bears select winter dens in tree cavities averaging about 11 meters (range = 5–20 m) above ground, which shield dormant bears against disturbances from humans, dogs, or floods caused by heavy winter rains. If the pelage of a bear becomes wet, the bear can lose 5–20 percent more body heat than one with a dry pelage (Hammel 1955). A tree den is also well insulated during winter, saving a bear about 15 percent more energy compared to an open, above-ground den.

In other southern locations, like the Great Dismay Swamp of Virginia and North Carolina and in the Osceola National Forest of Florida, bear dens may occur at or just above ground level if located in slightly elevated areas to reduce risks from winter floods (Hellgren and Vaughan 1989; Wooding and Hardisky 1992). These southern, ground-level dens also are generally surrounded by dense vegetation, which presumably provides a warm microclimate and concealment from enemies.

Black bears in more northerly latitudes, however, almost always use winter dens at or below (about 1 m) ground level (Tietje and Ruff 1980; Alt and Gruttadauria 1984). These dens may be under upturned roots or trunks of fallen trees, at the base of hollow trees, and in excavations, brushpiles, or rock crevices. Females typically use well-protected dens, for example, in hollow trees or rock crevices, whereas males use less concealed sites, such as under brushpiles or ground nests (Alt 1984).

Snow cover in northern latitudes helps conceal and insulate "hibernating" bears that use dens at or slightly below ground level. From an energetic perspective, dens covered with snow are about twice as insulated (27% energy savings) compared to those in tree cavity dens (15%). Dormant bears occupying dens at or near ground level in northern habitats are probably less susceptible to winter flooding compared to those in southern habitats; however, a ten-year study of bears in Pennsylvania indicated that 19 percent of the dens were abandoned and 5 percent of the cubs in these dens died because of floods caused by winter rains (Alt 1984).

Black bears use only a small number (5–9%) of the winter dens from one year to the next (Tietje and Ruff 1980; Alt 1984). When a den is reused, it usually by either the same bear or the daughters of the adult female who used that den in the previous year. In areas where dens are limited (e.g., in some southern states where large trees with cavities are scarce because of logging practices), bears may more likely reuse the same den in successive years (Lindzey and Meslow 1976; Johnson and Pelton 1981). Switching to new dens each winter is probably adaptive in bears because predators can learn the location of dens and because disease transmission may be reduced (Alt 1984).

Humans should make every effort to avoid disturbing a black bear in winter lethargy (Tietje and Ruff 1980). If a bear is aroused and forced to abandon the den, it may lose over 56 percent more of its body weight compared to normal weight loss. If a female with cubs is disturbed, weight loss associated with the disturbance can profoundly lower her energy levels for lactation and thereby reduce cub survival. Furthermore, black bears in winter lethargy shunt blood away from skeletal muscles and into vital organs to better ration stored fat reserves (Rogers and Durst 1987). Thus, if "awakened" by a predator during winter lethargy, a black bear is quite sluggish and, hence, very susceptible to predators.

In summary, the black bear is truly a metabolic marvel during winter. Physiological and behavioral changes, coupled with strategic den-site selection, have evolved in black bears to enhance their survival and care of young during winter lethargy. As we walk through the woodlands of the mid-eastern states during winter, take a moment to reflect on how our largest carnivore is coping with the rigors of winter. We also can do our part in conserving this magnificent mammal by staying clear of their dens while they are "asleep" over winter.

13

Raccoon and Allies

Family Procyonidae

Description of the Family Procyonidae

The family Procyonidae is in the order Carnivora and includes nineteen species. Only one procyonid species, the lesser (or red) panda, is found in the Old World; it occurs in the wild in limited numbers in Nepal, China, and surrounding countries. The remaining eighteen species are New World in distribution, with three species present in North America: white-tailed coati, ringtail, and common raccoon. Raccoons are common in all eight mid-eastern states (see table 1).

Procyonids are medium-sized carnivores that evolved from the canid family. The pelage of procyonids varies from reddish brown (e.g., lesser pandas) to grayish (common raccoons). The common raccoon is representative of many procyonids in terms of body size (66–101 cm in total length and 5–16 kg in weight). Most species have facial markings, as with the familiar mask in raccoons, and tails are usually ringed with alternating light and dark bands. The ears of procyonids are short and rounded, muzzles are relatively short, and faces are broad. The typical number of teeth is forty; carnassials (see chap. 11) are developed only in ringtails.

Procyonids are terrestrial and very good climbers; most have a bear-like, plantigrade gait, using both heels and toes while walking (see chap. 12). They prefer a variety of home sites, such as tree cavities and rock crevices. Procyonids are principally omnivorous, although lesser pandas rely heavily on bamboo as food.

Common raccoons are found in wooded and brushy areas, especially near water. They also occupy agricultural, urban, and suburban habitats (Kaufmann 1982). Raccoons are mainly active at night (see essay 35 below) and feed on a broad range of animal and plant matter, such as crayfish, bird eggs, insects, acorns, and corn, depending on seasonal availability. Raccoons do not hibernate but may spend extended periods of winter inactivity in tree cavities or other sheltered areas once permanent snow cover is present.

Raccoons are promiscuous, with mating occurring from January to March. Young are born in early spring after a gestation of about sixty-three to sixty-five days. Most young are weaned within sixteen weeks. However, the family may remain intact through autumn, and often family groups in northern latitudes overwinter communally in the same tree cavity or in cavities of several nearby trees.

ESSAY 35

The Invasion of the Raccoon Rabies —

History, Distribution, and Concerns

Rabies is one of the most dreaded infectious diseases known to humans (see essay 29 in chap. 11). The major vectors of rabies in North America traditionally have been foxes, striped skunks, and bats (J. Smith 1989; Krebs, Wilson, and Childs 1995). However, since the early 1990s, the raccoon has become the major wild vector of this disease in the United States (Krebs, Wilson, and Childs 1995). For example, of 7,124 cases of rabies in the United States in 1996, 52 percent were attributed to raccoons (http://www.cdc.gov/ncidod/dvrd/rabies).

The potential for human contacts with rabid raccoons is of particular concern because raccoon populations are often high in cities and suburbia (Anthony, Childs, Glass, Korch, Ross, and Grigor 1990). Also, humans often show little fear of raccoons—we might see them in our backyard raiding the garbage or know of someone who has kept a young raccoon as a pet. Furthermore, a rabid raccoon exhibits docile behavior and is visibly weakened (Kaufmann 1982) rather than showing a furious form of rabies, which is seen often in canids and is characterized by aggressive attacks and biting. Thus, an unsuspecting person may interpret a docile rabid raccoon as simply being friendly and initiate contact with the animal (Bruggemann 1992).

Although raccoon rabies became common in the 1990s, it has been recorded in Florida since the early 1950s (http://www.wadsworth.org/rabies) and in some other southeastern states (e.g., Alabama, Georgia, and South Carolina) for the past few decades (Bruggemann 1992; Krebs, Wilson, and Childs 1995). But a renewed concern in raccoon rabies surfaced in 1977 when rabid raccoons were found in eastern West Virginia near

Family Procyonidae

177

the border of northern Virginia; these records were much further north than previous known incidences of raccoon rabies (Jenkins and Winkler 1987; Krebs, Wilson, and Childs 1995). The infected raccoons in the West Virginia–Virginia area may have been animals that were captured in the southeastern United States and later released by hunters into this more northerly location (http://www.wadsworth.org/rabies).

Since 1977, the invasion of raccoon rabies into eastern West Virginia has proceeded northward and eastward at a steady rate of about sixteen to thirty-two kilometers per year. Raccoon rabies was initially documented, for example, in the south central counties of Pennsylvania in 1982 and in the northern counties of the state by 1988 (J. T. Rankin, personal communication, 1995). By 1989 raccoon rabies probably dispersed northward into New York state, although no cases were documented during that year (Reid-Sanden, Dobbins, Smith, and Fishbein 1990; http://www.wadsworth.org/rabies). Thus, in the early 1990s, raccoon rabies existed in two rather distinct areas: one in the southeastern states and another in the mid-Atlantic states (Krebs, Wilson, and Childs 1995). However, now in the twenty-first century, the distribution of raccoon rabies has become contiguous throughout all of eastern North America, extending from Florida to at least southeastern Canada and southern Maine (http://www.wadsworth.org/rabies).

The rise in the number of cases of raccoon rabies has paralleled its spread in the mid-eastern states. For instance, in 1978, only a few cases of raccoon rabies were reported in West Virginia and Virginia; but within four years, approximately 1,000 cases were reported annually in both states combined (Bruggemann 1992). The number of raccoon rabies cases in Pennsylvania rose from 74 possible cases in 1982 to a peak of 702 cases in 1989, with declines thereafter (Iampietro 1998).

During the period spanning 1991–97, incidences of raccoon rabies was commonplace in several mid-eastern states (Krebs, Holman, Hines, Strine, Mandel, and Childs 1992; Krebs, Strine, and Childs 1993; Krebs, Strine, Smith, Rupprecht, and Childs 1994, 1995; Krebs, Strine, Smith, Noah, Rupprecht, and Childs 1996; Krebs, Smith, Rupprecht, and Childs 1997, 1998; see also table 2). A total of 17,903 cases was reported during this seven-year period, with most (45.1%) in New York, followed by Maryland (17.4%), New Jersey (12.9%), Virginia (10.7%), and Pennsylvania (9.0%).

Table 2. The number of cases of raccoon rabies reported in each of the eight mideastern states from 1991 to 1997.

Year	DE	MD	NJ	NY	OH	PA	VA	WV	Total
				Number of Cases					
1991	143	467	787	666	0	219	167	17	2,466
1992	162	413	579	1,392	1	208	203	23	2,981
1993	100	501	332	2,369	0	229	213	35	3,779
1994	38	412	194	1,284	0	222	251	0	2,401
1995	53	326	219	846	0	219	271	64	1,998
1996	52	511	76	688	1	250	383	63	2,024
1997	40	494	124	836	59	272	429	0	2,254
Total	**588**	**3,124**	**2,311**	**8,081**	**61**	**1,619**	**1,917**	**202**	**17,903**
	(3.3%)	(17.4%)	(12.9%)	(45.1%)	(0.3%)	(9.0%)	(10.7%)	(1.1%)	

Conversely, the number of cases of raccoon rabies was considerably lower in West Virginia, Delaware, and Ohio (range = 0.3–3.3%). Most raccoon rabies cases in the mid-eastern states were noted in 1993, largely because of a peak in New York state (n = 2,369 cases).

In the 1990s, the number of rabies cases in raccoons far exceeded those in other wild or domestic animals in the eight mid-eastern states. In 1997, for instance, 68.1 percent of the 3,312 cases of rabies in the mid-eastern states were those in raccoons, 17.3 percent (n = 574) in skunks, 6.1 percent (n = 202) in bats, and 5.5 percent (n = 184) in foxes (Krebs et al. 1998). In contrast, only 6.4 percent (n = 212) of the rabies cases during 1997 were in domestic animals, giving a sixteen- to seventeenfold higher rate of rabies in wild versus domestic animals.

Only eighteen humans have been diagnosed with various strains of rabies from 1980 to 1999, and the cost of its prevention in humans is in the millions of dollars (http://ntri.tamuk.edu). For example, in New York state alone, about 2,500 persons were treated for rabies as of 1999 because of potential contact with rabid raccoons at a cost of about $1,000/person (total = $2.5 million) (http://www.wadsworth.org/rabies). Fortunately, no one has yet acquired rabies from a rabid raccoon in the United States.

So what is the solution to raccoon rabies and its invasion in eastern North America? First, some may feel that raccoon-removal programs, for example, trapping or use of poison baits, are a logical solution. Removal

Family Procyonidae

programs for raccoons, however, are usually unsuccessful and can have an impact on nontarget wildlife (Jenkins, Perry, and Winkler 1988; Bruggemann 1992). Second, although large-scale vaccination of wild raccoon populations has been somewhat successful (Johnston, Voigt, MacInnes, Bachmann, Lawson, and Rupprecht 1988; Bruggemann 1992; http://www. wadsworth.org/rabies), the density of rabid raccoons in a population does not begin to decline until about 95 percent of the raccoons are annually vaccinated. This percentage obviously is difficult to achieve because raccoon populations can turn over as much as 80 percent per year (Coyne, Smith, and McAllister 1989; Bruggemann 1992). Hence, the vaccination of wild raccoon populations for rabies may not be a practical alternative. A third and best solution is to take personal measures to reduce this disease. We can achieve this by vaccinating our pets and becoming more educated about the necessary precautions to take when a docile, "cute," yet potentially rabid raccoon is encountered in the wild or in our backyard.

14

Weasels and Allies

Family Mustelidae

Description of the Family Mustelidae

The family Mustelidae (order Carnivora) is composed of fifty-nine species that inhabit all parts of the world, with the exception of several areas, for example, Australia, Madagascar, West Indies, and most of the Philippine Islands. Eight mustelid species occur in the mid-eastern states; of these, only long-tailed weasels and mink are ubiquitous (see table 1). All mustelids in the mid-eastern states are native.

The family Mustelidae formerly included weasel-like mammals (e.g., weasels, otters), skunks from North America, and stink badgers from Asia. Recently, however, mitochondrial-DNA data and morphological data have been used to separate the weasel-like mammals from the skunks and stink badgers, giving two families, Mustelidae and Mephitidae, respectively (see chap. 15) (Dragoo and Honeycutt 1997; Jones et al. 1997).

Most mustelids have elongated bodies, but wolverines and American badgers are stocky. The ears of mustelids are short and either rounded or pointed. Claws are compressed and curved but are particularly large in badgers for digging purposes. Digits in the northern river otter are webbed for swimming.

The pelage of mustelids is usually uniformly colored, but three species (ermine, long-tailed weasel, and least weasel) in the mid-eastern states are brown in summer and white in winter. The least weasel is the smallest carnivore in the world (16–20 cm in total length and 38–63 g in weight); the giant otter of South America is the largest mustelid (1.2–2.4 m and 22–34 kg). Mustelids exhibit sexual dimorphism, with males being about one-fourth larger than females. The eight mustelid species in the mid-eastern states have thirty-four to thirty-eight teeth and well-developed carnassials and canines.

Mustelids occupy a range of terrestrial and aquatic habitats. Certain species, such as martens, are agile tree climbers, whereas others (northern river otters) are adept at swimming. Mustelids are either nocturnal or diurnal. They are flesh-eaters and hunt principally by olfaction, although visual and auditory senses are well developed.

Most mustelids have two features that are shared with the closely related mephitids: production of potent smelling secretions and delayed implantation (see also bears, chap. 12). Mustelids have anal glands that produce secretions for intraspecific communication or when alarmed. When handled, these secretions have a pungent odor that is quite offensive to humans. In contrast, secretions produced by mephitids (e.g., skunks) are well known for their extremely noxious odor, which is used as a defensive weapon (see essay 39 in chap. 15).

Delayed implantation is a widespread phenomenon in

mustelids (Weir and Rowlands 1973). During delayed implantation, the fertilized egg remains in the uterus as a hollow ball of cells, known as the blastocyst. The blastocyst does not immediately implant in the lining of the uterus because low levels of the hormone progesterone are produced with reduced daylength, thereby curtailing further development of the embryo. However, as daylength increases the following spring, progesterone levels rise, which then initiates the implantation of the embryo into the uterine lining and subsequent rapid growth of the embryo. The period of delayed implantation varies with species. It may last six to seven months in northern river otters and less than one month in mink, but is absent in least weasels. In the closely related North American mephitids, only the western spotted skunk exhibits delayed implantation.

Mustelids usually produce one litter of two to five young. In contrast, least weasels are more rodent-like by producing two litters of three to ten young per litter. Gestation ranges from around one month in least weasels to nearly one year in fishers. Only the adult female cares for the young.

Family Mustelidae

ESSAY 36

Conservation of Northern River Otters and Fishers

The conservation status of two large mustelid species in the mid-eastern states, northern river otters and fishers, has been a major concern over the past several decades. Otters were once found throughout all the major waterways of Canada and the United States, with the exception of those in the arid southwestern states and frozen Arctic (Hall 1981). As a result of excessive trapping during the nineteenth century, human encroachment on habitat, and habitat loss or degradation, otters were extirpated or became rare in many areas of North America by the early to mid-1900s (Toweill and Tabor 1982; Melquist and Dronkert 1987; Serfass, Brooks, and Rymon 1993).

Otter habitats were lost or degraded because waterways and riparian areas were developed for recreation, industry, agriculture, or residential areas and because water quality declined as a result of pesticides, increased siltation, or acid-mine drainage. Only a decade or so ago in the mid-eastern states otters were present in low numbers only in eastern Maryland, northeastern Pennsylvania, and eastern New York, and were extirpated in Ohio and West Virginia. However, since 1976 (in Colorado), otter reintroduction projects have been initiated by numerous state and provincial wildlife agencies, enabling populations of this aesthetic mustelid to make a remarkable comeback in the mideastern states and elsewhere in North America (Melquist and Dronkert 1987; Serfass, Peper, Whary, and Brooks 1993).

Two established and successful reintroduction projects for northern river otters in the mid-eastern states are those in Pennsylvania and West Virginia. The Pennsylvania River Otter Reintroduction Project began in 1982 with the major objective to restore otters in watersheds within their historic range of north central and western Pennsylvania (Serfass, Peper, Whary, and Brooks 1993; Serfass, Lovallo, Brooks, Hayden, and Mitcheltree 1999). These animals were live-trapped from established populations in northeastern Pennsylvania and eastern Maryland or were obtained from commercial dealers and trappers in Louisiana, Michigan, New Hampshire, and New York. Since 1982 the range of river otters in Pennsylvania has expanded considerably because of the reintroduction project, dispersal of animals northward from the Chesapeake Bay area in Maryland and eastward from Ohio. Otters from Ohio were originally introduced by the state near the Ohio-Pennsylvania border (Serfass et al. 1999).

The West Virginia River Otter Reintroduction Project was initiated in 1984 with the intention of restoring otters to watersheds once occupied by this mammal prior to the 1950s (Allen 1997). Otters for the West Virginia project were acquired by live-trapping along coastal areas of Maryland, North Carolina, and Virginia, trading wild turkeys for otters with state wildlife agencies in North Carolina and Texas, and purchasing otters from private suppliers in North Carolina. Other otter restoration efforts also have begun in the mid-eastern states, for example, the New York River Otter Reintroduction Project in 1995 (http://www.nyotter.org). Like the other projects, the New York otter project has already been successful in returning this mustelid to its historic range.

A successful otter reintroduction program is contingent on several factors (Serfass, Brooks, Swimley, Rymon, and Hayden 1996). First, to ensure that the population becomes established, an adequate number of animals must be released in a given watershed; for example, twenty to thirty animals, evenly divided between the sexes, are recommended for release at each site (Serfass et al. 1996; http://www.nyotter.org). Second, every effort should be made to keep trap-related injuries to a minimum, and animals housed prior to release in the wild should be kept in sanitary housing and be provided with nutritional food (Serfass et al. 1993, 1996). Third, when otters are released, wildlife biologists should avoid periods of high human activity (e.g., weekends) and inclement weather at release sites (Serfass et al. 1996). Finally, the cost of reintroducing river otters does not come cheap. For instance, about $1,000 was spent for each otter reintroduced into New York (http://www.nyotter.org).

Family Mustelidae

The fisher is another aesthetic mustelid reintroduced by wildlife biologists into its former range in North America (Douglas and Strickland 1987). Fishers historically occurred throughout much of Canada and northern United States, but populations were decimated in the nineteenth and twentieth centuries worldwide and in the mid-eastern states (Ohio, Pennsylvania, Virginia, and West Virginia) by timber removal in large forested tracts, agriculture, excessive trapping, and use of strychnine as harvest and predator control methods (Strickland, Douglas, Novak, and Hunziger 1982; Douglas and Strickland 1987; Buskirk 1992). State and provincial wildlife agencies, however, have successfully reintroduced fishers since the mid- to late 1950s, enabling this mustelid to expand into its former range in some areas of North America. For example, fishers were introduced in West Virginia in 1969, and these animals now have spread into parts of Virginia. Fishers were released into the Catskill Mountains of New York in 1976, and populations spread so rapidly that fisher trapping is now permitted in New York.

The Pennsylvania Fisher Reintroduction Project, which began in 1994, is representative of efforts by wildlife agencies to restore this beautiful mustelid into its former range (Serfass, Brooks, Tzilkowski, and Mitcheltree 1994; Serfass 1998). The fisher was last documented in Pennsylvania in 1921, although viable breeding populations were probably extirpated by the end of the twentieth century (Genoways and Brenner 1985). Wildlife biologists in Pennsylvania began this project by selecting five release sites on forested, public (state and federal) lands with minimal development. Fishers were purchased from trappers in New Hampshire and New York, and twenty-three to forty-seven animals were stocked at each site.

The Pennsylvania fisher reintroduction project initially got off on the right footing using four important steps (Serfass et al. 1994; Serfass 1998). First, wildlife biologists spent a considerable amount of time generating public support for the reintroduction project. An informed, supportive public is more likely to report sightings of released fishers and be intolerant of the illegal killing of fishers. Second, those trappers who provided the biologists with fishers for release were required to use box or cage traps and specially designed transport containers to minimize injury to the animals. Third, each captive animal was held for a ten- to fourteen-day period where it was given a comprehensive veterinary evaluation before release to ensure that the animal was in good health. Fourth, some of the released animals were fitted with a transmitter attached to a radio collar and radio-tracked after release to determine their long-term survival.

Fishers are very susceptible to overharvest by trapping (Powell 1979; Paragi, Krohn, and Arthur 1994). Thus, once fishers have been established in a given state or province, wildlife agencies must be conservative when establishing trapping regulations for this mustelid.

The reintroduction projects for otters and fishers in North America are perfect examples of positive wildlife conservation in action. We are fortunate to live in an era in which scientists and the public alike appreciate the role and beauty of these aesthetic carnivores in our aquatic and forested ecosystems. Only a century or so ago, some large predators, such as gray wolves and mountain lions (see essay 30 in chap. 11 and essay 42 in chap. 16), were feared and indiscriminantly killed. Hence, as a society, we have become more "conservation mature" and better stewards of our wildlife resources compared to several decades in our recent past.

E S S A Y 3 7

Sexual Dimorphism in Weasels and Other Mammals

In most mammalian species, males tend to be at least slightly larger than females, whereas in most invertebrates, in many fishes, amphibians, and reptiles, and in some birds, females are larger than males (Ralls 1977). A surprising number of mammalian species exhibit extreme dimorphism in body size, whereby one sex is on average 1.6 times heavier than the other

Family Mustelidae

sex. The mustelids are excellent examples of mammals that show extreme sexual dimorphism. Here I survey the occurrence of this phenomenon and explore why it may be adaptive in mammals.

To begin with, extreme sexual dimorphism in body size in favor of females is uncommon in mammals, occurring only in the vespertilionid bats (see chap. 5) (Ralls 1976). Two hypotheses have been given for the "big mother" hypothesis in these bats. First, a larger female may be at an advantage by being able to produce more offspring than a smaller female. Second, and probably more important, larger body size in females enables them to produce more milk; greater milk production would allow young bats to gain body weight more quickly (Findley and Trout 1970; Ralls 1976). This is adaptive because vespertilionid bats have a limited amount of time in the spring and summer to raise their young to adult size, and young must gain weight rapidly in preparation for winter hibernation.

Conversely, extreme sexual dimorphism in favor of males is found in large aquatic species (e.g., sperm whale, northern elephant seal, northern fur seal, and walrus), large terrestrial species (e.g., great red kangaroo, orangutan, gorilla, and African elephant), and small mustelids (Ralls 1977). The evolution of large males seems to be associated with adult body size and the type of mating system (monogamy versus polygyny), at least in the larger mammalian species. For instance, the male harbor seal is only slightly larger than the female, and it is monogamous. On the other hand, the northern elephant seal is sexually dimorphic and polygynous, with males mating with more than one female and investing no time in care of young. For some unexplained reason, however, body size and type of mating system are not related in small mammals, such as rodents and insectivores. In these taxonomic groups, extreme sexual dimorphism is absent, yet these small mammals are polygynous.

Why is extreme sexual dimorphism in favor of males adaptive? Larger body size may better enable a male to mate and subsequently defend his harem and young from rival males, as in northern elephant seals and gorillas (Ralls 1977). In another species, the walrus, harem defense is not the issue because copulation takes place in the water; instead, large body size better ensures that large, dominant males occupy the best position on land within large amorphous groups along the shore (Ronald, Selley, and

Healey 1982). These males are then located in safer, central positions, whereas the smaller, subordinate males are positioned along the periphery of the colony where they are more susceptible to predators, such as killer whales.

The elongated mustelids give us some additional insight into the adaptiveness of extreme sexual dimorphism in favor of males. Ermine, for instance, rely heavily on small mammals, for example, voles (see essay 38 below). The smaller female ermine is especially capable of following small mammals into runways and tunnels, but the larger male cannot fit into these areas and relies more on somewhat larger prey. Thus, differential body size enables male and female mustelids to partition food resources, thereby reducing intraspecific competition between the sexes (Brown and Lasiewski 1972).

Two additional reasons for sexual dimorphism in elongated weasels are related to mobility and dominance. The more mobile male weasel has a much larger home range than the less mobile female (Simms 1979; Svendsen 1982). Because of a relatively large territory size, males probably encounter several mates (Erlinge 1979; Simms 1979). Moreover, when males encounter each other, the largest of the two is likely to be dominant over the smaller individual; therefore, larger body size allows a male to better defend his territory or an estrous female from a smaller rival male (Simms 1979). Also, the size advantage of a male over a female enables him to physically dominate her, which involves vigorous fighting (Svendsen 1982); prior to mating, the male subdues the female by grabbing her by the back of the neck with his teeth and clasping her lower abdomen with his forelegs.

In conclusion, extreme sexual dimorphism has at least five possible explanations for its evolution, depending on the species. Much needs to be learned regarding its adaptiveness across the spectrum of mammals exhibiting this interesting phenomenon.

How Do Mammals Minimize Competition?

Examples from Mustelids

Competition may occur between two individuals of the same or different species, which is termed *intraspecific* and *interspecific* competition, respectively. Furthermore, competition may be subdivided into two types: interference or exploitative (Miller 1967). Interference competition involves aggression between individuals and occasionally death. Conversely, exploitative competition occurs when an individual gains access to a resource before another and does not involve overt aggressive behavior.

We are familiar with some examples of interference and exploitative competition between individuals of the same species. Each spring, many of us witness interference competition when two male American robins sing simultaneously in neighboring backyards as a means of establishing and maintaining territorial boundaries. Another example is when an adult male white-tailed deer spars with a rival in an effort to defend and mate with an estrous female. Exploitative competition can be readily seen in cavity-nesting bird species—the first bluebird that finds the nest box is often the one that becomes the tenant of the box. Similarly, the first red fox to encounter a road-killed cottontail is the one that makes a meal of the rabbit.

We have already discussed examples of interference competition involving aggression and even death between two species, for example, co-existing canids and ursids (see essay 27 in chap. 11 and essay 32 in chap. 12). A considerable amount of published literature dealt with ways in which sympatric mammals minimize exploitative competition and thereby partition food resources (Grant 1972). In the desert Southwest, for instance, sympatric Arizona pocket mice and Merriam's kangaroo rats feed at different times of the day and on slightly different food resources to reduce exploitative competition (Reichman 1975). Closer to home, sympatric white-footed and deer mice partition space by foraging at different heights in deciduous trees; the white-footed mouse tends to spend more time nearer to ground level than the deer mouse (Barry, Botje, and Grantham 1984). As other examples, eastern chipmunks rely on smaller-sized food resources compared to larger gray squirrels (see essay 9 in chap. 7). Flying squirrels, although feeding on many of the same food resources as chipmunks and gray squirrels, are active at night rather than during the day to reduce competition for food with these diurnal sciurids (see essay 11). The potential for interspecific competition also exists in sympatric mustelids of the mid-eastern states. I would like to explore competition between two semiaquatic mustelids, northern river otter and mink, and among three terrestrial mustelids, long-tailed weasel, ermine, and least weasel.

Northern river otters are associated with aquatic habitats, especially larger streams, rivers, and estuaries (Toweill and Tabor 1982). Mink also occur in these aquatic habitats, as well as in lakes, ditches, swamps, and marshes (Linscombe, Kinler, and Aulerich 1982). Furthermore, both mustelid species feed on aquatic vertebrates and invertebrates. Thus, a perfect scenario exists for potential interspecific competition between these two closely related mustelids for either space or food in the mid-eastern states, for example, Maryland, New York, Pennsylvania, and Virginia (table 1).

Interspecific competition between northern river otters and mink, however, is probably nonexistent, or at best minimal, for several reasons. Let's start by comparing their aquatic adaptations. Otters have cylindrical body shape, small ears relative to body size, a dorso-ventrally flattened tail serving as a rudder, webbed feet acting as paddles, waterproof fur, equivalent vision above and below water, and a well-developed lung capacity to forage for food underwater (Dunstone and O'Conner 1979; Toweill and Tabor 1982; Powell and Zielinski 1983; Melquist and Dronkert 1987). Mink, on the other hand, have typical weasel-like features (e.g., elongated body and small ears), semiwebbed feet, and waterproof fur (Melquist, Whitman, and Hornocker 1981; Linscombe, Kinler, and Aulerich 1982). Thus, of the two species, the adaptations of otters make them much better specialized for an aquatic way of life.

Second, despite sometimes coexisting in the same habitat, northern river otters and mink exhibit spatial and temporal differences in foraging activity (Melquist, Whitman, and Hornocker 1981). Otters always forage in the water, and mink almost exclusively forage along the shoreline. Furthermore, otters may forage at any time of the day, but mink forage at night.

Third, when analyzed in detail, the food preferences of otters and mink are quite different. Otters are larger (5–13.7 kg in weight) than mink (0.7–1.6 kg) and, thus, differ in selection of prey type and size. Indeed, nearly the entire diet of otters consists of fish (93–100%) (Melquist, Whitman, and Hornocker 1981; Melquist and Hornocker 1983). In contrast, mink are more generalist predators, with a diet of about 7 to 59 percent fish (Melquist, Whitman, and Hornocker 1981; Gilbert and Nancekivell 1982; Eagle and Whitman 1987). Otters also usually feed on fish that are at least fifteen centimeters, and mink prey on much smaller fish.

Otters tend to forage on slow-moving, bottom-dwelling, and schooling fish species, many of which are weakened or injured (Melquist, Whitman, and Hornocker 1981; Toweill and Tabor 1982; Melquist and Hornocker 1983). Fish species commonly preyed upon by otters are sucker, carp, dace, catfish, sunfish, and sculpin, whereas fast-moving species, like trout and pike, are relatively unimportant as food. Mink, on the other hand, rely on a mix of aquatic and terrestrial prey items, for example, small fishes, crayfish, amphibians, birds, bird eggs, small mammals (voles, mice, and shrews), which varies with season, location, and prey availability (Sargeant, Swanson, and Doty 1973; Burgess and Bider 1980; Melquist, Whitman, and Hornocker 1981; Linscombe, Kinler, and Aulerich 1982).

In short, interspecific competition is negligible between northern river otters and mink. Even within the same habitat, these two mustelids tend to restrict foraging activities to certain areas and times of day and have relatively little overlap in prey species.

As with the otter-mink scenario, the setting is perfect for interspecific competition to potentially exist among long-tailed weasels, ermine, and least weasels. The range of these three species overlaps in four mid-eastern states (table 1); but in North America the distribution is more southerly in long-tailed weasels versus more northerly in the other two species (Simms 1979; Svendsen 1982). Furthermore, two or more of these species may inhabit the same woodland or grassland. Thus, how are food resources partitioned among these species?

There are some distinct differences in the body sizes of these three weasels. The long-tailed weasel is the largest (279–418 mm total body length), the ermine intermediate (181–332 mm), and the least weasel smallest (165–203 mm). Therefore, long-tailed weasels tend to prefer larger prey, for example, cottontails, although they are also known to feed on voles (Simms 1979). Female ermine and both sexes of the least weasel, on the other hand, are vole specialists. But because male ermine are about 10 to 15 percent larger that female ermine (see essay 37 above), males are sometimes unable to forage for voles in smaller tunnels and must rely on larger prey.

In northern latitudes with winter snow cover, the smaller ermine and least weasel easily exploit the subnivean environment, which is the zone between the ground and the snow layer (Simms 1979). In winter, most activity of small mammals is confined to this zone. Hence, the northward distribution of the larger long-tailed weasel is restricted because it is too large to forage within this subnivean environment. In more northerly latitudes, the long-tailed weasel is "replaced" by the larger marten, which is an arboreal mustelid that is not only very adept at hunting for red squirrels in trees but also capable of hunting long-tailed weasels.

Conversely, in southern latitudes, the distribution of ermine and least weasels is restricted, despite the presence of voles, for two possible reasons (Rosenweig 1966; Simms 1979). First, the larger long-tailed weasel can exclude or kill these two smaller weasel species; thus, without a predictable layer of snow in southern latitudes, these smaller weasels lack refugia from predation by their larger cousin. Of the two smaller weasels, the range of the least weasel extends further southward into the range of the long-tailed weasel. Perhaps this is because the least weasel has a very high reproductive potential, which partially offsets predation pressures imposed on it by the long-tailed weasel and other predators. Second, all three of these weasels are capable of changing coat color from brown in summer to white in winter. Ermines in eastern North America always change to a white coat color in winter regardless of latitude, whereas southern populations of long-tailed weasel remain brown year-round. Therefore, eastern populations of ermine found in southerly latitudes where snow cover is lacking or scarce during winter would be very susceptible to a variety of predators such as long-tailed weasels and great horned owls.

Family Mustelidae

15

Skunks and Stink Badgers

Family Mephitidae

Description of the Family Mephitidae

Skunks from North America and stink badgers from Asia originally were placed in the family Mustelidae with weasels, otters, and allies (see chap. 14). However, based on an in-depth examination of mitochondrial-DNA and morphological data, these animals recently have been classified as a new family, Mephitidae (Dragoo and Honeycutt 1997; Jones et al. 1997).

There are eight species of mephitids: six skunks and two stink badgers. Striped and spotted skunks occur in the mideastern states (see table 1). The striped skunk is ubiquitous in the eight mideastern states, with its range extending from southern Canada to northern Mexico. The eastern spotted skunk is common in two of the mideastern states (Maryland and Virginia) and is rare or at risk in two others (Pennsylvania and West Virginia). The geographic distribution of the spotted skunk is more restrictive than that of the striped skunk, extending from southcentral Pennsylvania, Minnesota, and eastern Wyoming to Florida and northeastern Mexico.

Unlike the elongated mustelids, skunks are stout carnivores with long, bushy tails. Mephitids have small and rounded ears and pointed noses. Their pelage has a striking black-and-white pattern. Striped skunks usually have a distinctive forked white dorsal stripe, but some individuals may have only a white spot at the base of the neck; sometimes a white stripe is found between the eyes. Conversely, eastern spotted skunks have a more complicated black-and-white pattern, consisting of a white spot on the forehead and small white spots in front of each ear, plus four white stripes extending down the back. These stripes are broken into spots on the rump, and tails are white-tipped.

Our two skunks are representative of mephitids in terms of size and weight. The striped skunk is larger (51–71 cm and 2.7–6.3 kg in total body length and weight, respectively) than the eastern spotted skunk (34–57 cm and 0.4–1.0 kg). Mephitids have either thirty-two or thirty-four teeth, and carnassials are not well developed; our two skunk species have thirty-four teeth.

Skunks occur in a variety of habitats from woodlots to grasslands and may be encountered along fencerows or woodlot edges, in rocky outcrops, and even beneath houses or vacant buildings. Skunks sometimes dig their own burrows, but cavities or spaces under fallen trees, old stumps, rocks, or buildings may serve as dens. Skunks often den communally, especially during winter. Skunks do not exhibit true hibernation in winter (see essay 10 in chap. 7); however, they may undergo an extended period of inactivity or shallow torpor lasting 75–100 days. Stored body fat is used as an energy source during torpor.

Skunks are nocturnal, typically traveling relatively short

Family Mephitidae

distances from a den to the same feeding area for several consecutive nights. They are omnivorous, feeding opportunistically on insects, small mammals, bird nests, fruit, grains, and other food items. Olfactory and auditory senses are important for prey capture; because skunks are slow-moving, they sometimes lie in wait or slowly stalk animal prey. Perhaps in part because of their slow movements, mephitids are conspicuously colored and produce powerful pungent secretions as a defensive weapon (see essay 39 below).

Only one skunk species, the western spotted skunk, exhibits delayed implantation (see chap. 14). Hence, the western spotted skunk is considered by most authorities to be a separate species from its eastern counterpart (Weir and Rowlands 1973). Striped and spotted skunks produce one litter per year of about four to seven young. Depending on the species, gestation is about seven to nine weeks, and the young are weaned in seven to ten weeks. Only the female cares for the young.

Skunks and Stink Badgers

ESSAY 39

Why Do Skunks Stink?

A variety of organisms are conspicuously colored or patterned: yellow jackets, coral snakes, skunks, zebras, to name a few. With the exception of zebras, conspicuous coloration or patterns apparently signal a warning to a potential predator to "stay away or suffer the consequences." In yellow jackets, the consequence is a sting; in coral snakes, poisonous venom; and in skunks, a pungent secretion. Before discussing why skunks stink, we will first diverge for a moment to discuss why another group of mammals, the zebras, are black-and-white patterned.

Color patterns in zebras are interesting from an evolutionary perspective because ancestors of all horses (including zebras) were striped, yet this characteristic is retained only in extant zebras and not in modern horses (Nowak 1999). Two tempting explanations for zebra color patterns are camouflage and temperature regulation (Kingdon 1984). But camouflage does not seem to be the answer because zebras are often found in open country away from vegetation. The alternating dark or light stripes of zebras probably do not assist in regulating body temperatures (see essay 32 in chap. 12) because they occupy areas with a range of climatic conditions in Africa.

Stripes in zebras instead seem to have some value in deterring predation (Kingdon 1984). The stripes of individual zebras fleeing from a predator may act to dazzle the predator, much like the visual illusion created by a spinning kaleidoscope. Perhaps the primary reason for zebra striping, however, is to aid in group cohesion. The black-and-white striping pattern has been found to stimulate nerve cells in the visual system of zebras. Thus, a current hypothesis for stripes is that it helps zebras maintain cohesive herds when fleeing from predators. Herd formation also is adaptive because zebras share limited resources, such as water at a watering hole, and it enables them to better detect potential danger.

Family Mephitidae

Returning to skunks, if the message "stay away or suffer the consequences" sent by the black-and-white pattern fails, a skunk will resort to other predator deterrents (Godin 1982; Howard and Marsh 1982). When approached by an enemy, a skunk will make noise by stamping its front feet quickly, hissing, growling, or clicking its teeth. A threatened skunk may also use visual displays that make it appear larger by arching its back, standing on its front feet, or walking a short distance on its front feet. The use of its musk is the last resort. Just before spraying, the skunk forms a U-shape with both its head and rump held high and facing the enemy. In this attack position, the skunk pulls back its tail and aims the nipples on the musk glands in the direction of the enemy. The skunk can accurately discharge the musk as a stream of tiny to rain-sized droplets for distances of usually two to three meters and up to about five meters. The attacker hit by the spray can experience nausea and burning eyes and nostrils. The entire contents of the scent glands may not be discharged in the initial spray, allowing the skunk to spray the attacker more than once. A skunk can spray when it is about six to seven weeks old, which is prior to being weaned (Nowak 1999).

The skunk's musk is contained within scent glands located just inside the anus; each gland contains around fifteen centimeters of the fluid (Blackman 1911; Lowery 1974). The fluid is white to yellowish and has the appearance of skim milk with cream curds (Crabb 1948). The smell of skunk musk is caused by a chemical called mercaptan, which is a sulfide in an oil base. Thus, the fluid is not easily washed away by rain or with soap and water. This potent-smelling liquid can be detected downwind for distances of two and a half kilometers from discharge (Nowak 1999).

Perhaps we can view our skunks as the yellow jackets or coral snakes of the mammal world, in that, if the color pattern and behavior do not deter the attacker, then a sting or bite is to follow. The effectiveness of the pungent scent of skunks is an amazing example of how skin glands in mammals have evolved for defensive purposes. This secretion can deter even the most determined farm dog from escalating an attack, and its odor is one that even the most city-bound person never forgets once exposed to it—hopefully from a distance!

16

Cats

Family Felidae

Description of the Family Felidae

The cats include thirty-eight species in the family Felidae (order Carnivora). Felids occur as natural populations on most land areas, with the exception of Antarctica, Australia, Madagascar, New Zealand, New Guinea, Taiwan, and various oceanic and arctic islands; however, feral or free-ranging populations of the domestic cat have been introduced by humans into these areas and elsewhere throughout most of the world.

Felids can be divided into large and small cat groups, with seven and thirty-one species per group, respectively (Kerby 1984). This distinction is based on the presence of elastic cartilage at the base of the tongue in large cats. As a result, large cats roar but cannot purr; conversely, small cats cannot roar but can purr continuously. Examples of big cats are African lions, tigers, jaguars, and cheetahs; representative small cats are domestic (feral) cats, mountain lions, lynx, and bobcats. Interestingly, some authorities consider the cheetah from Africa to be closely related to our mountain lion (Adams 1979; Nowak 1999). This is not surprising when we realize that the cheetah historically roamed throughout much of North America with the mountain lion; the cheetah also extended its range into Europe, Asia, and Africa (O'Brien et al. 1985).

Three felid species occur in the mid-eastern states: domestic (feral) cats, bobcats, and lynx (see table 1). Domestic cats, including feral and free-ranging populations (see essay 40 below), are found in all mid-eastern states, bobcats in all states but Delaware, and lynx only in New York. Of these three felids, only the feral cat is exotic (see essay 40); lynx and bobcats (and perhaps mountain lions) are of considerable conservation concern (see essays 41 and 42 below).

Like canids, felids are well adapted to a cursorial way of life, having relatively long, slender legs and compact, deep-chested, muscular bodies. They range in size from the domestic cat (averaging about 76 cm and 3.3 kg in total length and weight) to the tiger from Siberia and Manchuria (2–3.9 m and 100–306 kg). Felids have short muzzles and rounded heads. Their ears are erect but may be rounded or pointed, and the eyes have pupils that contract to form vertical slits. Pelages range from gray to reddish or yellowish brown in color, with some species spotted or striped. Tail lengths vary, being short in bobcats but long in mountain lions. All cats, except the cheetah, have retractable claws. Felids have well-developed carnassials and large canines; the number of teeth is either twenty-eight or thirty. Tongues are rough and covered with sharp-pointed, horny, recurved projections of skin (papillae) to cut and retain food in the mouth.

Felids occur in a variety of habitats, for example, lynx are found in northern boreal forests and jaguars in tropical forests. Compared to canids, however, most species of felids are associated with tropical and subtropical regions rather than temperate or polar regions of the world. Felids often use trees, hollow logs, rock crevices, caves, or dense vegetation as home sites. Most cats hunt by stalking prey or waiting in ambush and attack their prey using short bursts of speed; on the other hand, cheetahs hunt using high-speed chases.

Felids, like canids and mustelids, are active year-round; activity is generally crepuscular or nocturnal. Cats are carnivorous, with plant material representing only a fraction of their diet. Larger species, like mountain lions, are capable of killing large prey, for example, white-tailed deer. Intermediate-sized species, such as bobcats, feed largely on leporids. Smaller species, like feral cats, rely mainly on small mammals as food. Cats are solitary; only the African lion and the extinct saber-toothed cat are (were) group forming.

Felids generally produce one litter of one to six young per year, but if the litter is lost, females may become estrus and mate again. Larger species breed only every two to three years. Gestation ranges from about 55 to 119 days, and the young are born blind and helpless. Only the female cares for the young. The young stay with the female until they are capable of hunting on their own; in the feral cat, for example, the young become independent of the mother at about six months old. Most felids are sexually mature at one or two years, and their lifespan is at least fifteen years.

Family Felidae

ESSAY 40

Domestic (Feral) Cats —

Ancestry, Domestication, and Ecology

Domestic (or feral) cats are closely related to two wild subspecies of small cats (*Felis silvestris*) from the Old World, African wild cats and European wild cats (Randi and Ragni 1991). Although some authorities consider these three cats as the same species (Ragni and Randi 1986), the American Society of Mammalogists lists the domestic cat as a separate species (*Felis catus*) (Jones et al. 1997).

The ranges of African and European wild cats are restricted today, with scattered populations in Africa and southwestern Asia and in Europe, respectively (Nowak 1999). Both wild subspecies have been subjected to excessive hunting and trapping pressure. Domestic, African wild, and European wild cats readily interbreed; hence, our domestic cat is clearly similar to the wild "Sylvester the Cat" from the Old World! The domestic cat has probably interbred with these wild cats for centuries, and today this hybridization continues as an additional threat to the conservation of both wild subspecies (Yurco 1990). Since the 1980s African and European wild cats have been given legal protection in most countries (Nowak 1999).

Of the two wild subspecies, the African wild cat appears to be the most direct ancestor of the domestic cat because it is phenotypically more similar to our domestic cat than the European wild cat (Ragni and Randi 1986). The African wild cat is believed to have lived in close association with humans in Middle East towns as long as 7,000 years ago, and Egyptians finally domesticated it about 4,000 years ago (Nowak 1999). As with the domestic dog (see essay 25 in chap. 11), the domestic cat has became a distinct species (or subspecies) only after being kept by humans in isolation from wild cats for a sufficient time period.

Unlike gray wolves, which were ancestors of the domestic dog and domesticated by humans for their companionship, hunting skills, and protection, African wild cats were domesticated primarily because of their religious significance. They were considered sacred by the Egyptians until at least the time of the Roman Empire (Ewer 1973; Nowak 1999). Egyptian followers of Bastet, the goddess of pleasure, mummified and buried cats as part of their religious beliefs; they also put bronze statues of cats in their sanctuaries. In fact, the Egyptian city of Bubastis was specifically dedicated to cat worship. Egyptian paintings of domesticated cats depict an animal with ginger color, dark markings on forelimbs and ears, and a dark-ringed tail, which resembles extant African and European wild cats.

In addition to their religious value, cats were domesticated to control rodent populations. People kept cats in villages and towns to help control populations of Old World rats and mice (e.g., the Norway rat), which spread dreaded diseases and damaged valuable stores of grain used by humans as food (see essay 19 in chap. 9).

The geographic range of the domestic cat rapidly spread, beginning about 3,000 years ago, as they accompanied humans in their voyages and migrations to other parts of the world (Randi and Ragni 1991). Cats arrived in the New World on ships with the first European traders and colonists. Today, the domestic cat is one of the most widespread mammals in the world, consisting of over thirty different breeds (National Geographic Society 1981). Interestingly, regardless of breed, domestic cats have remained between three and five kilograms in size (Nowak 1999), whereas dog breeds vary tremendously in size and appearance. Thus, have you ever wondered why domestic cat breeds do not vary in size from "chihuahua-sized" on one end of the scale to "St. Bernard–sized" on the other? Perhaps this is because the ancestor of our domestic dog was a rather large ancestor, the gray wolf, rather than a four- to five-kilogram African wild cat. In other words, given the physical size of their respective ancestors, it was presumably easier to breed smaller domestic dogs than larger domestic cats!

Numbers of domestic cats in the United States have increased 100 percent over the past two decades, approximately doubling from about 30 million cats in the 1970s to 60 million in the 1990s (Nassar and Mosier 1991). Conversely, there are about 52 million domestic dogs in the United States. Because cats are the most common domesticated animal in the

United States and because some states lack cat-vaccination programs, they are a serious health threat as a potential carrier of rabies (see essay 29 in chap. 11) (Krebs, Wilson, and Childs 1995).

The ecology and behavior of domestic cats are very similar to their cousins, the African and European wild cats. Domestic cats are solitary, but individuals in a given area may coexist in a dominance hierarchy that is established by fighting (Ewer 1973). Many of us own house cats, but some cats are termed *free-ranging*, which means they live in loose association with humans in residential areas or on farms and return home only to obtain food and shelter (Haspel and Calhoon 1993). Densities of free-ranging cats can range from thirty-eight cats per square kilometer in non-farm rural areas to forty to forty-four cats per square kilometer in rural areas with farms (Coleman and Temple 1993); higher densities of cats in rural areas with farms are probably tolerated because they help control rodent populations. In contrast to house or free-ranging cats, feral cats have little or no dependency on humans for food or shelter and may be found either near humans (e.g., among multiple rental dwellings in cities) or well away from humans in remote rural areas.

All domestic cats (house, feral, and free-ranging) exhibit a bimodal activity pattern, with most activity occurring just after midnight and again at sunrise (Haspel and Calhoon 1993). Free-ranging and feral cats generally hunt along forest-field interfaces and roadsides (Warner 1985). They are opportunistic predators and typically feed mainly on mice, followed by small birds, cottontails, and larger birds (Parmalee 1953; Warner 1985). These cats also can have a major negative impact on songbird populations in farmland and residential areas (Lowery 1974), and sometimes rely on garbage or human handouts as food sources. Domestic (house) cats often continue to hunt for food and routinely deposit the prey at their owner's residence even when fed by humans (Warner 1985).

Feral or free-ranging cats are of considerable conservation concern because they can negatively impact native bird populations on islands. When intentionally or accidentally introduced to islands, they (like rats; see essay 19 in chap. 9) can virtually decimate the island birdlife (Diamond 1985). Island birds and other fauna are relatively tame and unaccustomed to efficient mammalian predators, like domestic cats.

In summary, the domestic cat, which is rivaled only by the domestic dog in being America's most favorite pet, remains remarkably similar in appearance, behavior, and ecology to its extant ancestor, the African wild cat. Like the domestic dog, its range has been expanded to all corners of the world as a companion of humans. Cat populations are expected to continually increase in the years to come, requiring special attention to effective means of population control, for example, via neutering (Coleman and Temple 1993), in order to mitigate the negative impacts of these aesthetic carnivores on native wildlife and to reduce the incidences of rabies.

ESSAY 41

The Conservation of Bobcats

We have two species of small "wild" cats, the bobcat and the lynx, in the deciduous and coniferous forests of North America. In the mid-eastern states bobcats are much more widely distributed than lynx (see table 1). Bobcats occur in each of the mid-eastern states, except Delaware; lynx are restricted to northern New York. This is not surprising because the extant distribution of bobcat is from southern Canada southward into Central America, whereas the range of lynx in North America extends from the northern United States and in the Rockies northward into Canada and Alaska (Hall 1981; Bailey 1984).

Bobcats and lynx are similar in many ways. They are comparable in size (3–15 kg), being about twice the size of domestic cats (see essay 40 above), although lynx are slightly larger (Bailey 1984; Rolley 1987). Both species have very short tails, but tails of lynx are somewhat shorter. Lynx also have densely furred foot pads that act as snowshoes while walking or hunting in deep snow. Bobcats have a black-spotted brown pelage, which

Family Felidae

blends well with dense brushy vegetation and rocky outcrops in the eastern deciduous forest; lynx are brownish-gray without spots, which provides camouflage in dense coniferous forests and swamps. Because bobcats and lynx are relatively small cats, their prey consists mainly of eastern cottontails and snowshoe hares (McCord and Cardoza 1982). They also are known to feed on smaller (mice) or larger prey (deer) (Fuller, Berg, and Kuehn 1985; Litvaitis, Clark, and Hunt 1986).

Historically, large charismatic carnivores, such as gray wolves and mountain lions, were hunted relentlessly until they were extirpated by the turn of the twentieth century in much of eastern North America (see essay 30 in chap. 11 and essay 42 below). But bobcat and lynx populations were not subject to this relentless level of exploitation. Yet over the last century or so, the abundance and distribution of both bobcats and lynx were reduced appreciably with the loss of the eastern deciduous forest to agricultural, industrial, and urban land uses subsequent to European settlement (Yahner 2000). Southerly populations of lynx have disappeared from many states, for example, Pennsylvania, and bobcat numbers have been reduced throughout the region (Whitaker and Hamilton 1998; Woolf and Hubert 1998).

In addition to habitat loss, bounties were another factor affecting bobcat populations. Bounties were paid on bobcats, beginning in 1727 in Massachusetts and continuing in many states during the nineteenth and early twentieth centuries (Rolley 1987); by the 1960s and 1970s, bounties on bobcats were eliminated in most states. However, relative to habitat loss, the historic payment of bounties had relatively little impact on bobcat abundance. In this essay, I would like to focus on the conservation story surrounding the bobcat in eastern North America.

Public concern for carnivores, such as bobcats, began to change around the 1970s from one largely characterized as indifference toward predators to one of considerable interest and support for their conservation (see essay 30 in chap. 11). The Endangered Species Act of 1973, for instance, gave protection to the gray wolf and other threatened and endangered carnivores. In the mid-1970s, however, another very interesting but lesser known legal event began to stir an awareness among conservationists and wildlife biologists because of its indirect implications to the future fate of bobcats. At this time, the Convention on International Trade in Endangered Species of Wild Fauna and Flora (CITES) prohibited trade of the pelts of many large endangered cats in the world (Woolf and Hubert 1998). As a result, unprotected populations of bobcats in North America became an alternative source of pelts on the international trade market. For instance, prior to the CITES ruling, only about 10,000 to 36,000 bobcats per year were harvested (hunted or trapped) in the United States from 1967 to 1976. But when the market and price of bobcat pelts increased during the late 1970s, over 86,000 bobcats were being harvested annually (today, the number of bobcats harvested is about 34,000, based on figures from 1995–96).

Increased harvests of bobcats in North America during the late 1970s led to a major shift in the management philosophy for this species (Rolley 1987; Woolf and Hubert 1998). Wildlife biologists immediately became concerned that this species would be overharvested. Also, CITES in 1975 ruled that countries harvesting and exporting bobcat pelts must determine if these activities negatively affect bobcat populations. Therefore, the U.S. Fish and Wildlife Service mandated that state wildlife agencies must determine the status of bobcats in their states. Some wildlife biologists also recommended that critical habitat, for example, white cedar stands, for bobcat prey such as white-tailed deer be preserved for the benefit of bobcat populations (Fuller, Berg, and Kuehn 1985).

Today, the outlook for bobcat populations in North America is very promising. Bobcats can be harvested in thirty-eight states, but they are completely protected in nine states. They are classified as state-endangered in four states (Indiana, Iowa, New Jersey, and Ohio) and state-threatened in one (Illinois). We can attribute the success of bobcat conservation to swift and positive action by wildlife biologists that began in the late 1970s. Fortunately, this wild cat has also been able to coexist with humans because of its secretive and solitary existence. Hence, we can be fairly confident that bobcats will remain as an aesthetic component of forested and brushy habitats in the mid-eastern states well into the twenty-first century.

History and Conservation

of Mountain Lions in the East

Mountain lions, sometimes referred to as catamounts, cougars, panthers, or pumas, have a certain mystique about them. First, the size of this animal is impressive; it is comparable in size to the leopard of Africa (36–103 kg) but is somewhat smaller than the biggest cat in North America, the jaguar (36–158 kg) (Nowak 1999). Second, mountain lions were revered by Native American cultures as the Ghost or Cat of the Great Spirit and were believed to provide protection against evil (Lutz and Lutz 1996). Third, because of the mountain lion's secretive, elusive, and solitary way of life coupled with its low numbers, very few people have ever caught a glimpse of one of these cats (Downing 1996). Fourth, in the eastern United States, the only documented breeding population of mountain lions occurs in Everglades National Park and Big Cypress Swamp (Dixon 1982; Belden and Hagedorn 1993). This highly publicized remnant population consists of only about thirty to fifty animals, locally known as Florida panthers, which is of tremendous conservation concern because of its endangered status (Matthews 1991). Finally, the authenticity of mountain lion sightings throughout the eastern United States seems to be an ongoing and favorite topic of debate (Downing 1996).

Mountain lions were once widespread throughout North America, ranging from southern Canada and southward into South America (Dixon 1982), although populations in the eastern United States were probably never very high in pre- or post-European times (McGinnis 1996). By the 1880s these cats were extirpated in the eastern United States (Brocke 1996). With the exception of the Florida population, they are now restricted to suitable habitat in the western United States and Canada where adequate numbers of major prey, white-tailed and mule deer, exist.

We have to go back to the mindset of the eighteenth-century culture to understand the demise of mountain lion populations in much of North America. Like the gray wolf (see essay 30 in chap. 11), this impressive cat was hunted and trapped relentlessly for at least two centuries because it was viewed as a dangerous, fierce enemy and potential competitor for game and livestock. In other words, the public's attitude was that "the only good mountain lion was a dead lion," and disdain and fear of this animal were exaggerated via local folklore (Altherr 1996). As early as 1758, bounties were paid on mountain lions in British Columbia, and payment of bounties in North America continued until 1970 in Arizona (Dixon 1982).

Today, there is little evidence that mountain lions occur as viable populations in the mid-eastern states. Hence, we are left with anecdotal tales of eastern mountain lions from the past, a remnant extant population in Florida (which, incidentally, is not truly a "pure" eastern mountain-lion population; Hedrick 1995), and an occasional mounted specimen as reminders of this impressive eastern cat. In Pennsylvania, for example, the last known eastern mountain lion was killed in 1871 (Doutt, Heppenstall, and Guilday 1977), which is represented today by a single mounted specimen called the Brush Panther (Esposito and Herb 1997). This specimen is on display at the Pennsylvania State University and has special significance, not only from a conservation perspective, but because it is responsible for the Penn State mascot being the Nittany Lion.

The story of the Brush Panther is one well worth telling. This cat was heard one evening back in 1856 by a local hunter, and so the hunter set out with his dogs the following day in pursuit of the animal. The cat was tracked, eventually treed by dogs, and then killed by the hunter. The facial expression of the mounted Brush Panther is very different from that seen on modern-day mounted specimens. The Brush Panther has its teeth bared, giving it a fierce look, thereby reflecting the historic fear that people had of these cats.

A renewed conservation effort for mountain lions in the eastern United States began a few decades ago among biologists interested in the long-term survival of Florida panthers. Several studies have focused on the extent and the effects of inbreeding and reduced genetic variation in this Florida population (O'Brien et al. 1990), the number of translocated animals needed to maintain genetic variation in the southern Florida population (Hedrick 1995; Maehr and Caddick 1995), the feasibility of expanding the range of mountain lions in the state by translocating mountain lions from Texas into northern Florida (Belden and Hagedorn 1993), and the importance of landscape features and land ownership on the distribution of mountain lions in southern Florida (Maehr 1990; Maehr and Cox 1995). These studies have confirmed that the future outlook for Florida panthers is not optimistic unless genetic variation is maintained (or better yet, enhanced) in the population and unless adequate habitat and protection are ensured.

Given the tenuous future of this small population of mountain lions in south Florida, can other populations of this large cat be introduced into the eastern United States? A first step in a reintroduction program would be to determine the present status of mountain lions in the eastern United States (Frome 1979). Various centers have already been established to catalog and investigate reports of mountain-lion sightings in the East (Dixon 1982). Reports of mountain-lion sightings in the mid-eastern states (e.g., Maryland, New York, Pennsylvania, Virginia, and West Virginia) since 1983 are not uncommon, including those of adult females with kittens (Lutz and Lutz 1996). In Pennsylvania alone 325 sightings of mountain lions were reported from 1890 to 1981 (McGinnis 1996).

Sightings of mountain lions, however, must be viewed with caution. Some of these could be those of fishers, which are relatively large, dark, weasel-like animals with long tails (see essay 36). Imagine catching a glimpse of a fisher in a dense stand of hemlock from a distance at dawn. Without field glasses and some knowledge of this mustelid, a person may be fooled into thinking that the fisher was a mountain lion.

Authentic sightings of mountain lions may be attributed to three potential sources: survivors from a remnant nineteenth-century population of eastern mountain lions, individuals that dispersed from a source population (e.g., Florida or Minnesota), or those that escaped from or were released by private sources, such as a privately owned zoo) (Dixon 1982; Brocke 1996; McGinnis 1996). Because mountain lions were probably extirpated from much of the eastern United States by the late nineteenth century (Brocke 1996), there is little credence given to an eastern population surviving into the twentieth century in the East. Moreover, because the major mortality factor of the Florida panther is collisions with vehicles (Matthews 1991), a road-killed mountain lion almost certainly would have been reported by now if a remnant population of mountain lions were present in states with heavy vehicular traffic, like New York or Pennsylvania (Downing 1996). In fact, vehicular collisions with mountain lions in southern Florida would even be higher if it were not for the construction of highway underpasses specifically designed for movements by mountain lions and other wildlife (Foster and Humphrey 1995).

A second key step in a restoration program for mountain lions would be to find suitable habitats of adequate size to sustain viable populations. In southern Florida mountain lions occupy an area of about 8,810 square kilometers (Maehr 1990), although this area is continually being degraded because of surface mining and water-manipulation activities (e.g., ditching, diking) (Matthews 1991). Thus, if we assume that there are fifty Florida panthers, the area required for each mountain lion is 176 square kilometers (0.56 mountain lions/100 km^2). This is a somewhat simplistic calculation because not all habitat in this 8,810-square-kilometer area is equally suitable for mountain lions, and because the size of home ranges varies by sex class (larger in males), season (smaller in winter-spring), and prey density (smaller with higher density). This home-range requirement, however, is within those needed by individual mountain lions in Idaho (Seidensticker, Hornocker, Wiles, and Messick 1973). Furthermore, based on computer models, ten to twenty mountain lions can be sustained in suitable habitat of at least 2,200 square kilometers, which equates to one mountain lion per 110–220 square kilometers (Beier 1993). A previous attempt to reintroduce mountain lions in northern Florida concluded that fifty animals could be supported in a 2,200-square-kilometer area provided that adequate deer populations were present (>3 deer/km^2) and human populations were minimal within sixty-four kilometers of a release site (Belden and Hagedorn 1993). Incidentally, the recent reintroduction of seven mountain lions from Texas into northern Florida failed because too few animals were introduced, some were killed by hunters, and others abandoned home ranges and moved into urban and agricultural areas.

Family Felidae

In an earlier essay (see essay 30 in chap. 11), we discussed a relatively contiguous, undisturbed area consisting of 77,000 square kilometers as a potential location for gray wolf reintroductions into the northeastern United States (Mladenoff and Sickley 1998). This area extends from upstate New York to northern Maine and is nearly ninefold larger than that occupied by the remnant population of mountain lions in southern Florida. Mountain lions could conceivably be reintroduced into this northeastern area, provided that adequate prey (deer) populations are present and human populations are low. As proposed for northern Florida, the initial release should consist of ten to twenty individuals, and the size of each release site should be at least 2,200 square kilometers (Belden and Hagedorn 1993). A goal would be to eventually maintain a population of fifty mountain lions at each site. Animals should be released after major hunting seasons, such as deer seasons, to minimize encounters with hunters, which could disrupt the establishment of permanent home ranges.

A third consideration for a mountain lion reintroduction program is to ensure adequate gene flow and genetic variation via periodic introductions of new individuals into the population. Theoretical models, for instance, have suggested that gene flow and genetic variation can be achieved in the isolated Florida population by immediately adding eight young, nonpregnant females obtained from a Texas population, followed by the introduction of one new female per subsequent generation (Hedrick 1995). Ideally, gene flow could naturally occur by natural dispersal of individuals if connectivity in the landscape were ensured via habitat corridors free of human disturbance, for example, residential areas, highways, and extensive logging (Van Dyke, Brocke, Shaw, Ackerman, Hemker, and Lindzey 1986; Beier 1993).

Fourth, a reintroduction effort also should involve a radio-tracking program to determine movements and survivorship of individual cats (Belden and Hagedorn 1993). In addition, an inventory and monitoring program should be established, thereby creating a long-term database on the distribution and abundance of mountain lions at each site. This program should include systematic searches for mountain-lion signs, such as tracks or scratch sites (Paradiso and Nowak 1982; Van Dyke and Brocke 1987) and mail questionnaires that document authentic sightings (Berg, McDonald, and Strickland 1983).

A fifth requisite for the recovery of mountain lions in the East would require considerable coordination and cooperation among personnel from various wildlife agencies (federal and state) and private landowners (Dixon 1982; Maehr 1990; Belden and Hagedorn 1993). In particular, public acceptance of any recovery or management plan for mountain lions is crucial to its success (Manfredo, Zinn, Sikorowski, and Jones 1998). Mountain lions are wide-ranging and obviously do not recognize the boundaries between public and private lands. Some may venture onto farms or into residential areas, resulting in potential problems whose resolution will require understanding and support from the general public.

A mountain lion is a formidable predator; hence, a sixth consideration would be how to deal with the likelihood of serious conflicts between mountain lions and humans, for example, predation on game species or livestock and possible attacks on humans or pets. Some segments of the hunting population, for instance, may resist the reintroduction of mountain lions because they fear that this cat would negatively affect prey populations, such as white-tailed deer. However, in northern Florida, wildlife agency personnel found little resistance from hunters to reintroduction efforts because deer densities at the release site could support both mountain lions and recreational hunting (Belden and Hagedorn 1993).

Some populations of mountain lions feed extensively on deer and livestock. Of forty-five confirmed kills by mountain lions in northern Florida, thirty (67%) were white-tailed deer, ten (22%) were pigs, and five (11%) were goats (Belden and Hagedorn 1993). In several western locations in North America, livestock occurred in only 4 percent of the mountain-lion diets (Dixon 1982). However, mountain lions occasionally may exhibit surplus killing on livestock, like sheep, which means that they kill more than they can eat at any one time; in contrast, surplus killing of wild prey, such as deer, has rarely been recorded in mountain lions. Mountain lions preying on livestock tend to be young transient males or old lions in poor physical condition (Paradiso and Nowak 1982). If mountain lions prey on livestock, landowners could be reimbursed for damages (Belden and Hagedorn 1993), much like compensation that is paid to landowners who experience predation by gray wolves on livestock (Paradiso and Nowak 1982) or excessive damage caused by deer on farm crops (see essay 46 in chap. 19).

Mountain lions can be potentially dangerous to humans and pets. In contrast to no documented case of gray wolves attacking humans in North America (Paradiso and Nowak 1982; see essay 29 in chap. 11), unprovoked attacks by mountain lions on humans are a very real phenomenon, especially in the last few decades (Beier 1991; Black 1996). Ten human fatalities and forty-eight nonfatal injuries have been attributed to mountain lions from 1890 to 1990 (Beier 1991). In particular, 50 percent of these fatal attacks and 65 percent of the nonfatal attacks have occurred since 1970, prompting wildlife agency personnel to warn humans about the dangers of attacks by mountain lions in some parts of the United States (e.g., southern California, eastern Colorado, and western Texas).

The recent increase in mountain-lion attacks on humans may be caused by two factors (Beier 1991). First, states and provinces in the West have changed the status of mountain lions from a bountied predator to either a game or fully protected species, which has allowed their numbers to increase. Second, with growing human populations, residential expansion, and greater recreational opportunities, humans have dramatically encroached on habitat once occupied by mountain lions free of human disturbance. Interestingly, a disproportionate number of mountain-lion attacks continues to occur on Vancouver Island, British Columbia—there are other possible reasons for this phenomenon. It may be caused by a lack of smaller-sized prey, such as rabbits, on the island, which otherwise would sustain a mountain lion between kills of larger prey in mainland Canada. In addition, the population of Vancouver mountain lions probably has become very aggressive and more apt to attack dogs and humans because they have been hunted by humans with dogs for many years. When a mountain lion becomes a problem to livestock, pets, or humans, a professional hunter using hounds should quickly deal with the cat (Belden and Hagedorn 1993).

We have discussed how a person can reduce incidences of attacks or reduce injuries when attacked by bears (see essay 31 in chap. 12), but how can we avoid attacks by mountain lions? Most mountain-lion attacks on humans involve children, and nearly all human fatalities are children who were alone or accompanied by other children (Beier 1991). Thus, as an important precaution, adults should keep children in sight at all times when in mountain-lion habitat; if a child is attacked, the adult can aid in repulsing the attack. If an attack by a mountain lion is imminent, passive resistance (e.g., playing dead) is not a recommended strategy as with bear attacks. Instead, if a person is attacked by a mountain lion, the best thing to do is to maintain eye contact with the cat, shout, clap hands, and aggressively fight back with fists, kicks, and any makeshift weapon (a rock or stick). Unless the person is near the safety of a car or other shelter, he or she should not run away but rather retreat at a moderate or slow speed— running away can elicit more aggression.

Someday, we may witness the return of our largest cat into the mid-eastern states or elsewhere in eastern North America. If this reintroduction is to take place, we must give careful considerations to the experiences and the problems encountered by wildlife agency personnel involved with the reintroduction and management of mountain-lion populations in Florida and western North America over the past few decades. Conceivably, this cat may someday find a home in the East, but wildlife agencies, private and public landowners, and the general public must work together to make this effort succeed with the least amount of mountain lion–human conflicts.

17

Horses and Other Equids

Family Equidae

Description of the Family Equidae

*T*wo mammalian orders, Perissodactyla and Artiodactyla (see chap. 18), include species referred to as odd-toed and even-toed ungulates, respectively. The term *ungulate* has no taxonomic basis but is simply used to describe an animal that walks on a hoof at the tip of its toes. Hooves are hard, thick, and keratinized; keratin is widespread in mammals, comprising claws in many mammals, horns in rhinos, and fingernails in humans and other primates.

The order Perissodactyla, which contains the family Equidae, once thrived in the early to mid-Tertiary period (about 40–60 million years ago). By the Oligocene epoch (about 30 million years ago), however, the diversity of perissodactyls began to decline worldwide. Coinciding with this decline in the perissodactyls, artiodactyls became the prominent ungulate group in the Miocene epoch (about 20 million years ago). Today, the order Perissodactyla consists of only three families and seventeen extant species; in contrast, the order Artiodactyla is represented by ten families and 221 species.

The family Equidae contains eight species or nearly one-half of the extant perissodactyls. Wild equids occur in Africa, Arabia, and central and western Asia. Horses and burros have been introduced to various parts of the world, such as North America (see essay 43 below). Wild (feral) populations of domestic horses can be found in two mid-eastern states, having been introduced to coastal areas of Maryland and Virginia (see table 1).

Equids vary from stocky, thick-headed, short-legged animals (e.g., feral horses, burros, and zebras) to long-legged and graceful animals (domestic racehorses). They are odd-toed, with only the third digit being functional as its hoof. Depending on the species, wild equids range from about 2.4 to 3.9 meters in total length and 175 to 400 kilograms in weight; they usually are about 1 to 1.6 meters tall at the shoulder. These ungulates have tails that reach to at least midleg, a mane of hair on the neck, and often a "forelock" or tuft of hair on the forehead. The pelage of equids is of variable length and color —the three zebra species are black-and-white striped (see essay 39 in chap. 15), whereas the other five wild equid species are typically brownish or grayish.

The long legs and hooves of equids make them very suitable to a cursorial way of life. They use speed to escape danger and can kick with their hindfeet and forefeet to effectively ward off enemies. Biting also can be used as a defensive tactic. The number of teeth varies from forty to forty-two; the upper canines are absent or vestigial in females.

Family Equidae

Wild equids prefer short grasslands and desert scrublands as habitats and they feed on a variety of plant material. They are active day or night but most often during the evening. Equids are social animals, living as bachelor groups or in mixed groups composed of an adult male (stallion), several adult females (mares), and their offspring (foals). Olfaction and hearing are excellent.

Depending on the species, gestation averages from 340 to 409 days. Usually only one foal is produced at intervals of one to three years. Foals are precocial, being capable of standing and following the mother almost immediately after birth. Young equids are able to graze at one month and are weaned within about eight to twelve months. They reach sexual maturity at about three years of age and may live as long as forty to forty-five years (particularly in captivity).

Horses

ESSAY 43

History and Ecology of Feral Horses

Horses are one of the most aesthetic mammals, both from a wild and domestic perspective. They were very much a part of the Old West and our country's heritage; horses remind some of us of the cowboy movies that were common in theaters and on television during our childhood days. Worldwide, the 58 million or so domestic horses provide numerous services (Nowak 1999)—many serve as "machines" and transportation, while others are valuable for recreational and sporting reasons. Horseback riding on weekends is a favorite pastime for many people; others use horses in sports, like polo and equestrian competitions. As amazing running machines (Nowak 1999), horses provide entertainment in the annual march to the Triple Crown of horse racing and in the many other lesser-known horse races across the country.

Although viewed as an exotic species, horses have evolutionary roots in North America. The earliest horse-like mammals belonged to the genus *Hyracotherium*, which appeared during the Eocene (about 54 million years ago) in both North America and Asia (Nowak 1999). These equids were herbivores, like modern horses, but they were only about twenty to thirty-five kilograms in weight or at least five times smaller than the smallest extant equid. Over evolutionary time, the legs of these horse-like mammals began to show signs of elongation, but each foot had three to four toes rather than the single digit seen in today's horse.

In the Miocene (about 8–24 million years ago), the horses of North America began to diversify into several species (Nowak 1999). These new species were larger than *Hyracotherium*, with some equal in body weight to that of modern equids (50–400 kg). However, by the Pleistocene (about 8,000–11,000 years ago), horses disappeared from the continent, coinciding with the invasion of humans into parts of North America occupied by

Family Equidae

horses (Garrott, Siniff, and Eberhardt 1991). The domestic horse later re-turned to our continent with Europeans in the sixteenth century.

The domestic (feral) horse is related to three historic subspecies of horses: Przewalski's wild horse or takhi (local name of this horse given by Mongolians), forest horse, and tarpan (Slade and Godfrey 1982; Nowak 1999; see also Groves 1994). The domestic horse probably diverged from the takhi about 12,000 to 18,000 years ago (Forstén 1991). Takhi are stocky horses, with large heads, short and erect manes, and long tails. They once were found in Russia, Mongolia, and China but went extinct in the wild in the 1960s (Nowak 1999). Today, over 1,000 takhi are found in zoos and field stations worldwide. Attempts to reestablish takhi populations in Mongolian deserts are ongoing using animals raised in captivity (Ryder 1993; Van Dierendonck and Wallis de Vries 1996).

The forest horse, which once inhabited much of central Europe, went extinct in the early nineteenth century (Nowak 1999). This equid was the likely progenitor of modern draft horses (Slade and Godfrey 1982). The tarpan of Russia and Ukraine went extinct a little later in the early twen-tieth century (Nowak 1999). This subspecies was probably the principal ancestor of the light-legged, domestic breeds of modern horses. Tarpans were relatively small horses (about 1.3 m at the shoulder), with gray col-oration and black manes and tails. Today, about 200 tarpan-like horses are found in field stations in Poland and in zoos across the United States and Europe; these animals are a product of horse breeders who have at-tempted since the 1930s to "breed back" a tarpan from domestic horses.

The location and timing of horse domestication are somewhat un-clear (Nowak 1999). Domestication probably occurred in a few different places, including China, Mesopotamia, and Russia, about 5,100 to 6,000 years ago. Over the centuries, at least 515 horse breeds have been pro-duced by domestication, but eighty-eight (17%) of these breeds have gone extinct in the last 100 years. Horse breeds range is size from the large Bel-gian and Shire draft horses (e.g., 1.86 m tall at the shoulder) to the small Falabella and Shetland ponies (1.02 m tall at the shoulder); the term *pony* is given to breeds that measure less than 1.32 meter at the shoulder. Today's horses and ponies vary tremendously in color, ranging from chestnuts to pintos.

Feral horse populations occur in Africa, the former USSR, and the

Horses

Figure 19. Wild horses (ponies) of Assateague Island off the coast of Maryland and Virginia. *(Photo by author.)*

United States (Slade and Godfrey 1982). There are about 45,000 feral horses in the United States, with the vast majority in western states, such as Nevada, Oregon, and Wyoming (Garrott, Siniff, and Eberhardt 1991); a couple hundred wild horses also inhabit Assateague Island along the Maryland and Virginia coasts (Keiper 1976) (see fig. 19). Horses were brought back into North America by the Spaniards around 1530, but it was not until the 1850s that horses became widespread in the United States (Seegmiller and Ohmart 1981; Berger 1986). Over the past few centuries, horses in the West escaped from ranches and Native American reservations; those along the East Coast probably originated from shipwrecks, escaped from farms, or were released intentionally.

Prior to the 1970s, local ranchers managed feral horse and burro populations. This localized control nearly led to the extirpation of horse populations in the western United States. Many equids were shot indiscriminantly by persons belonging to the "100-burro club"; the goal of each of these persons was to shoot 100 feral horses or burros (Seegmiller and Ohmart 1981). Then, feral horses and burros in the United States were

Family Equidae

given complete protection by the passage of the 1971 Wild Horse and Burro Act. This act authorized the U.S. Forest Service and the Bureau of Land Management, rather than ranchers, to manage equids on federal lands in the West.

The Wild Horse and Burro Act was controversial from the start. Given protection, feral horse and burro populations rapidly increased about 20 percent a year because they can essentially double their population in four to ten years (Eberhardt, Majorowicz, and Wilcox 1982). High populations of equids resulted in overgrazing of sensitive ecosystems (e.g., deserts), and competition for food resources with native mammals (e.g., desert bighorn sheep) (Seegmiller and Ohmart 1981; Slade and Godfrey 1982). As a consequence, wildlife biologists were forced to develop safe and humane ways to control equid populations within acceptable ecological levels on federal lands in the West.

Wild horses were readily captured by biologists using tranquilizer guns from helicopters or vehicles, and soon a need arose to dispose of these captured animals humanely (Slade and Godfrey 1982; Boyles 1986). Hence, a program called Adopt-a-Horse was developed, which transferred the ownership of a horse to a private person for a fee of $200. This program, although well intended, backfired because more horses were being captured than those being adopted (Boyles 1986; Garrott, Siniff, Tester, Eagle, and Plotka 1992). The cost of humanely maintaining the unwanted horses in captivity by federal agencies, such as the Bureau of Land Management, exceeded $6 million per year, which detracted considerably from the monies available to these agencies for the management and conservation of other wildlife species.

A viable alternative to the Adopt-a-Horse program has been the development and use of contraception technologies for wild horses (Kirkpatrick, Liu, and Turner 1990; Turner and Kirkpatrick 1991; Garrott et al. 1992). Vaccines can be remotely injected into horses from the ground using dart guns (Kirkpatrick, Liu, and Turner 1990), or they can be implanted into the neck (Eagle, Siniff, Tester, Garrott, and Plotka 1992). Neck implants, for instance, can reduce reproduction rates for three to five years. Contraceptive programs hold promise as a means of controlling feral horse populations in the future by minimizing population fluctuations, extending the interval between captures of individual animals, and reducing overall management costs (Garrott et al. 1992; Garrott 1995). The technologies developed for contraception in horses may someday be valuable in addressing another serious issue facing wildlife biologists today, namely the control of high populations of nonhunted deer populations, such as those in suburbia and other areas posted from hunting (Warren 1995) (see essay 45 in chap. 19).

Feral horse populations will remain in our western- and eastern-seaboard landscapes for many generations to come, thanks to the efforts of wildlife biologists and federal agencies. The challenge, however, is to find ways to economically control these feral populations before they reach numbers that cause serious negative impacts on the ecosystem. There is an aesthetic value in knowing that horses, which were once absent from North America for thousands of years (perhaps because of humans), are once again present for our enjoyment. I recommend taking a ride along the coast of Maryland and Virginia to see and photograph the wild horses (ponies) on Assateague Island.

18

Pigs and Hogs

Family Suidae

Description of the Family Suidae

$\mathcal{T}$he family Suidae is found in the order Artiodactyla (see chap. 17) and consists of fourteen species of even-toed ungulates, known as pigs and hogs. Wild suids occurred originally in Europe and Asia. Feral populations of Eurasian wild hogs (or wild boars), which is the same species as the domestic pig, have been introduced to mainland North America and many islands, for example, Hawaii, New Guinea, and New Zealand (see essay 44 below). Feral populations of wild pigs now are found in three mid-eastern states: Ohio, Virginia, and West Virginia (see table 1).

Suids are barrel-shaped mammals, with short necks, long, pointed heads, and blunt, mobile snouts made of cartilages. This snout is valuable as a tool to turn the surface soil while

Figure 20. Foraging by domestic pigs results in upturned soil. *(Photo by author.)*

looking for food (see fig. 20). Depending on the species, the
total body length is 0.5 to 1.9 meter, a body weight of 50 to 350
kilograms, and a tail of 0.4 meters or less. Unlike the long-
legged equids (see chap. 17), suids have relatively short legs,
but they are swift runners. The skin of some suids is virtually
hairless, whereas others have a limited amount of brown or
black bristly hair. Young suids are striped, except those of the
domestic (feral) pig and babirusa from Asia.

The skulls of suids are high, sloping, and contain either
thirty-four or forty-four teeth. The upper canines (or tusks) are
large and grow outward and backward; they are used as effective defensive weapons or to dig for food. In males, upper and
lower tusks are also used as offensive weapons during intraspecific combat (Barrette 1986).

Wild suids generally occupy wooded habitats. They are
nocturnal or crepuscular and feed on both plant and animal

Family Suidae

material, such as green vegetation, bulbs, fungi, invertebrates, small vertebrates, and bird eggs. Suids often live in herds of about twenty individuals or more, consisting of several mother and young groups; adult males, on the other hand, are typically solitary. Olfaction and audition are acute in suids.

Gestation in pigs and hogs varies from 100 to 140 days. The number of young is usually four to eight, but one to twelve piglets may occur in a litter. The young stay are born and remain in nests, unlike the precocial equids (see chap. 17), until being weaned in three to four months. Sexual maturity is achieved as early as eight to ten months of age. Thus, compared to other ungulates, pigs and hogs have a very high reproductive potential. The average life span of suids is about ten years.

Pigs and Hogs

Origins of Feral Pig Populations

and Impacts on Ecosystems

When speaking of feral or wild pigs in North America, we are actually referring to a single species with an Old World origin. They include domestic pigs gone feral, Eurasian wild boars (or pigs), and hybrids between
domestic and Eurasian wild boars, each of which readily interbreed (Wood
and Barrett 1979; Gipson, Hlavachick, and Berger 1998; Nowak 1999).
Feral pigs are somewhat different in appearance from domestic pigs (see
fig. 21). The pelage of feral pigs is usually blackish and more coarse than

Figure 21. A feral pig, showing the blackish, coarse pelage and more streamlined
body, compared to the domestic pig. *(Photo by R. H. Barrett and maintained by the
Mammal Images Library of the American Society of Mammalogists.)*

Family Suidae

domestic pigs; in addition, feral pigs are thinner and more streamlined in body shape and have longer and sharper tusks than their domestic counterparts (Hanson and Karstad 1959).

Domestic pigs are virtually worldwide in distribution because humans valued them as food and because pigs mature faster and have larger litters than other domestic ungulates. The history of its domestication began about 8,500 to 9,000 years ago, with the Eurasian wild boars in Asia (Nowak 1999). Domestic pigs of Eurasian wild boar stock were subsequently introduced into the New World and the United States several times over the past centuries. Initially, the Polynesians brought pigs into Hawaii about 1,000 years ago. Later, Christopher Columbus introduced pigs to the West Indies in 1493, and Hernando de Soto brought this species to Florida in 1539 (Towne and Wentworth 1950). Expeditions led by both Francisco Coronado from Mexico City in 1540 and de Soto from Florida in 1541 into Arkansas, Kansas, Texas, and other states relied on pigs as food; these pigs often escaped or were stolen by Native Americans and released to form free-ranging populations. From the 1700s until the mid-twentieth century, feral pigs were introduced into various states, for example, Ohio, Kansas, and Missouri, by European settlers. Until the mid-twentieth century, pigs were often allowed to range freely in woodlots surrounding many towns and villages; when this practice became illegal, many of these free-ranging pigs were unclaimed and became feral.

European wild boars were introduced into a shooting preserve in North Carolina in 1912 (Wood and Barrett 1979). During the 1920s and 1930s, most of these wild boars escaped, dispersed into other areas of the Appalachians, and interbred with other feral pigs (Godin 1977). In addition, feral pigs were trapped and transferred for sport hunting in the southeastern United States, thereby expanding the range of this species (Howe and Bratton 1976; Sweeney and Sweeney 1982).

Today, feral pig populations occur in four major locations in the United States: southeastern United States, California, eight islands in Hawaii, and Puerto Rico/Virgin Islands (Wood and Barrett 1979). Prior to 1981 the range of feral pigs in the lower forty-eight states was confined to fifteen states, ranging from California eastward to Virginia; since this time, however, pigs have rapidly become established in eight additional states, extending from Colorado eastward to Ohio and West Virginia (Gipson,

Hlavachick, and Berger 1998). The most plausible explanation for this range expansion is clandestine trap-and-transfer of feral pigs for hunting purposes. Feral hogs illegally transported in livestock trailers to release sites are often very difficult to distinguish from hogs being shipped to production or slaughter facilities, thereby making it hard to monitor and control this practice. Recent expansions in the range of feral pigs also can be attributed to animals that have dispersed from established populations, escaped from properties owned by hunting clubs for sport hunting, or escaped from domestic swine producers and pet owners.

Wildlife biologists are in general agreement that feral pig populations have been detrimental to native fauna and flora. Feral pigs may have direct negative effects on other wildlife by feeding on small vertebrates, such as frogs, snakes, and salamanders, and on nests of ground-nesting birds (Henry 1969; Wood and Barrett 1979). Pigs can also compete with native wildlife, like white-tailed deer and wild turkey, for acorn crops in the fall (Wood and Roark 1980).

Feral pigs may also have indirect negative impacts on native fauna and flora in forests. The foraging activity of pigs, which includes uprooting and digging in the soil (see fig. 20 above) can reduce the diversity and abundance of soil arthropods, which are vital to the health of a forest ecosystem (Vtorov 1993). In some areas, like the Great Smoky Mountains National Park, foraging feral pigs consume and trample seedlings and herbaceous vegetation (wildflowers) (Bratton 1975; Howe and Bratton 1976).

Feral pigs can cause problems for the agricultural industry. For example, feral male pigs occasionally break into pens of domestic pigs, breeding with the females and injuring the males (Mayer and Brisbin 1991). Foraging by pigs can severely damage agricultural crops (Pine and Gerdes 1973). In addition, fatal diseases, such as brucellosis and trichinosis, can be transmitted from feral pigs to domestic pigs and to other livestock and humans (Wood and Brenneman 1977; Wood and Barrett 1979; Gipson, Hlavachick, and Berger 1998).

On the positive side, uprooting of forest soils by foraging pigs can increase growth rates of some tree species, such as American beech (Lacki and Lancia 1986). Rooting of soil by pigs can also facilitate the cycling of soil nutrients and thereby enhance the decomposition of the forest leaf litter (Lacki and Lancia 1983; Singer, Swank, and Clebsch 1984). More-

Family Suidae

over, feral hogs provide recreational opportunities for hunters in a few states, such as California, North Carolina, and West Virginia, where they are considered a game species (Sweeney and Sweeney 1982).

Because of potential and actual impacts of feral pig populations on native fauna and flora, control of pig populations is warranted in some areas (Sweeney and Sweeney 1982). Management options at federal, state, and private levels include hunting, trap-and-transfer programs, and eradication. On public lands, such as national parks and national forest lands, the feral pig is an exotic species, which mandates control of this species because of its disruptive effect on native ecosystems (Katahira, Finnegan, and Stone 1993). A comprehensive control program for feral pigs must involve population monitoring, use of fencing to reduce movements into unoccupied areas, and population reduction methods (Hone and Stone 1989; Katahira, Finnegan, and Stone 1993). At Hawaii Volcanoes National Park (HAVO), for instance, over 11,000 feral pigs were eliminated from the 1930s to 1980, but complete eradication was not achieved. Hence, control of feral pig populations is difficult, if not impossible. Control of pig populations is also costly; the annual cost (in 1989 dollars) of the ongoing pig-control program at HAVO was over $270,000.

In conclusion, the pig in its domestic form is one of the most important sources of food for humans worldwide. The feral version of the pig, however, is much like the commensal Old World rodents (see essay 19 in chap. 9) in that its distribution has been dramatically expanded by humans, which in turn has caused considerable problems. Thus, the feral pig is a classic example of an exotic species that has ecologically backfired. If national trends in feral pig populations are any indication, we can expect feral pig populations in the mid-eastern states to not only expand but also be a conservation issue in the years to come.

19

Deer

Family Cervidae

Description of the Family Cervidae

The family Cervidae contains forty-one species of deer; this family, like Suidae (see chap. 18), is in the order Artiodactyla. Deer species have a natural distribution that includes North America, South America, Europe, Asia, and northern Africa; some also have been introduced by humans into Australia and New Zealand. Five species of cervids are found in the mid-eastern states, varying from four in New York to only one in Delaware (see table 1). White-tailed deer are ubiquitous in our region, elk and the exotic sika deer from Asia are found in only two mid-eastern states, and moose and woodland caribou occur only in New York.

Deer range in size from two species of pudus from Central and South America, which may be as small as sixty-two centimeters in total body length and five to thirteen kilograms in weight, to moose from North America and Eurasia, which can be over 2.4 meters in total body length and weigh at least 200 kilograms. Regardless of species, males tend to be slightly larger and more stocky than females. During the breeding season (termed the *rut*), the necks of males are larger than those of females.

Deer are brownish in color, although the young (e.g., fawns of white-tailed deer) and adults in some species (e.g., sika deer) are spotted. In temperate areas the winter coats of deer are darker than summer coats. The winter pelage of white-tailed deer, for instance, is drab brown, but the summer pelage is reddish brown.

The presence of antlers in cervids is the principal characteristic separating this family from other ungulates. All deer species have antlers, with the exception of Chinese water deer. Antlers grow from pedicels, which are two permanent, skin-covered projections on the skull (see essay 47 below). Only males have antlers, but they occur also in female caribou and occasionally in aberrant females of other species.

Antlers are shed annually and, hence, are deciduous; in contrast, the horns of the family Bovidae (see chap. 20) are permanent structures. The Père David's deer, which is native to China, is the only deer that grows and sheds two different sets of antlers per year. Antler size varies widely among deer species; for example, they are relatively inconspicuous (e.g., 10 cm long) in muntjac (or barking deer) from Asia and pudus but are very large in moose and elk.

Deer have either thirty-two or thirty-four teeth. In three genera of small deer from China (Chinese water deer, muntjac, and tufted deer), the upper canines are relatively large and saber-like; these canines serve as very effective defensive weapons.

Deer are long-legged, relatively slim ungulates, which makes them very well adapted to a cursorial way of life. They occur in a variety of habitats, ranging from forests to arctic tundra. Some species, such as caribou, undergo extensive migrations; others, such as elk in western mountainous areas, migrate to higher elevations in spring and summer and to lower elevations in fall and winter. Deer are herbivorous, and some species, such as our whitetail, occasionally cause considerable damage to agricultural crops and forested ecosystems when populations are high (see essay 46 below).

Deer vary in their degree of sociality. Certain deer of tropical forests, like muntjac, are solitary, whereas some species of temperate regions are more social. Elk, for example, are very gregarious and may form groups numbering in the hundreds. The breeding season (or rut) for deer species occupying temperate latitudes occurs in late autumn or winter. During the rut, males spend considerable energy in male-male competition for mates (see essay 50). Deer typically produce 1–2 young; the gestation is usually 6–9 months. Most young-of-the-year stay with the mother until the following spring.

Family Cervidae

History and Economics of

White-Tailed Deer Populations

As a boy growing up in western Pennsylvania, I often saw deer in relatively high numbers in forested areas interspersed with farmlands. Moreover, I and others felt that deer in the more southerly (agricultural) counties of Pennsylvania seemed to be larger than deer in the more northerly (extensively forested) counties. My impressions of deer in Pennsylvania and elsewhere in the mid-eastern states, however, changed over the years. First, as part of my collaborative research studies with colleagues at Penn State on deer biology in Valley Forge National Historical Park and Gettysburg National Military Park (Cypher, Yahner, and Cypher 1988; Storm, Cottam, and Yahner 1995), I began to appreciate that high deer populations were quite common on public and private lands throughout much of the mid-eastern states.

Second, I also learned that deer present in today's eastern forest are probably smaller than those encountered by Europeans settlers. This became evident to me on a visit to the Carnegie Museum in Pittsburgh several years ago. The museum had a magnificent mount of a male white-tailed deer, which was larger than any deer I had ever seen. The mammal curator of the museum explained to me that the large size of this mounted deer was representative of extirpated eastern whitetails that once roamed the eastern United States. Thus, today's mid-eastern landscape is characterized not only by high deer populations but also smaller-sized deer compared to a century or so ago.

In order to appreciate the history of white-tailed deer populations, let's go back to the sixteenth century. Estimates of the historical abundance of white-tailed from this time period are few and conjectural but

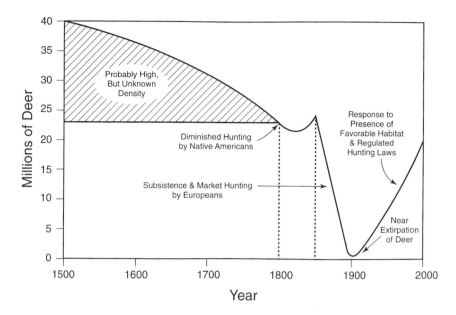

Figure 22. Historical trends in populations of white-tailed deer in North America from 1500 to the present. *(http://www/aqd.nps.gov/facts/wtdeer.htm. Modified from McCabe and McCabe 1984.)*

probably were about four to eight deer per square kilometer in the eastern United States (Seton 1909, cited in McCabe and McCabe 1984; Elder 1965). In some localized areas, however, deer populations were likely much higher, at least 19 deer per square kilometer, because the distribution of deer was not uniform through the entire range of the species and varied with natural events and hunting pressures by Native Americans (McCabe and McCabe 1984). Given the fact that the North American landscape in the sixteenth century was not dotted with urbanization and agricultural land uses as it is today, estimates of deer populations during the 1500s may have ranged as high as 23–40 million in North America (see fig. 22) (McCabe and McCabe 1984; Nowak 1999; http://www/aqd.nps.gov/facts/wtdeer.htm). Unfortunately, we will never know exactly how many deer existed in the mid-eastern states in pre-European times.

White-tailed deer were the most common source of protein for many tribes and cultural groups of Native Americans in North America, including those that relied also on agriculture or fishing as a livelihood (McCabe and McCabe 1984). Deer also provided hides for the manufacture of clothing (moccasins and leggings) and other essential items (blankets and quivers) for the Native American way of life. Other parts of deer had numerous uses; for instance, sinew was used for bowstrings, bones for arrowheads and utensils, and antlers as symbols of social status or for the production of objects (e.g., knife handles or children's toys). Based on remains at archaeological sites, Native Americans relied considerably more on deer than on other wildlife in the eastern forests, such as wild turkey and black bear (Guilday 1971, cited in McCabe and McCabe 1984).

Land-use activities by Native Americans, such as agriculture and burning, created suitable habitat for deer (McCabe and McCabe 1984). Deer populations in pre-European times probably also were benefited by natural events, such as uncontrolled fires, tornadoes, and insect damage (Cronon 1983). These human-induced and natural disturbances created early successional and edge habitats in a relatively continuous mature forested habitat. Hence, when Europeans settled on the East Coast of our continent in the early seventeenth century, they noted that "the most usefull and most beneficiall beast which is bredd in those parts is the Deare. There are in the Country three kindes of Deare of which there are great plenty" (Morton 1883, cited in McCabe and McCabe 1984). The three "kindes" of deer presumably refer to white-tailed deer, elk, and moose.

Prior to the early seventeenth century, Native Americans hunted deer without firearms (McCabe and McCabe 1984). But as firearm technology increased, large numbers of deer could efficiently be exploited. Deer hides then became an important form of currency for Native Americans in their trade with European settlers; hence, the term *buck* was coined in reference to the exchange value (one dollar) of a deer hide during colonial times (Allen 1929). On the frontiers of North America, deerskins and venison also were vital to the European way of life throughout the late seventeenth and early eighteenth centuries (Barber 1984). Hence, by the end of the eighteenth century, the outlook for white-tailed deer became bleak (McCabe and McCabe 1984). This aesthetic mammal soon vanished from much of New England because of excessive hunting pressures, combined with habitat changes and competition from domestic livestock (Cronon 1983). As a result, deer became a scarce commodity of diminished value in European markets (McCabe and McCabe 1984).

Throughout the nineteenth century in eastern North America, some events occurred simultaneously, thereby favoring white-tailed deer populations for a short time period (McCabe and McCabe 1984). First, because deer numbers were low at this time, Europeans reduced the hunting pressure on deer. Second, the unfortunate near-extirpation of native peoples in eastern North America further reduced deer harvests. As a consequence, white-tailed deer populations began to rebound from 1800 to 1900 throughout much of eastern North America. Deer, which were once scarce in the eighteenth century, now became a more common sight in the eastern forests and farmlands. Market hunting of deer was a profitable venture for Europeans and reached its peak after the Civil War with the widespread availability of the repeating rifle. Venison was a frequent menu item in many of the fashionable restaurants of Chicago, New York, and Philadelphia. This overwhelming market demand for venison coupled with subsistence hunting resulted in deer populations once again dropping rapidly by the beginning of the twentieth century. Once-common whitetails now were rarely seen, being locally extirpated and numbering only about 300,000 in the United States by the 1890s (McCabe and McCabe 1984; Marchinton, Miller, and McDonald 1995). This latest widespread decline in deer populations at the end of the twentieth century was a prime impetus for the origin of modern wildlife conservation and management as we know it today.

The resilient white-tailed deer made a remarkable turnaround again in the early decades of the twentieth century. Deer populations have continued to increase as we enter the new millennium, and their populations are considered overabundant in many areas of the mid-eastern states and elsewhere (Warren 1997). Five factors have contributed to the rise in deer increase in deer populations. First, deer were protected from uncontrolled hunting. Many state wildlife agencies were established near the turn of the twentieth century with mandates to establish hunting regulations for the protection of deer and other consumptive wildlife (Mattfield 1984; Diefenbach and Palmer 1997). Therefore, landowners could no longer hunt deer year-round; instead, carefully regulated hunting seasons and harvest limits were imposed to prevent deer from being overexploited. Second, natural predators of deer, for example, gray wolves and mountain lions, were eliminated from much of the eastern landscape (Yahner 2000). Third, land-use changes, such as extensive logging of the eastern forest in the late nineteenth and early twentieth centuries, created favorable deer habitat by providing abundant early successional habitat in the ensuing years. In addition, many farms were abandoned and converted to early successional habitat in the East. Fourth, large numbers of deer were stocked throughout many areas of the mid-eastern states in the early decades of the twentieth century (Barber 1984; Shrauder 1984; Marchinton, Miller, and McDonald 1995); Pennsylvania, for example, received deer trapped and transferred from other states, such as Michigan, North Carolina, Texas, and Wisconsin (Marchinton, Miller, and McDonald 1995). Finally, in the last few decades, hunting pressures on deer have shown a gradual decline because of fewer hunters than in previous decades and because of reduced opportunities for hunting in many urban-suburban-agricultural landscapes with more acreage posted off-limits to hunting (Coffey and Johnston 1997; Lund 1997).

The number of deer present in the United States in the latter years of the twentieth century is conjectural, but it probably ranged between 14 and 20 million (http://www/aqd/nps.gov/facts/wtdeer.htm). At the turn of the twenty-first century, the total population of this deer in North America probably exceeds 20 million and may be as high as 28.5 million (Crête and Daigle 1999); furthermore, the distribution of whitetails continues to expand and now extends into southern Canada (Hesselton and Hesselton 1982). Let's conservatively assume that currently there are 17 million white-tailed deer in the United States. Given this estimate, what is the monetary value of this resource from recreational and aesthetic perspectives? This is a difficult question to answer because assigning a value to wildlife species, which are owned by society rather than individuals, cannot be determined by an economic market system as it can for domesticated animals (Conover 1997a).

One way of determining the total monetary value of a wildlife species, however, is to determine the amount spent on that species for recreational or aesthetic purposes minus the amount spent on damage incurred by this species. Using this approach the net positive monetary value of white-tailed deer in the United States is estimated to be at least $12 billion, which includes expenditures by deer hunters such as travel, equipment, food, and lodging (Conover 1997a). Thus, according to my calculations, each deer in the United States is worth about $706, which is similar to $780 per head of beef cattle (1999 figures, http:www.beef.org). From a total population and economical perspective, beef cattle are about six times more valuable that white-tailed deer because there are about 98.5 million beef cattle (in 1999), which equates to about $77 million. Yet from an aesthetic perspective, I and most others interested in the outdoors would rather view a doe and her fawn in the wild rather than a cow and her calf in a pasture. Hence, the white-tailed deer is perhaps the best example of a charismatic wildlife species that provides both positive economical and intangible values to society in the mid-eastern states and North America in general (Conover 1997a).

Concurrent with a growing deer herd in the last few decades is considerable controversy about three deer issues: disease transmission, vehicular collisions, and damage to vegetation (Baker and Fritsch 1997; deCalesta and Stout 1997). Deer are major hosts of Lyme disease, and, thus, higher deer populations can pose a very serious health threat to humans and pets (see essay 22 in chap. 9).

Deer-vehicular collisions, especially during the fall rut when deer are quite active and wide-ranging, can be another major problem, with an estimated 1.5 million collisions occurring per year in the United States. Each collision carries an average price tag of $1,500 or $1 billion in total annual damage to vehicles (Conover, Pitt, Kessler, DuBow, and Sanborn 1995). Deer-vehicular collisions also can result in possible injury or loss of human life (Hansen 1983). As a means of reducing deer-vehicular collisions in the mid-eastern states, deer-proof fencing has been placed along collision-prone sectors of highways, such as those with high speed limits that border wooded areas (Bashore, Tzilkowski, and Bellis 1985). Deer may be an additional problem along airport runways because landing areas often are planted with succulent grasses that provide food for deer and because some may be placed near wooded areas (Bashore and Bellis 1982).

Homeowners, foresters, and farmers often feel the economic brunt of high deer populations. An estimated $250-million loss is caused by deer eating shrubbery and other vegetation around homes (Conover 1997a). In addition, feeding by deer is responsible for millions of dollars in damage to the agricultural and timber industries (see essay 46 below).

In my opinion, the white-tailed deer (which, incidentally, is the state mammal of my home state of Pennsylvania) epitomizes the beauty of our natural world and has played a major role in the lives of peoples that historically occupied our region. Only a century or so ago, this charismatic mammal was virtually eliminated from the mid-eastern states. Deer numbers have now rebounded to the point that this mammal has become an unwanted pest in some locations. Yet today its estimated positive monetary value ($12 million/year) easily outweighs its estimated negative value ($2 million/year) by six to one (Conover 1997a). But many of us are convinced that high deer populations have, and will continue to have, a substantial and deleterious ecological impact on other fauna and flora. Some of these impacts will be explored in the next essay.

ESSAY 46

Impacts of Deer on Crops and Forest Resources

White-tailed deer can have a major negative impact on agricultural crops, commercially important seedlings, and orchard trees. Although deer typically are considered browsers, meaning they feed on tender, high-energy tips of woody stems, they also graze on agricultural crops. Since the early 1900s, deer have learned to feed on large quantities of agricultural crops, which historically represented negligible or nonexistent food resources for most deer (Calhoun and Loomis 1975). In the mid-eastern states, farmers growing important crops, like alfalfa, corn, and winter wheat, have experienced considerable economic loss (Palmer, Kelly, and George 1982; Vecellio, Yahner, and Storm 1994). Taken collectively, the estimated annual damage by deer to agricultural crops and forest seedlings in the United States is at least $100 million and $750 million respectively (Conover 1997a).

In recent studies at Gettysburg National Military Park (GETT), small enclosures (fencing) were used in crop fields to estimate the extent of damage caused by deer to crops (Vecellio, Yahner, and Storm 1994; Storm, Cottam, and Yahner 1995). The average yield of field corn was 20 percent less in unfenced compared to fenced plots; damage to some corn grain in some plots was as high as fifty-five bushels per hectare. In some fields at GETT, the entire corn crop was consumed by deer. The average yield of winter wheat at GETT was 30 percent less in unfenced plots compared to fenced plots, with damage to wheat grain of 56 bushels per hectare in certain areas of the park. On both public and private agricultural lands, fencing and planting of alternate crops (e.g., milo) are not economically feasible options to reduce crop damage by deer; instead, a reduction of deer numbers is likely the most viable option (Erickson and Giessman 1989; Vecellio, Yahner, and Storm 1994). As of 1994 nineteen states and seven Canadian provinces have compensation programs for farmers who report damage to agricultural crops by wildlife (Wagner, Schmidt, and Conover 1997). However, of the eight mid-eastern states, only Virginia provides compensation for crop damage caused by white-tailed deer.

Deer browsing can have a major negative effect on the economics of the timber industry (Conover 1997a). Browsing on seedlings in the forest can reduce or even eliminate commercially important tree species, delay the time normally required for regeneration of a forest, and produce browse lines devoid of vegetation to about two meters above ground (Marquis 1981; Stromayer and Warren 1997; Waller and Alverson 1997; Yahner 2000). In the early 1980s the annual timber loss of hardwood tree species caused by deer browsing was estimated to be $56 per hectare (Marquis 1981). Intensive deer browsing at Cades Cove in the Great Smoky Mountains National Park changed the species composition from primarily deciduous trees to coniferous trees (Bratton 1979). The impact of deer on tree seedlings, however, can be mitigated to some extent with the use of fencing, such as five-wire Penn State Vertical Electric Deer Fence (Palmer, Payne, Wingard, and George 1985).

Unfortunately, the deleterious effects of deer browsing in forest ecosystems goes well beyond the direct effects on commercially important tree species. Other integral components of a functional forested ecosystem (e.g., wildflower and songbird populations) can be impacted (Yahner 2000).

Family Cervidae

Because deer rely on herbaceous plants as food in summer (McCaffery, Tranetzki, and Piechura 1974; Cypher, Yahner, and Cypher 1988), populations of many rare and endangered wildflowers have been reduced or eliminated (Miller, Bratton, and Hadidian 1992; Waller and Alverson 1997). At Presque Isle State Park in northwestern Pennsylvania, for instance, seed production by an endangered perennial, the hairy puccoon, has been reduced 90 percent by deer grazing (Campbell 1993).

Extensive browsing by deer in managed forest stands has reduced the abundance and diversity of many songbird species and the abundance of snowshoe hares (a species of special concern in Pennsylvania) by reducing cover used by these coexisting wildlife species as home, nest, or foraging sites (Casey and Hein 1983; Dessecker and Yahner 1987; Scott and Yahner 1989; deCalesta 1994). Deer also compete with snowshoe hares for food resources (Scott and Yahner 1989). The effects of high deer populations on other aspects of a forested ecosystem, such as nutrient cycling or net primary production, are only beginning to be understood and need further research (Hobbs 1996).

Fruit growers often experience extensive damage by white-tailed deer (Decker and Brown 1982). Damage to orchard trees is typically caused when deer feed on the dormant twigs of trees, which then stunts woody growth and reduces the number of leaves (Swihart and Conover 1990; Mower, Townsend, and Tyznik 1997). Deer most often damage orchard trees within the first three years of planting (Scott and Townsend 1985); thus, protection from deer browsing using protective wire cylinders is especially important and effective during the first season after planting (Mower, Townsend, and Tyznik 1997).

Deer may damage orchard trees by creating buck rubs (Nielsen, Dunlap, and Miller 1982). Male deer often select small, smooth barked trees (16–25 mm in diameter, 15 cm above ground) as rubs (see essay 49 below). Once a rub is created by a dominant buck on a nursery tree, it generally no longer meets the quality standards for nursery stock. Trees damaged most often by buck rubs in an Ohio nursery were mountain ash, river birch, and flowering cherry. Some ways to minimize damage to preferred nursery trees are to plant nonpreferred species (e.g., crabapple and hawthorn), use chemical repellents and protective fencing on preferred trees, and implement deer-reduction programs (Decker and

Brown 1982; Swihart and Conover 1990; Mower, Townsend, and Tyznik 1997).

In summary, populations of white-tailed deer are much too high in many suburban, agricultural, and forested landscapes of the mid-eastern states. Wildlife agencies will need to use both traditional and nontraditional means of controlling deer populations (DeNicola, Weber, Bridges, and Stokes 1997; Diefenbach and Palmer 1997). Most important, a major responsibility of state wildlife agencies is to inform and educate hunters, metropolitan residents, and others interested in seeing more deer (see Conover 1997b) that high deer populations cannot be ecologically sustained in our forests without having serious negative impacts on other plants and animals (Diefenbach, Palmer, and Shope 1997; Yahner 2000).

ESSAY 47

"Quality" White-Tailed Deer—

Biological and Management Implications

Earlier, we compared the value of individual white-tailed deer and beef cattle ($706 versus $780, respectively) (see essay 45 above). Wildlife biologists, however, strive to maintain a population of healthy deer, not in terms of a dollar value but rather based on physical attributes of individual animals, such as body, litter, or antler size. For example, a deer population with lower average body weights may be considered to be in poorer health than a population with higher body weights (Cook 1984).

Body weights of white-tailed deer may not necessarily be the best measure of health because weights can vary regionally. For instance, body weights of deer generally vary along a latitudinal gradient, with the heaviest deer found in the northern United States and southern Canada and the lightest deer occurring in more southerly latitudes (Baker 1984; Sauer 1984). As an extreme example, deer in Ontario are four- to sixfold heavier than those in the Florida Keys (91–137 versus <23 kg, respectively).

Weights of deer also differ among seasons, with both males and females losing weight during autumn and winter but gaining weight in spring and summer. However, long-term declines in the average body weights of a deer population in a given region can mean one of two things: either the population is too large for the amount of food resources available or the young are for some reason getting less or poorer quality food (Sauer 1984). For instance, an individual adult deer weighing about seventy kilograms requires about 2.5 to 2.7 kilograms of food per day (10,000 calories), with 13–16 percent of the diet consisting of protein, in order to remain healthy (French, McEwen, Magruder, Ingram, and Swift 1955). Thus, there is a direct relationship between the health of deer, as measured by average body size, and what wildlife biologists refer to as the carrying capacity of the habitat. In other words, a habitat with abundant food resources would have a higher carrying capacity, meaning it would be able to sustain a higher deer population, than a habitat with reduced food resources.

Reproductive rates, as measured by the number of fawn to doe ratio, can vary with the health of individual deer (Sauer 1984). On average, two-year-old does in good health are about 50 percent heavier in body weight than one-year-old does (Moen and Severinghaus 1981); these older does typically have two fawns per year compared to younger does producing one fawn per year; younger, smaller females have less energy to expend in raising young. In habitats with adequate food supplies, healthy, older females always produce twins and sometimes triplets (10–15% of the time) (Hesselton and Hesselton 1982). As an interesting aside, females in poor health typically produce disproportionately more male fawns than female fawns, whereas the reverse is true in females in good health (Verme 1969). Essentially, young males may be more expendable than young females in a polygamous species, like the white-tailed deer, when habitat and health conditions are reduced.

Antlers are the most prominent feature of white-tailed deer and other members of the cervid family (see essay 50 in chap. 20), and the size of antlers can be an indicator of deer health. As indicated earlier, antlers are deciduous bony structures that grow from permanent bony pedicels on the frontal bones of males, beginning at about three to five months of age (Waldo and Wislocki 1951; Hesselton and Hesselton 1982).

Antlers undergo four phases during the annual cycle: growth, mineralization, hardening (death), and polished (Hesselton and Hesselton 1982; Sauer 1984; Weeks 1995). The initial growth phase begins each spring (around April) with a progressive increase in day length and testosterone levels. The growing antler is composed of spongy bone and a central marrow space, consisting of protein, calcium, and phosphorus. The spongy character of young antlers in the growth phase increases the antlers' strength by preventing breakage—similar to a green tree branch bending rather than breaking. Moreover, the spongy nature of antlers permits deer to grow larger antlers because there is less energy drain than if a male were to grow antlers of solid bone. Antlers in the growth phase are covered with "velvet" (skin plus hair); the skin of velvet contains arteries and veins, which supply the growing antler with a rich blood supply.

Antlers continue to grow until about midsummer to late summer, at which time a one-month mineralization phase begins. During this relatively short phase, arteriosclerosis sets in as calcium and phosphorus are deposited in the blood vessels of the antlers. These deposits restrict blood flow and eventually cause the antler to "die" (harden). The hardened antler is about 50–60 percent minerals, with the remaining amount consisting of protein (Weeks 1995). In the early stages of the hardening phase, the velvet dries up, cracks, and peels (Hesselton and Hesselton 1982), and it takes about two to three days for all velvet to be removed from antlers (Hirth 1977). Some of the velvet is removed by pre-rut behavior when adult males rub their antlers and forehead glands on small trees to form "buck rubs" (see essay 49 below). Velvet-free, polished antlers then represent the last phase of the antler cycle; these antlers are used as sparring weapons during the rut (see essay 50).

Antlers are retained throughout all or most of the rut. Males begin to lose their antlers sometime between early December and early winter when testosterone levels rapidly decline (Hesselton and Hesselton 1982). Larger antlers tend to be retained for up to two months longer than smaller antlers (Zagata and Moen 1974; Forand, Marchinton, and Miller 1985). The size of antlers is determined by at least three factors: age, nutritional status, and genetics of individual deer (French et al. 1955; Severinghaus and Cheatum 1956; Hesselton and Sauer 1973; Sauer 1984).

Older male deer in good health produce larger antlers with more points than younger males in good health. For example, in New York, average diameter and number of points per antler were twenty-nine centimeters and eight points for 4.5-year-old males, respectively, compared to nineteen centimeters and four points for 1.5-year-old males. When food is scarce, however, an additional year or so may be required for a deer to attain antler size comparable to deer of the same age in habitat with adequate food (Sauer 1984). Furthermore, as deer age, their antlers typically continue to grow in diameter (Sauer 1984; Scribner, Smith, and Johns 1989). The maximum number of points and overall antler quality reach their peak when a buck is about 4.5–5.5 years old and plateau until about the age of 9.5 years, after which antler size and quality begin to decline (Scribner, Smith, and Johns 1989; Jacobson 1995). Older males are presumably unable to continually increase antler size and quality because of energy stresses related to increasing age.

Nutrition is critical to antler growth and size, regardless of buck age. Bucks require a diet of at least 16 percent crude protein, which can be obtained from some grasses in summer and terminal buds of trees (browse) in winter. A small amount of calcium and phosphorus (about 0.5–1.0 g/day) also helps to ensure better antler growth. Deficiencies in these minerals can cause reductions in the strength of antlers and increase the likelihood of breakage. When a habitat contains limited food resources, younger males in the population may often produce what are called spikes, that is, small antlers (<8 cm) with no branching; but when food is adequate, these same individuals may be very capable of growing relatively large antlers.

The occurrence of spike bucks in a population, however, is affected by genetics. For example, the offspring of bucks with "superior" genetics seldom have spiked antlers, whereas 50–60 percent of the offspring sired from bucks with spiked antlers exhibit inferior antler growth and size. This is an interesting statistic because at one time wildlife agencies prohibited the harvest of spike bucks in order to give these individual deer an opportunity to grow better antlers in the subsequent year. In reality, this management practice helped to perpetuate many spike bucks in the next generation by protecting those with inferior genetics! The notion, however, that "once a spike, always a spike" may not necessarily hold because antler development is a function of several interacting factors—age, nutrition, and genetics (Brothers, Guynn, Hamilton, and Marchinton 1995).

In summary, a "quality" deer herd might be defined as one consisting of large healthy individuals, with high reproductive rates and antler size. Today, wildlife agencies are giving considerable emphasis to a concept called *quality deer management* (Hamilton, Knox, and Guynn 1995; Regan, Gwynn, and Woods 1995). Quality deer management is not *trophy management*, meaning the management of bucks with the largest antlers. Instead, this new, sound approach to deer management includes the voluntary reduction in both the harvest of younger males combined with an appropriate harvest level of antlerless deer. The goal of this management strategy is to maintain a healthy deer herd that is in balance with resources (food) in the habitat. As a consequence, quality deer management is good stewardship of a valuable resource, the aesthetic whitetail, at a population level that minimizes or eliminates damage to other resources (wildflowers or songbirds) in the ecosystem (see essay 46 above).

ESSAY 48

Brainworm in Deer and

Its Implications for Conservation

Diseases and parasites are common phenomena in many species of wildlife (Davidson, Hayes, Nettles, and Kellogg 1981). We already have seen how the fatal disease, rabies, affects canid and raccoon populations (see essay 29 in chap. 11 and essay 35 in chap. 13). A parasite that has important implications to the biology and conservation of deer is the so-called brainworm (Anderson and Prestwood 1981). This parasite is a nematode worm that causes a disease popularly referred to as "moose sickness" (Coady 1982; Miller 1982). Curiously, however, the white-tailed deer does not contract moose sickness, even though it is the principal host of the brainworm (Hesselton and Hesselton 1982).

The brainworm is widespread in eastern populations of whitetails; for instance, it was found in 77 percent of the deer examined in New York (Behrend 1970), 80 percent of the deer in Pennsylvania (Mitchell 1982), and 100 percent of the deer in some Maine populations (Behrend and Witter 1968). Incidences of brainworm may not necessarily be related to deer population densities. For example, in Maine, brainworm occurred in 81 percent of the individual deer in low-density populations but in only 59 percent of the deer in high-density populations (Gilbert 1973). Furthermore, within the same population, incidences of brainworm can vary from year to year (e.g., 63–85% over a three-year period).

The life cycle of brainworms includes both white-tailed deer and terrestrial snails (Anderson and Prestwood 1981). Adult worms mature on the meningeal surfaces lining the brain or in the sinuses of the cranial cavity of the deer. The cycle begins when these adults deposit fertilized eggs in the blood of deer. These eggs then are transported via blood to the lungs, where they hatch into the first larval stage within the alveoli of the lungs. The brainworm larvae are coughed up, swallowed, digested, and passed in the feces of deer. Once the first-stage larvae are excreted by deer, terrestrial snails become the important host. A snail feeds on the feces of deer infected with brainworm larvae; these larvae molt twice inside the body of the snail, giving the third and infective stage of the snail.

The brainworms life cycle comes full circle when a deer is feeding on vegetation and accidentally ingests a snail containing third-stage larvae. The ingested larvae complete the cycle by penetrating the lining of the deer's stomach and migrating to the spinal cord over a period of about ten days. Within a couple months, the worms mature to the adult stage and harmlessly enter the meningeal lining of the brain and cranial sinuses of the deer. Based on a survey of several studies, the number of brainworms per infected white-tailed deer was two to twenty (Anderson and

Prestwood 1981), and as many as sixty-five worms caused negligible or no effect on individual deer (Samuel, Pybus, Welch, and Wilke 1992).

Other deer species, for example, mule deer, moose, elk, and caribou, can serve as hosts of the brainworm (Anderson and Prestwood 1981), but this parasite can be fatal to these species (Gilbert 1973). However, compared to rabies (see essay 29 in chap. 11 and essay 35 in chap. 13), moose sickness presumably is not an all-or-none, fatal disease (Samuel et al. 1992). For instance, elk infected with fifteen worms or less are relatively unaffected by brainworms, but individuals infected with at least twenty-five worms typically die. This may explain why remnant populations of elk can persist in similar habitat with white-tailed deer in some states, like Pennsylvania, Michigan, and Ontario.

Brainworms are fatal to other deer species because they simply do not stay within the meninges and cranial tissues of the brain but continue their penetration into the brain, spinal cord, and optic nerves. This often results in neurological disorders, blindness, fearlessness, circling, and even death (Samuel et al. 1992). Hence, a cervid inflicted with moose sickness often wanders aimlessly in a very disoriented fashion. Incidentally, brainworm can have similar negative health effects on domestic sheep and goats (Alden, Woodson, Mohan, and Miller 1975; Mahyhew, Delahunta, Georgi, and Aspros 1976).

There is no practical means of controlling brainworm in the wild, thereby making it difficult to reduce the impact of this parasite on other deer species (Anderson and Prestwood 1981). The occurrence of this nematode is probably related to several, poorly understood environmental factors, such as densities of terrestrial snail populations, suitability of habitat for both white-tailed deer and snails, and climatic effects on snail populations (Raskevitz, Kocan, and Shaw 1991; Gilbert 1992). For example, snow-melt during spring in regions with deep snow cover can wash larval brainworms from deer feces, which possibly can lower the rates of parasite transmission to other deer species.

The northern distribution of white-tailed has been limited historically by winter severity and habitat availability (Hesselton and Hesselton 1982; Gilbert and Bateman 1983). However, as mature forests were eliminated at the turn of the twentieth century in northern latitudes (Yahner 2000), regenerating forests became more favorable habitat for whitetails but less favorable for other species, like woodland caribou (Miller 1982). This habitat change allowed whitetail populations to expand their geographic range further north; with this range expansion came white-tailed deer infected with brainworm to the detriment of woodland caribou and moose populations. Today, in areas where both the ranges of white-tailed deer and moose overlap and the prevalence of brainworm in deer is high (e.g., in Ontario), populations of moose remain quite low (Saunders 1974). Hence, moose populations (and perhaps other deer species) may be held in check by white-tailed deer populations characterized by high incidences of brainworm (Gilbert 1974, 1992; but see Nudds 1992).

The presence of brainworm in white-tailed deer populations has potential, wide-ranging implications to wildlife agencies when translocating other deer species into areas already occupied by whitetails (Samuel et al. 1992). Although elk have been introduced successfully in some areas, like Pennsylvania (Woolf, Mason, and Kradel 1977), Michigan (Moran 1973), and Minnesota (Bryant and Maser 1982), other attempts have failed. Translocation failures in New York, for instance, have been directly attributed to brainworm transmission from native whitetails to translocated elk (Severinghaus and Darrow 1976; Raskevitz, Kocan, and Shaw 1991). Unsuccessful introductions of woodland caribou into historic range also have been attributed to transmission of brainworms from white-tailed deer to caribou (Dauphine 1975; Anderson and Prestwood 1981). Moreover, the continued range expansion of white-tailed deer and its parasite, the brainworm, into western states has probably caused population declines in mule deer (Anderson and Prestwood 1981). As a precaution against this happening, several wildlife biologists in western North America have banned the introduction of white-tailed deer in areas occupied by native populations of mule deer, moose, elk, or caribou (Samuel et al. 1992).

In conclusion, predator-prey interactions and environmental variables are major factors affecting the distribution and abundance of wildlife species (see essay 8 in chap. 6 and essay 21 in chap. 9). Yet many of us were probably unaware that an inconspicuous parasite, the brainworm, has been a major factor influencing historic and extant cervid populations in North America. Hence, this nematode must be considered by wildlife agencies when developing sound conservation strategies for other aesthetic cervids, such as mule deer, moose, elk, and woodland caribou.

ESSAY 49

Why Do Deer Create Buck Rubs and Buck Scrapes?

A conspicuous sign indicating the presence of white-tailed deer in a wood-lot is a buck (or antler) rub (see fig. 23). A *buck rub* is caused when a male deer strips the bark of a small tree with its antlers, which creates an obvi-ous visual signal to us and presumably to other deer in the area. A rub is usually placed at the shoulder height of a deer (1 m or less above ground) on a smooth-barked, small diameter (16–25 mm) tree (Kile and Marchin-ton 1977; Nielsen, Dunlap, and Miller 1982). The smooth bark of small red maples, for instance, makes this species ideal for buck rubs in the forests of the mid-eastern states (Shaffer and Rehnberg 1999). Small, smooth-barked nursery trees also are frequent targets of buck rubs, often resulting in considerable monetary damage to nursery stock (Nielsen, Dunlap, and Miller 1982) (see essay 46 above).

Adult male deer usually produce rubs in late summer or early autumn when the outer velvet layer is being shed from their antlers (see essay 47 above). Rubs are created about one to two months before the breeding season or rut (Kile and Marchinton 1977). Hence, for a long time, biolo-gists believed that male deer used buck rubs not only to clean and polish antlers but also to provide practice for the ensuing male-male combat during the rut (Atkeson and Marchinton 1982), like high school football linemen practicing their blocking prior to the first football game. How-ever, biologists also noted that deer sniff and lick a "strange rub," which suggests that this visual mark on a small tree plays a very important com-munication purpose in the social life of deer.

The importance of olfactory communication in the way of life of deer was documented by an interesting study of captive adult mule deer a few decades ago, which noted that males rubbed their foreheads on branches and twigs, especially as autumn approached (Müller-Schwarze 1972). A

Figure 23. Buck rub caused by a male deer stripping the bark of a small tree with its antlers. *(Photo by author.)*

decade later, another study reported that adult male white-tailed deer also exhibited forehead rubbing just before and during the rut (Atkeson and Marchinton 1982). It was found that when a whitetail buck makes a rub, it moves both antlers and forehead glands along the small tree in a vertical direction. This forehead rubbing behavior coincides with a high level of glandular activity in the modified scent glands found on the fore-heads of male deer; the glandular activity causes the forehead pelage of adult males to be distinctly darker than in other age and sex classes.

Forehead rubbing by male deer on buck rubs presumably sends a great deal of information to conspecifics (Atkeson and Marchinton 1982). First, the chemicals deposited on the rub provide information on the individ-ual identity of an animal; no two mammals produce the same scent (see Eisenberg and Kleiman 1972). For instance, as we all know, dogs recog-nize each other via smell. Second, because only male deer rub, the buck rub and its associated chemicals indicate the sex class of the deer produc-ing the rub. Third, older, more dominant buck produce more buck rubs and probably deposit more glandular secretions on a given rub (Miller, Marchinton, and Ozoga 1995). Thus, the presence of many well-marked rubs is indicative of older, higher-status males being in the general vicin-ity rather than simply being a crude measure of relative deer abundance in a given area. The information conveyed by the olfactory signals on a buck rub make it the social equivalent of some auditory signals in other deer species, such as "bugling" by bull elk (Müller-Schwarze 1972).

Because both sexes of whitetails respond to buck rubs by smelling and licking them, rubs may serve a very important additional function (Ozoga 1985). Fresher buck rubs (<2 days old), in particular, are visited more fre-quently by adult females than older rubs (Sawyer, Marchinton, and Miller 1989). Hence, a major communication function suggested for fresh buck rubs is that they may help to physiologically induce and synchronize es-trus in females that visit these rubs. This would be an obvious advantage to wide-ranging deer, especially to a socially dominant buck when court-ing several adult females during the autumn rut.

While walking in the eastern forest in autumn, we might also en-counter another visual signal produced by white-tailed deer, which has been termed a *buck scrape* (see fig. 24). Scrapes consist of a clearing (about 0.5 m diameter) and shallow depression made in the leaf litter by pawing; after making the scrape, the deer typically urinates in the depression (Atke-son and Marchinton 1982; Marchinton and Hirth 1984). Thus, like a buck rub, a scrape is both a visual and an olfactory signal.

Buck scrapes are generally created after leaf-fall in autumn (late October–early November), which is just before or during the rut (Ozoga

Family Cervidae

Figure 24. A buck scrape, which consists of a depression and clearing made in the leaf litter by pawing. Older adult males often mark a branch directly above the scrape (branch indicated by a former Penn State graduate student). *(Photo by author.)*

Deer

254

1989a). Scrapes are usually placed in open or conspicuous places, such as along a deer trail (Kile and Marchinton 1977). Most are made by older males (Miller, Marchinton, Forand, and Johansen 1987), although females and younger (≤2.5 years old) males occasionally make scrapes (Sawyer, Marchinton, and Berisford 1982). Those produced by older males also include an overhanging branch, which is located one to two meters directly above the scrape; this branch is marked by the male's forehead glands. Interestingly, adult male deer can be induced to form scrapes by attaching a single bowed stem to a nearby tree above a deer trail (Ozoga 1989b).

Scrapes apparently advertise the social status and physiological state of older males producing (Moore and Marchinton 1974; Miller et al. 1987), whereas the social significance of scrapes made by adult females is unknown (Sawyer, Marchinton, and Berisford 1982). Because adult females often sniff and occasionally urinate in scrapes produced by older males, these signposts may act like buck rubs to induce and synchronize estrus in adult females (Sawyer, Marchinton, and Miller 1989). Scrapes are occasionally made at other times of the year, like late spring or early summer. These scrapes may help segregate the sexes during the nonbreeding season and thereby reduce competition for food resources when antler development and fawn rearing are important activities (Ozoga 1989a).

In summary, the next time we observe a buck rub or scrape in a nearby woodlot, it should be viewed as a sophisticated signal in the life of deer. What may seem to us as a simple mark on a tree or a cleared area on the forest floor is instead a wealth of information for deer society. Because deer are wide-ranging and nocturnal, both buck rubs and buck scrapes help ensure an effective means of communication among members of a localized deer population, especially during the breeding season.

20

Bovids

Family Bovidae

Description of the Family Bovidae

The largest group of hooved mammals or ungulates is the family Bovidae, which contains 140 species. Like the preceding two families, Suidae and Cervidae (see chaps. 18 and 19, respectively), bovids are even-toed and hence in the order Artiodactyla. The natural distribution of bovids is similar to that of cervids, which includes North America, South America, Europe, Asia, and Africa; bovids also have been introduced into Australia, New Zealand, and many smaller islands.

The bovids are important components of many ecosystems, for example, wildebeest and impala of the African grasslands. Historically, bison were critical to the natural succession of prairie plant communities in the western plains of the United States and Canada. Today, many species, like domestic goats, sheep, and cattle, are extremely valuable to humans as sources of meat, milk, and clothing. About 600 million domestic goats, 1 billion domestic sheep, and 1.3 billion domestic cattle are found worldwide.

Only one feral bovid species is found in our region, the feral goat; it occurs as isolated wild populations in West Virginia (see table 1). In the United States, however, the feral goat is actually the most widespread feral ungulate; on islands, such as Hawaii and the Galapagos, goat populations can reach very high densities, causing considerable destruction to native vegetation and the endangerment or extinction of native birdlife.

Besides goats, two domestic bovids are present in the mideastern states, sheep and cattle. Feral sheep populations can affect native vegetation, cause the endangerment and extinction of island fauna, and spread disease to wild relatives. Modern domestic cattle contain over 1,000 breeds, including the aesthetic Texas longhorns, which were introduced to the American West by Spaniards. Scattered herds of feral cattle occur throughout many parts of the world and in parts of the United States.

Bovids vary in size from the very tiny pygmy antelope of Africa to various large members of the genus *Bos* (e.g., domestic cattle and American bison). The pygmy antelope is only fifty-seven centimeters in total length (body and tail combined) and weighs around two to three kilograms, which is considerably smaller than the smallest deer, the pudu (see chap. 19). Cattle and bison, on the other hand, can be over four meters in total length and weigh as much as 1,000 kilograms; thus, some bovid species are much larger in body weight than the largest deer, the moose. As in deer, male bovids are larger and more stocky in build than females. Many bovids (e.g., bison) are rather robust in body shape, whereas others (e.g., impala) are long-legged and sleek in body shape, giving a deer-like appearance. The pelage of bovids is often brownish but can be much lighter with beautiful markings, as in the gemsbok of Africa; it also may range from smooth to shaggy.

Horns are permanent structures found in males of most bovid species and in females of about 50 percent of the bovid species. They consist of body cores attached to frontal bones of the skull; hard keratin sheaths cover the cores. With the exception of the four-horned antelope from India and Nepal, two horns are the rule in bovids. Horns are not exclusive to bovids but can be found in pronghorns and other ungulates. Bovids have thirty to thirty-two teeth.

Bovids live in a variety of habitats; for instance, some populations of bighorn sheep are found in deserts of the southwestern United States, whereas, muskox inhabit tundra in the Arctic. Most bovids are gregarious, and some are territorial. Food consists of a variety of plant material, including grasses, stems, and leaves.

Bovids generally produce few young; as examples, American bison and bighorn sheep have a single young every one to two years. The gestation is 285 days in the American bison versus 174 days in the bighorn sheep. The time required for weaning of young can vary with species; using the same two wild species, young American bison are weaned seven to twelve months after birth, but young bighorn sheep are weaned four to six months after birth. Many bovids are long-lived, surviving in the wild for as long as twenty years.

Bovids

Why Have Ungulates Evolved Antlers and Horns?

As we survey the 4,800 or so species of mammals, we find that only a relatively small percentage have evolved antlers or horns. These bony structures are absent from species that exhibit a subterranean, aerial, or aquatic way of life. Antlers or horns also do not occur in many large orders of terrestrial mammals, such as rodents or carnivores. However, antlers and horns are prominent features of many terrestrial cervid and bovid species, respectively.

As we discussed in chapter 19, antlers are found in most deer species. Antlers are a male characteristic except in caribou, in which antlers occur in both sexes, and in a relatively small percentage of females of other cervid species (Nowak 1999). For instance, in white-tailed deer, antlers may be found in about one out of every 1,000 does (Hesselton and Hesselton 1982). Typically, antlers in female whitetails are retained for life (rather than being lost in winter; see essay 47 in chap. 19), remain in the velvet phase of development, and are unbranched. The occurrence of antlers in female deer is not a function of nutritional or health status but appears to be caused by abnormally high levels of testosterone (Sauer 1984). Antlered females are fertile and can produce young (Wislocki 1956).

In contrast to antlers being principally a male phenomenon in cervids, about 50 percent of the bovid species have horns in females (Packer 1983). Two interesting points should be made regarding the prevalence of horns in female bovids. First, horns in females are much more likely to occur in open-country species that have relatively large body weight (>40 kg). Conversely, forest-dwelling bovids tend to have hornless females and are usually smaller (<40 kg). Second, when horns are found in both males and females of the same species, the size and shape of the horns are considerably different between the sex classes; horns of males tend to be

Family Bovidae

curved or spiraled and thicker at the base, whereas horns of females are straighter and thinner (Packer 1983; Lundrigan 1996).

Why do deer have antlers and bovids horns? Let's begin with antlers. At least five hypotheses have been proposed for the evolution and, hence, role of antlers (Barrette 1977). A first hypothesis suggests that because antlers are highly vascularized during the growth phase, deer have evolved these structures to help dissipate body heat. If this were true, we would expect antlers to be growing during the hot summer months in all deer species. Yet antlers in roe deer of Europe, for instance, are still growing in winter. Moreover, the antlers of moose are already dead in summer, having gone through the mineralization and hardening phases of the antler cycle well in advance of the hottest times of the year. If antlers evolved for the dissipation of heat, we should expect the largest antlers to exist in tropical deer species rather than in temperate species (Barrette 1977). Instead, tropical deer, like the Reeve's muntjac of China, has very tiny antlers, and antlers of elk and moose in cooler temperate latitudes are quite large. In addition, female deer rarely have antlers, but females presumably generate a similar amount of body heat as males. Thus, the first hypothesis can be rejected.

A second hypothesis for the evolution of antlers is that large antler size in males attracts females (Barrette 1977). There is no evidence for this hypothesis; however, females perhaps select older, larger body-sized males over younger, smaller males.

A third hypothesis for the evolution of antlers is that they act as a means of assessing dominance status (Barrette 1977). In other words, males with larger antlers are typically older and more dominant than males with smaller antlers. If antlers were used to measure dominance, a male during the rut could assess age, social status, and strength of a rival without actually fighting and thereby risking injury and possible death. Male-male combat in cervids can be lethal; about 5 percent of deaths in adult male elk are attributed to combat injuries acquired during the rut (Leslie and Jenkins 1985). In reality, the behavior of deer during male-male encounters (e.g., use of vocalizations and ritualized parallel walks) are probably more indicative of a male's fighting ability than antler size. Thus, little credence is given to this third hypothesis.

A fourth hypothesis suggests that antlers have evolved for defense against predators (Barrette 1977). If antlers were used as a major weapon against predators, we would expect to find antlered females in all or most deer species because only females care for the young. In addition, if antlers are weapons, they would be present in winter and early spring when predation pressures are usually highest rather than being present in summer and autumn. Instead of using antlers as weapons, deer rely on other anti-predator strategies. Small deer (e.g., Reeve's muntjac) use their razor-sharp canines against enemies. Large deer (e.g., white-tailed deer and moose) use their hooves against predator attacks. In a twelve-year study of gray wolves on Isle Royale National Park, two of nine dead wolves died from malnutrition, which was likely related to broken ribs received by hooves of moose (Peterson and Page 1988).

A fifth and most plausible reason for the evolution of antlers is for use in male-male combat (Barrette 1977). In some small deer (e.g., muntjac), antlers are used to knock another male off balance, followed by attacks with the canines. In a larger deer, antlers are used to injure a rival male, protect it from blows delivered by a rival, and engage in pushing contests for establishment of dominance status. Hence, antlers are best developed in polygamous species in which individual males defend and mate with a large number of females; white-tailed deer and elk from the mid-eastern states are examples of these species.

In conclusion, the primary (or sole) reason for the evolution of antlers in male deer is likely to enhance fighting ability (Barrette 1977). The abnormal antlers in females of some species, such as white-tailed deer, probably serves no purpose but are simply a by-product of excessive secretions of the hormone testosterone (Sauer 1984). The relatively small antlers in female caribou may serve as an important source of calcium during winter; in this species, antlers in females are retained throughout winter (Miller 1982).

Let's turn to the evolution of horns. As mentioned earlier, horns are prevalent in many open-country bovid species where crypsis may not be a viable antipredator strategy. Thus, horns may help a female to defend her young from predators. In these females, horns are relatively thin and dagger-like, thereby specializing as effective stabbing weapons. The consensus is that in female bovids, horns have evolved for predator defense.

In contrast to the role of horns in female bovids, predator defense does not appear to be the primary reason for the evolution of horns in male bovids. This conclusion is based on an examination of the shape and size of male horns versus female horns. Rather than being dagger-like, horns of male bovids have some type of curvature or spiraling and are thick. This shape and size allow a male to deflect and absorb considerable force from blows of a rival male. The familiar ritualized head butting of rival bighorn sheep attests to the importance of horns in mitigating injury to combatants (Lawson and Johnson 1982). Therefore, horns in male bovids appear have evolved primarily for intrasexual combat and perhaps secondarily for predator defense (Packer 1983; Alvarez 1990).

One prominent exception to this male-female dichotomy in the shape and size of horns is nicely shown in mountain goats. Both sexes have dagger-like rather than curved or spiraled horns (Geist 1964). Male mountain goats do not exhibit ritualized male-male fights. Moreover, both males and females have unusually high levels of intrasexual aggression (Fournier and Festa-Bianchet 1995).

SCIENTIFIC NAMES OF ANIMALS AND PLANTS MENTIONED IN THE TEXT

Adelgid, Hemlock Woolly	*Adelgid tsugae*
Alder	*Alnus* spp.
Amphibia	(Class Amphibia)
Ant	(Order Hymenoptera)
Antelope, Four-horned	*Tetracerus quadricornis*
Antelope, Pygmy	*Neotragus pygmaeus*
Ape, Great	(Family Pongidae)
Aspen	*Populus* spp.
Babirusa	*Babyrousa babyrussa*
Bacterium, Bubonic Plague	*Pasteurella pestis*
Bacterium, Lyme Disease	*Borrelia burgdorferi*
Bacterium, New World Typhus	*Rickettsia mooseri*
Badger, American	*Taxidea taxus*
Badger, Stink	*Mydaus* spp.
Bamboo	(Family Gramineae)
Bat, Big Brown	*Eptesicus fuscus*
Bat, Brazilian Free-tailed	*Tadarida brasiliensis*
Bat, Eastern Red	*Lasiurus borealis*
Bat, Evening	*Nycticeius humeralis*
Bat, Free-tailed	(Family Molossidae)
Bat, Fruit	(Suborder Megachiroptera)
Bat, Hoary	*Lasiurus cinereus*
Bat, Northern Yellow	*Lasiurus intermedius*
Bat, Rafinesques Big-eared	*Plecotus rafinesquii*
Bat, Seminole	*Lasiurus seminolus*
Bat, Silver-haired	*Lasionycteris noctivagans*
Bat, Townsends Big-eared	*Plecotus townsendii*

Bat, Vampire	*Desmodus rotundus*
Bear	(Family Ursidae)
Bear, Black	*Ursus americanus*
Bear, Brown (or Grizzly)	*Ursus arctos*
Bear, Etruscan	*Ursus etruscus*
Bear, Polar	*Ursus maritimus*
Bear, Sloth	*Melursus ursinus*
Bear, Spectacled	*Tremarctos ornatus*
Bear, Sun	*Helarctos malayanus*
Beaver, American	*Castor canadensis*
Beaver, European	*Castor fiber*
Beaver, Mountain	*Aplodontia rufa*
Bee	(Order Hymenoptera)
Beech	*Fagus* spp.
Beech, American	*Fagus grandifolia*
Beetle	(Order Coleoptera)
Bison, American	*Bos bison*
Blackberry	*Rubus* spp.
Blight, Chestnut	*Endothia parasitica*
Bobcat	*Lynx rufus*
Brainworm	*Parelaphostrongylus tenuis*
Brucellosis	*Burcella* spp.
Bulrush	*Scirpus* spp.
Burro (or Donkey)	*Equus asinus*
Caribou	*Raniger tarandus*
Carp	*Cyprinus* spp.
Cat, African Wild	*Felis silvestris libyca*
Cat, European Wild	*Felis silvestris silvestris*
Cat, Feral (or Domestic)	*Felis catus*
Cat, Saber-toothed	*Smilodon fatalis*
Catfish	*Ictalurus* spp.
Cattail	*Typha latifolia*
Cedar, White	*Thuja occidentalis*
Cheetah	*Acinonyx jubatus*
Cherry, Black	*Prunus serotina*
Chestnut, American	*Castanea dentata*

Chickadee, Black-capped	*Poecile atricapillus*
Chipmunk, Eastern	*Tamias striatus*
Coati, White-nosed	*Nasua narica*
Corn	*Zea mays*
Cottontail, Appalachian	*Sylvilagus obscurus*
Cottontail, Eastern	*Sylvilagus floridanus*
Cottontail, New England	*Sylvilagus transitionalis*
Cow, Domestic	*Bos taurus*
Coyote	*Canis latrans*
Coyote, Ancestral	*Canis lepophagus*
Crayfish	*Cambarus bartoni*
Cuckoo, Black-billed	*Coccyzus erythropthalmus*
Cuckoo, Yellow-billed	*Coccyzus americanus*
Dace	*Cyprinus* spp.
Deer	(Family Cervidae)
Deer, Chinese Water	*Hydropotes inermis*
Deer, Mule	*Odocoileus hemionus*
Deer, Père Davids	*Elaphurus davidianus*
Deer, Roe	*Capreolus capreolus*
Deer, Sika	*Cervus nippon*
Deer, Tufted	*Elaphodus cephalophus*
Deer, White-tailed	*Odocoileus virginianus*
Dingo	*Canis familiaris dingo*
Dog, Feral	*Canis familiaris*
Dog, Prairie	*Cynomys* spp.
Duck	(Family Anatidae)
Echidna	(Family Tachyglossidae)
Elephant	(Family Elephantidae)
Elephant, African	*Loxodonta africanus*
Elk (or Wapiti)	*Cervus elaphus*
Ermine	*Mustela erminea*
Fennec	*Fennecus zerda*
Fish	(Class Chondrichthyes)
Fisher	*Martes pennanti*
Flea, Rat	*Xenopsylla cheopis*
Fly	(Order Diptera)

Fox, Arctic	*Alopex lagopus*
Fox, Bat-eared	*Otocyon megalotis*
Fox, Gray	*Urocyon cinereoargenteus*
Fox, Kit	*Vulpes macrotis*
Fox, Red	*Vulpes vulpes*
Gemsbok	*Oryx gazella*
Giraffe	(Family Giraffidae)
Goat, Feral	*Capra hircus*
Goat, Mountain	*Oreamnos americanus*
Gorilla	*Gorilla gorilla*
Goshawk	*Accipter gentilis*
Grape, Wild	*Vitis* spp.
Grouse, Ruffed	*Bonasa umbellus*
Hare, European	*Lepus europaeus*
Hare, Snowshoe	*Lepus americanus*
Hawk, Coopers	*Accipter cooperii*
Hawk, Red-tailed	*Buteo jamaicensis*
Hemlock, Eastern	*Tsuga canadensis*
Hickory	*Carya* spp.
Horse, Feral	*Equus caballus*
Horse, Forest	*Equus caballus sylvaticus*
Horse, Przewalski's Wild (or Takhi)	*Equus caballus przewalskii*
Impala	*Aepyceros melampus*
Insects	(Class Insecta)
Jackal	*Canis* spp.
Jacket, Yellow	(Order Hymenoptera)
Jackrabbit, Black-tailed	*Lepus californicus*
Jackrabbit, White-tailed	*Lepus townsendii*
Jaguar	*Panthera onca*
Jay, Blue	*Cyanocitta cristata*
Kangaroo, Red	*Megaleia rufa*
Lemming	*Dicrostonyx* spp.
Lemming, Southern Bog	*Synaptomys cooperi*
Lemur, Flying	(Family Cynocephalidae)
Leopard	*Panthera pardus*
Lily	*Erythronium* spp.

Lion, African	*Panthero leo*
Lion, Mountain	*Puma concolor*
Lynx, Canada	*Lynx canadensis*
Mallard	*Anas platyrhynchos*
Man, Cro-Magnon	*Homo sapiens sapiens*
Maple	*Acer* spp.
Maple, Red	*Acer rubrum*
Marten, American	*Martes americana*
Mink, American	*Mustela vison*
Mole, Eastern	*Scalopus aquaticus*
Mole, Golden	(Family Chrysochloridae)
Mole, Hairy-tailed	*Parascalops breweri*
Mole, Marsupial	*Notoryctes typhlops*
Mole, Star-nosed	*Condylura cristata*
Monster, Gila	(Family Helodermatidae)
Moose	*Alces alces*
Moth	(Order Lepidoptera)
Moth, Gypsy	*Lymantria dispar*
Mouse, Arizona Pocket	*Perognathus amplus*
Mouse, Cotton	*Peromyscus gossypinus*
Mouse, Deer	*Peromyscus maniculatus*
Mouse, Eastern Harvest	*Reithrodontomys humulis*
Mouse, Golden	*Ochrotomys nuttalli*
Mouse, House	*Mus musculus*
Mouse, Meadow Jumping	*Zapus hudsonius*
Mouse, Woodland Jumping	*Napaeozapus insignis*
Mouse, White-footed	*Peromyscus leucopus*
Muntjac (Barking Deer)	*Muntiacus* spp.
Muntjac, Reeve's (Chinese)	*Muntiacus reevesi*
Muskox	*Ovibos moschatus*
Muskrat, Common	*Ondatra zibethicus*
Myotis, Eastern Small-footed	*Myotis leibii*
Myotis, Gray	*Myotis grisescens*
Myotis, Indiana	*Myotis sodalis*
Myotis, Little Brown	*Myotis lucifugus*
Myotis, Northern	*Myotis septentrionalis*

Myotis, Southeastern	*Myotis austroriparius*
Nematode	(Phylum Nematoda)
Nuthatch, White-breasted	*Sitta carolinensis*
Nutria	*Myocastor coypus*
Oak	*Quercus* spp.
Oak, Chestnut	*Quercus prinus*
Oak, Northern Red	*Quercus rubra*
Oak, Scarlet	*Quercus coccinea*
Oak, White	*Quercus alba*
Oilbird	*Steatornis caripensis*
Opossum, Common	*Didelphis marsupialis*
Opossum, Virginia	*Didelphis virginiana*
Orangutan	*Pongo pygmaeus*
Otter, Giant	*Pteronura brasiliensis*
Otter, Northern River	*Lontra canadensis*
Owl, Great Horned	*Bubo virginianus*
Panda, Giant	*Ailuropoda melanoleuca*
Panda, Lesser	*Ailurus fulgens*
Phalanger	(Family Phalangeridae)
Pig, Feral	*Sus scrofa*
Pika, American	*Ochotona princeps*
Pika, Collared	*Ochotona collaris*
Pike	*Esox* spp.
Pinniped	(aquatic carnivores, Suborder Pinnipedia)
Pipistrelle, Eastern	*Pipistrellus subflavus*
Platypus, Duck-billed	*Ornithorhynchus anatinus*
Pokeweed	*Phytolacca americana*
Poplar, Tulip	*Liriodendron tulipifera*
Porcupine, Common	*Erethizon dorsatum*
Primate	(Order Primate)
Pronghorn	*Antilocapra americana*
Pudu	*Pudu* spp.
Rabbit, Domestic (European)	*Oryctolagus cuniculus*
Rabbit, Marsh	*Sylvilagus palustris*
Raccoon, Common	*Procyon lotor*

Rat, Black	*Rattus rattus*
Rat, Hispid Cotton	*Sigmodon hispidus*
Rat, March Rice	*Oryzomys palustris*
Rat, Merriam's Kangaroo	*Dipodomys merriami*
Rat, Norway	*Rattus norvegicus*
Rat, Pack	*Neotoma* spp.
Reptile	(Class Reptilia)
Rhino	(Family Rhinocerotidae)
Ringtail	*Bassaricus astutus*
Roadrunner, Greater	*Geococcyx californianus*
Robin, American	*Turdus migratorius*
Rodent	(Order Rodentia)
Roundworm, Raccoon	*Baylisascaris procyonis*
Sculpin	*Cottus* spp.
Seal	(Family Phocidae)
Seal, Harbor	*Phoca vitulina*
Seal, Northern Elephant	*Mirounga angustirostris*
Seal, Northern Fur	*Callorhinus ursinus*
Sheep, Bighorn	*Ovis canadensis*
Sheep, Domestic	*Ovis aris*
Shrew	(Family Soricidae)
Shrew, Least	*Cryptotis parva*
Shrew, Long-tailed	*Sorex dispar*
Shrew, Maryland	*Sorex fontinalis*
Shrew, Masked	*Sorex cinereus*
Shrew, Northern Short-tailed	*Blarina brevicauda*
Shrew, Pigmy	*Sorex hoyi*
Shrew, Smokey	*Sorex fumeus*
Shrew, Southeastern	*Sorex longirostris*
Shrew, Southern Short-tailed	*Blarina carolinensis*
Shrew, Water	*Sorex palustris*
Skunk, Eastern Spotted	*Spirogale putorius*
Skunk, Striped	*Mephitis mephitis*
Skunk, Western Spotted	*Spirogale gracilis*
Snake, Coral	(Family Elapidae)
Songbird	(Passerine or Perching Bird)

Scientific Names

Spicebush	*Lindera benzoin*
Spruce	*Picea* spp.
Squid	(Class Cephalopoda)
Squirrel, Eurasian Red	*Sciurus vulgaris*
Squirrel, Fox	*Sciurus niger*
Squirrel, Gray	*Sciurus carolinensis*
Squirrel, Northern Flying	*Glaucomys sabrinus*
Squirrel, Red	*Tamiasciurus hudsonicus*
Squirrel, Scaly-tailed	(Family Anomaluridae)
Squirrel, Southern Flying	*Glaucomys volans*
Squirrel, Thirteen-lined Ground	*Spermophilus tridecemlineatus*
Stonefly	(Order Plecoptera)
Sucker	*Catostomus* spp.
Sunfish	*Lepomis* spp.
Swiftlet, Cave	*Collacalia fuciphaga*
Tarpan	*Equus caballus gmelini*
Teal, Blue-winged	*Anas discors*
Tick, Deer	*Ixodes scapularis*
Tick, Wood (American Dog)	*Dermacentor variabilis*
Tiger	*Panthera tigris*
Trout	*Salmo* spp.
Trout, Brook	*Salvelinus fontinalis*
Turkey, Wild	*Meleagris gallopavo*
Viper, Pit	(Family Viperidae)
Virus, Rabies	*Lyssavirus* spp.
Vole, Beach	*Microtus breweri*
Vole, California	*Microtus californicus*
Vole, Meadow	*Microtus pennsylvanicus*
Vole, Prairie	*Microtus ochrogaster*
Vole, Rock	*Microtus chrotorrhinus*
Vole, Southern Red-backed	*Clethrionomys gapperi*
Vole, Woodland	*Microtus pinetorum*
Walrus	*Odobenus rosmarus*
Wasp	(Order Hymenoptera)
Weasel, Least	*Mustela nivalis*
Weasel, Long-tailed	*Mustela frenata*

Scientific Names

Weevil, Acorn	(Family Curculionidae)
Whale, Blue	*Balaenoptera musculus*
Whale, Humpback	*Megaptera novaeangliae*
Whale, Killer	*Orcinus orca*
Whale, Sperm	*Physeter catadon*
Whale, Toothed	(Suborder Odontoceti)
Wildebeast	*Connochaetes* spp.
Willow	*Salix* spp.
Wolf, Falkland Island	*Dusicyon australis*
Wolf, Gray (or Timber)	*Canis lupus*
Wolf, Red	*Canis rufus*
Wolverine	*Gulo gulo*
Woodchuck (or Groundhog)	*Marmota monax*
Woodrat, Appalachian	*Neotoma magister*
Woodrat, Eastern	*Neotoma floridana*
Worm, Parasitic Nematode	(*Strongyloides robustus*)
Worm, Trichinosis	*Trichinella spiralis*
Yellow Jacket	(Order Hymenoptera)
Zebra	*Equus* spp.

GLOSSARY OF TERMS

Altricial: Young born in a relatively underdeveloped condition (e.g., eyes closed and minimal hair) and requiring extended parental care.

Arthropod: An animal of the phylum Arthropoda, which are invertebrates with jointed legs and segmented body parts.

Auditory sense: The sense of hearing.

Browse: Twigs and leaves of woody vegetation used as food by animals.

Cache: To store or hoard food for later use.

Canine: Usually elongated, single-cusped teeth that are anterior to the premolars.

Carnassials: Shearing teeth of carnivores, consisting of last upper premolar and the first lower molar.

Carnivorous: Meat eating.

Carrying capacity: The maximum population size that can be sustained by available resources in a habitat.

Chitin: The hard outer exoskeleton of insects and crustaceans.

Clearcutting: An even-aged system of forest management in which all large trees of a given area are harvested.

Climate: The long-term weather patterns characteristic of a given area.

Conspecific: An individual of the same species.

Continental drift: The movement of large masses of the earth's surface over geological time as a result of plate tectonics.

Convergent evolution: The development of similar adaptations by distantly related species with a similar way of life.

Crepuscular: Active at dawn and dusk.

Cursorial: Adapted to running.

Dentition: Teeth.

Dispersal: The process in which an organism typically moves from its place of birth (natal site) to a permanent site where it reproduces when mature.

Diurnal: Active during the daylight hours.

Echolocation: The emission of high-frequency sounds that is used to obtain information on the surrounding environment by the interpretation of the returning echoes.

Endemic: Native to a restricted geographic range.

Endothermy: The maintenance of a relatively constant internal body temperature by the production of heat within the body.

Even-aged management: A system of forest management in which trees of the same age and size are maintained.

Exotic species: A nonnative species that has become established in a given area from which it did not occur before human introductions or influences.

Extant: Currently living on earth today.

Extirpation: A process whereby a species or population becomes extinct in a given geographic area.

Fecundity: The addition of new animals to a population by birth.

Forb: A nonwoody plant (herb) other than grass or grass-like plants.

Fossorial: An underground way of life.

Forest fragmentation: A process whereby a large, forested stand is converted into smaller, more isolated stands as a result of human land uses.

Functional response: A change in the rate of prey consumption by a predator as a result of the change in prey density.

Gene flow: The movement of genetic material between populations of the same species by interbreeding or between different species by hybridization.

Gestation: The period of time from fertilization to birth of young.

Herbivorous: Plant eating.

Hibernation: An extended period of winter inactivity characterized by a reduction in physiological processes, such as breathing and heart rates.

Home range: An area normally traversed by an animal in its daily activities.

Incisor: Unicuspid tooth located anterior to the premolars.

Invertebrate: An animal without a spinal cord (backbone).

K-strategist: A species that has relatively slow rates of growth and reproduction.

Lactation: The production of milk by the mammary glands.

Marsupium: An abdominal pouch used to carry young.

Mast: Fruit produced by trees and shrubs.

Metapopulation: A group of populations that is interconnected via dispersal.

Migration: A predictable seasonal movement as from habitats used during winter and breeding seasons.

Molar: Permanent cheektooth with cusps that is posterior to premolars.

Nocturnal: Active at night.

Numerical response: A change in the population size of a predator as a result of a change in prey density.

Olfactory sense: The sense of smell.

Omnivore: An animal that feeds on plant and animal material.

Patagium: A thin layer of skin that forms the membrane of the wing of a bat.

Pelage: The hair of a mammal.

Pheromone: A chemical that elicits a response in another individual, usually of the same species.

Pinnae: The external ears of mammals.

Placenta: The structure or connection that permits the exchange of nutrients from the mother to the young and of waste materials from the young to the mother in the uterus.

Plant succession: The change in plant species composition and abundance over time in a given area, sometimes in a predictable fashion.

Plantigrade: Walking with the entire foot touching the ground.

Precocial: Young born in a relatively developed condition (e.g., eyes open and considerable hair) and requiring minimal parental care.

Predation: The process of killing and feeding on an animal.

Prehensile: Tail or digits used to grasp or hold objects.

Premolar: Permanent and deciduous cheektooth with cusps that are anterior to molars but posterior to canines.

Primitive: An organism that has not changed much from its ancestral form.

r-strategist: A species that has relatively high, slow rates of growth and reproduction.

Riparian: Referring to the shoreline or bank of a river, stream, or lake.

Savannah: A grassland covered in part with trees and shrubs.

Shelterbelt: Rows of trees and shrubs planted on the windward side of a farmstead to protect the farmstead from high winds and snowdrifts.

Snag: A dead or nearly dead tree.

Steppe: A grassland devoid of trees and shrubs.

Submaxillary gland: Gland located at the base of the incisors in the lower jaw.

Sympatric: Populations or species that occupy the same or overlapping geographic range.

Tactile sense: The sense of touch.

Territory: The portion of a home range defended from animals of the same or different species.

Torpor: A period of inactivity characterized by a reduction in physiological processes, such as breathing and heart rates but which is not as pronounced as in hibernation.

Tragus: Fleshy projection in the external ear of most microchiropteran bats.

Vertebrate: An animal with a spinal cord (backbone).

Weather: Short-term changes in precipitation, temperature, wind speed, and other atmospheric conditions.

REFERENCES

Abrams, M. D., and G. J. Nowacki. 1992. Historical variation in fire, oak recruitment, and post-logging accelerated succession in central Pennsylvania. *Bulletin of the Torrey Botanical Club* 119:19–28.

Abramsky, Z., and C. R. Tracy. 1979. Population biology of a noncycling population of prairie voles and a hypothesis on the role of migration in regulating microtine cycles. *Ecology* 60:349–61.

Adams, D. B. 1979. The cheetah: Native American. *Science* 205:1155–58.

Adams, R. A. 1997. Onset of volancy and foraging patterns of juvenile little brown bats, *Myotis lucifugus. Journal of Mammalogy* 78:239–46.

Albert, D. M., and R. T. Bowyer. 1991. Factors related to grizzly bear–human interactions in Denali National Park. *Wildlife Society Bulletin* 19:339–49.

Alden, C., F. Woodson, R. Mohan, and S. Miller. 1975. Cerebrospinal nematodiasis in sheep. *Journal of the American Veterinary Medical Association* 166:784–86.

Aleksuik, M. 1968. Scent-mound communication, territoriality, and population regulation in beaver (*Castor canadensis* Kuhl). *Journal of Mammalogy* 49:759–62.

———. 1970a. The seasonal food regime of Arctic beavers. *Ecology* 51:264–70.

———. 1970b. The function of the tail as a fat storage depot in the beaver (*Castor canadensis*). *Journal of Mammalogy* 51:145–48.

Aleksuik, M., and I. M. Cowan. 1969a. The winter metabolic depression in Arctic beavers (*Castor canadensis* Kuhl) with comparisons to California beavers. *Canadian Journal of Zoology* 47:965–79.

———. 1969b. Aspects of seasonal expenditure in the beaver (*Castor canadensis* Kuhl) at the northern limit of its distribution. *Canadian Journal of Zoology* 47:471–81.

Allen, G. M. 1929. History of the Virginia deer in New England. *The Game Breeder* 203–56.

Allen, T. J. 1997. River otter reintroduction. Final Report, Department of Natural Resources, West Virginia.

Allman, J. M. 1998. *Evolving brains*. Scientific American Library. New York: W. H. Freeman.

Alt, G. L. 1980. Rate of growth and size of Pennsylvania black bears. *Pennsylvania Game News* 51(12):7–17.

———. 1982. Reproductive biology of Pennsylvania's black bear. *Pennsylvania Game News* 53(2):9–15.

———. 1984. Black bear cub mortality due to flooding of natal dens. *Journal of Wildlife Management* 48:1432–34.

Alt, G. L., and J. M. Gruttadauria. 1984. Reuse of black bear dens in northeastern Pennsylvania. *Journal of Wildlife Management* 48:236–39.

Altherr, T. L. 1996. The catamount in Vermont folklore and culture. In *Proceedings of the Eastern Cougar Conference,* ed. J. W. Tischendorf and S. J. Ropski, 50–91. Fort Collins, Colo.: American Ecological Research Institute.

Alvarez, F. 1990. Horns and fighting in male Spanish ibex, *Capra pyrenaica. Journal of Mammalogy* 71:608–16.

American Kennel Club, The. 1973. *The complete dog book.* New York: Howell Book House.

Andersen, D. C., and M. L. Folk. 1993. *Blarina brevicauda* and *Peromyscus leucopus* reduce overwinter survivorship of acorn weevils in an Indiana hardwood forest. *Journal of Mammalogy* 74:656–64.

Anderson, J. E. 1991. A conceptual framework for evaluating and quantifying naturalness. *Conservation Biology* 5:347–52.

Anderson, P. K. 1964. Lethal alleles in *Mus musculus:* Local distribution and evidence for isolation of demes. *Science* 145:177–78.

Anderson, R. C., and A. K. Prestwood. 1981. Lungworms. *In Diseases and parasites of white-tailed deer,* ed. W. R. Davidson, F. A. Hayes, V. F. Nettles, and F. E. Kellogg, 266–317. Miscellaneous Publication No. 7. Tallahassee, Fla.: Tall Timbers Research Station.

Anthony, E. L., and T. H. Kunz. 1977. Feeding strategies of the little brown bat, *Myotis lucifugus,* in southern New Hampshire. *Ecology* 58:775–86.

Anthony, J. A., J. E. Childs, G. E. Glass, G. W. Korch, L. Ross, and J. K. Grigor. 1990. Land use associations and changes in population indices of urban raccoons during a rabies epizootic. *Journal of Wildlife Diseases* 26:170–79.

Anthony, R. G., L. J. Niles, and J. D. Spring. 1981. Small mammal associations in forested and old-field habitats—a quantitative comparison. *Ecology* 62:955–63.

Anthony, R. G., D. A. Simpson, and G. M. Kelly. 1986. Dynamics of pine vole populations in two Pennsylvania orchards. *American Midland Naturalist* 116:108–17.

Armitage, K. B., and K. S. Harris. 1982. Spatial patterning in sympatric populations of fox and gray squirrels. *American Midland Naturalist* 108:389–97.

Armstrong, E. 1983. Relative brain size and metabolism in mammals. *Science* 220:1302–4.

Arthur, S. M., W. B. Krohn, and J. R. Gilbert. 1989. Habitat use and diet of fishers. *Journal of Wildlife Management* 53:680–88.

Atkeson, T. D., and R. L. Marchinton. 1982. Forehead glands in white-tailed deer. *Journal of Mammalogy* 63:613–27.

Bailey, E. D., and D. E. Davis. 1965. The utilization of body fat during hibernation of woodchucks. *Canadian Journal of Zoology* 43:701–7.

Bailey, J. A. 1968. Regionwide fluctuations in the abundance of cottontails. *Transactions of the North American Wildlife and Natural Resources Conference* 33:265–77.

Bailey, T. N. 1984. Bobcat and lynx: Habitat and physique. In *The encyclopedia of mammals*, ed. D. Macdonald, 51. New York: Facts on File Publications.

Baker, R. H. 1984. Origin, classification and distribution. In *White-tailed deer ecology and management*, ed. L. K. Halls, 1–18. Harrisburg, Pa.: Stackpole Books.

Baker, S. V., and J. Fritsch. 1997. New territory for deer management: Human conflicts on the suburban frontier. *Wildlife Society Bulletin* 25:404–7.

Balcom, B. J., and R. H. Yahner. 1996. Microhabitat and landscape characteristics associated with the threatened Allegheny woodrat. *Conservation Biology* 10:515–25.

Banfield, A. W. F. 1974. *The mammals of Canada.* Toronto: University of Toronto Press.

Barash, D. P. 1974. The evolution of marmot societies: A general theory. *Science* 185:415–20.

Barber, H. L. 1984. Eastern mixed forest. In *White-tailed deer ecology and management*, ed. L. K. Halls, 345–54. Harrisburg, Pa.: Stackpole Books.

Barbour, A. G., and D. Fish. 1993. The biological and social phenomenon of Lyme disease. *Science* 260:1610–16.

Barbour, R. W., and W. H. Davis. 1969. *Bats of America.* Lexington: University of Kentucky Press.

Barclay, R. M. R. 1982. Interindividual use of echolocation calls: Eavesdropping by bats. *Behavioral Ecology and Sociobiology* 10:271–75.

Barclay, R. M. R., D. W. Thomas, and M. B. Fenton. 1980. Comparison of methods used for controlling bats in buildings. *Journal of Wildlife Management* 44:502–6.

Barnes, D. M., and A. U. Mallik. 1997. Habitat factors influencing beaver dam establishment in a northern Ontario watershed. *Journal of Wildlife Management* 61:1371–77.

Barrette, C. 1977. Fighting behavior of muntjac and the evolution of antlers. *Evolution* 31:167–79.

———. 1986. Fighting behavior of wild *Sus scrofa. Journal of Mammalogy* 67:177–79.

Barry, R. E., Jr., M. A. Botje, and L. B. Grantham. 1984. Vertical stratification of *Peromyscus leucopus* and *maniculatus* in southwestern Virginia. *Journal of Mammalogy* 65:145–48.

References

Bashore, T. L., and E. D. Bellis. 1982. Deer on Pennsylvania airfields: Problems and means of control. *Wildlife Society Bulletin* 10:386–88.

Bashore, T. L., W. M. Tzilkowski, and E. D. Bellis. 1985. Analysis of deer-vehicle collision sites in Pennsylvania. *Journal of Wildlife Management* 49:769–74.

Beck, A. M. 1973. *The ecology of stray dogs: A study of free-ranging urban animals.* Baltimore: York Press.

———. 1975. The ecology of feral and free-roving dogs in Baltimore. *In The wild canids,* ed. M. W. Fox, 380–90. New York: Van Nostrand-Reinhold.

Beer, J. 1955. Movements of tagged beavers. *Journal of Wildlife Management* 19:492–93.

Behler, J. L., and F. W. King. 1995. National Audubon Society field guide to North American reptiles and amphibians. New York: Knopf.

Behrend, D. F. 1970. The nematode *Pneumostrongylus tenuis* in white-tailed deer in the Adirondacks. *New York Fish and Game Journal* 23:101–37.

Behrend, D. F., and J. F. Witer. 1968. *Pneumostrongylus tenuis* in white-tailed deer in Maine. Pittman-Robertson Project W-37-R.

Beier, P. 1991. Cougar attacks on humans in the United States and Canada. *Wildlife Society Bulletin* 19:403–12.

———. 1993. Determining minimum habitat areas and habitat corridors for cougars. *Conservation Biology* 7:94–108.

Bekoff, M. 1982. Coyote. In *Wild mammals of North America,* ed. J. A. Chapman and G. A. Feldhamer, 447–59. Baltimore: Johns Hopkins University Press.

Belden, R. C., and B. W. Hagedorn. 1993. Feasibility of translocating panthers into northern Florida. *Journal of Wildlife Management* 57:388–97.

Bellrose, F. C., and L. G. Brown. 1941. The effect of fluctuating water levels on the muskrat population of the Illinois River Valley. *Journal of Wildlife Management* 5:206–12.

Bendel, P. R., and J. E. Gates. 1987. Home range and microhabitat partitioning of the southern flying squirrel (*Glaucomys volans*). *Journal of Mammalogy* 68:243–55.

Berchielli, L. 1994. Regulating the legal sale of bear gallbladders and other parts in New York. In *Proceedings of the International Symposium on the Trade of Bear Parts for Medicinal Use,* ed. D. A. Rose and A. L. Gaski, 110–12. Washington, D.C.: TRAFFIC USA/World Wildlife Fund.

Berg, R. L., L. L. McDonald, and M. D. Strickland. 1983. Distribution of mountain lions in Wyoming as determined by mail questionnaires. *Wildlife Society Bulletin* 11:265–68.

Berger, J. 1986. Wild horses of the Great Basin. Chicago: University of Chicago Press.

Berry, S. S. 1923. Observations on a Montana beaver canal. *Journal of Mammalogy* 4:92–103.

Betts, B. J. 1998. Effects of interindividual variation in echolocation calls on identification of big brown and silver-haired bats. *Journal of Wildlife Management* 62:1003–10.

Birch, J. M. 1997. Comparing wing shape of bats: The merits of principal-components analysis and relative-warp analysis. *Journal of Mammalogy* 78:1187–98.

Black, M. 1996. Public attitudes toward mountain lions *(Felis concolor)* and their implications for education about the eastern panther. In *Proceedings of the Eastern Cougar Conference*, ed. J. W. Tischendorf and S. J. Ropski, 200–239. Fort Collins, Colo.: American Ecological Research Institute.

Blackman, M. W. 1911. The anal glands of *Mephitis mephitica. Anatomical Review* 5:491–504.

Boardman, L. A., and R. H. Yahner. 1999. Wildlife communities associated with even-aged reproduction stands in two state forests of Pennsylvania. *Northern Journal of Applied Forestry* 16:1–7.

Bomford, M., and P. O'Brien. 1995. Eradication or control for vertebrate pests? *Wildlife Society Bulletin* 23:249–55.

Boonstra, R., and C. J. Krebs. 1979. Viability of large- and small-sized adults in fluctuating vole populations. *Ecology* 60:567–73.

Booth, D. C. 1991. Seriousness of Lyme disease prompts effort to reduce the abundance of deer ticks. *Journal of Forestry* 89(1):27–29.

Boutin, S., and D. E. Birkenholz. 1987. Muskrat and round-tailed muskrat. In *Wild furbearer management and conservation in North America*, ed. M. Nowak, J. A. Baker, M. E. Obbard, and B. Malloch, 214–325. Toronto: Ministry of Natural Resources.

Bowen, W. D., and I. T. Cowan. 1980. Scent marking in coyotes. *Canadian Journal of Zoology* 58:473–80.

Boyles, J. S. 1986. Managing America's wild horses and burros. *Journal of Equine Veterinary Science* 6:261–65.

Brady, C. A., and G. E. Svendsen. 1981. Social behaviour in a family of beaver, *Castor canadensis. Biology of Behaviour* 6:99–114.

Brand, C. J., L. B. Keith, and C. A. Fischer. 1976. Lynx responses to changing snowshoe hare densities in central Alberta. *Journal of Wildlife Management* 40:416–28.

Bratton, S. P. 1975. The effect of the European wild boar, *Sus scrofa*, on gray beech forest in the Great Smoky Mountains. *Ecology* 56:1356–66.

———. 1979. Impacts of white-tailed deer on the vegetation of Cades Cove, Great

Smoky Mountains National Park. *Proceedings of the Annual Conference of the Southeastern Association of Fish and Wildlife Agencies* 33:305–12.

Brenner, F. J., and P. D. Lyle. 1975. Effect of previous photoperiodic conditions and visual stimulation on food storage and hibernation in the eastern chipmunk (*Tamias striatus*). *American Midland Naturalist* 93:227–34.

Brocke, R. H. 1970. The winter ecology and bioenergetics of the opossum, *Didelphis marsupialis*, as distributional factors in Michigan. Ph.D. diss., Michigan State University, East Lansing.

———. 1996. The prognosis for cougar restoration in northern North America—an abstract. In *Proceedings of the Eastern Cougar Conference*, ed. J. W. Tischendorf and S. J. Ropski, 240–42. Fort Collins, Colo.: American Ecological Research Institute.

Brody, A. J., and M. R. Pelton. 1989. Effects of roads on black bear movements in western North Carolina. *Wildlife Society Bulletin* 17:5–10.

Brooks, R. P., and W. E. Dodge. 1986. Estimation of habitat quality and summer population density for muskrats on a watershed basis. *Journal of Wildlife Management* 50:269–73.

Broschart, M. R., C. A. Johnston, and R. J. Naiman. 1989. Predicting beaver colony density in boreal landscapes. *Journal of Wildlife Management* 53:929–34.

Brothers, A., D. C. Guynn Jr., J. Hamilton, and R. L. Marchinton. 1995. The spike question. In *Quality whitetails: The why and how of quality deer management*, ed. K. V. Miller and R. L. Marchinton, 112–17. Harrisburg, Pa.: Stackpole Books.

Brown, J. H., and R. C. Lasiewski. 1972. Metabolism in weasels: The cost of being too long and thin. *Ecology* 53:939–43.

Brown, J. L. 1964. The evolution of diversity in avian territorial systems. *Wilson Bulletin* 76:160–69.

Brownlow, C. A. 1996. Molecular taxonomy and the conservation of the red wolf and other endangered carnivores. *Conservation Biology* 10:390–96.

Bruggemann, E. P. 1992. Rabies in the mid-Atlantic states—Should raccoons be vaccinated? *BioScience* 42:694–99.

Bryant, L. D., and C. Maser. 1982. Classification and distribution. In *Elk of North America: Ecology and management*, ed. J. W. Thomas and D. E. Toweill, 1–59. Harrisburg, Pa.: Stackpole Books.

Buckley, J. L. 1950. The ecology and economics of the beaver (*Castor canadensis* Kuhl) with a plan for its management on the Huntington Wildlife Forest Station. Ph.D. diss., State University of New York, Syracuse.

Bunnell, F. 1984a. Grizzly bear. In *The encyclopedia of mammals*, ed. D. Macdonald, 88–91. New York: Facts on File Publications.

———. 1984b. American black bear. In *The encyclopedia of mammals*, ed. D. Macdonald, 94–95. New York: Facts on File Publications.

Burgess, S. A., and J. R. Bider. 1980. Effects of stream improvements on invertebrates, trout populations, and mink activity. *Journal of Wildlife Management* 44:871–80.

Burt, W. H., and R. P. Grossenheider. 1976. *A field guide to mammals.* 3d ed. Boston: Houghton Mifflin.

Buskirk, S. W. 1992. Conserving circumboreal forests for martens and fishers. *Conservation Biology* 6:318–23.

Calhoun, J., and F. Loomis. 1975. *Prairie white-tails.* Springfield: Illinois Department of Conservation.

Campbell, J. M. 1993. Effects of grazing by white-tailed deer on a population of *Lithospermum caroliniense* at Presque Isle. *Journal of the Pennsylvania Academy of Science* 67:103–8.

Campbell, R. W., and R. J. Sloan. 1976. Influence of behavioral evolution on gypsy moth pupal survival in sparse populations. *Environmental Entomology* 5:1211–17.

Carbyn, L. N. 1982. Coyote population fluctuations and spatial distribution in relation to wolf territories in Riding Mountain National Park, Manitoba. *Canadian Field-Naturalist* 96:176–83.

———. 1989. Coyote attacks on children in western North America. *Wildlife Society Bulletin* 17:444–46.

Carey, A. B. 1982. The ecology of red foxes, gray foxes, and rabies in the eastern United States. *Wildlife Society Bulletin* 10:18–26.

Carey, A. B., R. H. Giles Jr., and R. G. McLean. 1978. The landscape epidemiology of rabies in Virginia. *American Journal of Tropical Medicine and Hygiene* 27:573–80.

Casey, D., and D. Hein. 1983. Effects of heavy browsing on a bird community in deciduous forest. *Journal of Wildlife Management* 47:829–36.

Chapman, J. A., K. L. Cramer, N. J. Dippenaar, and T. J. Robinson. 1992. Systematics and biogeography of the New England cottontail, *Sylvilagus transitionalis* (Bangs, 1895), with the description of a new species from the Appalachian Mountains. *Proceedings of the Biological Society of Washington* 105:841–66.

Chapman, J. A., A. L. Harman, and D. E. Samuel. 1977. Reproductive and physiological cycles in the cottontail complex in western Maryland and nearby West Virginia. *Wildlife Monographs* 56:1–73.

Chapman, J. A., J. G. Hockman, and W. R. Edwards. 1982. Cottontails. In *Wild mammals of North America*, ed. J. A. Chapman and G. A. Feldhamer, 83–123. Baltimore: Johns Hopkins University Press.

Chapman, J. A. and J. R. Stauffer. 1981. The status and distribution of the New England cottontail. In *Proceedings of the World Lagomorph Conference*, ed. K. Myers and C. D. MacInnes, 973–83. Guelph, Ontario.

Chapman, R. C. 1978. Rabies: Decimation of a wolf pack in arctic Alaska. *Science* 201:365–67.

Charney, J. D. 1980. Hemlock-hardwood community relationships in the Highlands of southeastern New York. *Bulletin of the Torrey Botanical Club* 107:249–57.

Clark, F. W. 1972. Influence of jackrabbit density on coyote population change. *Journal of Wildlife Management* 36:343–56.

Clark, J. D., and M. R. Pelton. 1999. Management of a large carnivore: Black bear. In *Ecosystem management for sustainability*, ed. D. Peine, 209–23. Boston: Lewis Publishers.

Clutton-Brock, J. 1977. Man-made dogs. *Science* 197:1340–42.

Clutton-Brock, J., G. B. Corbet, and M. Hills. 1976. A review of the family Canidae, with a classification by numerical methods. *Bulletin of the British Museum of Natural History, Zoology* 29:117–99.

Coady, J. W. 1982. Moose. In *Wild mammals of North America*, ed. J. A. Chapman and G. A. Feldhamer, 902–22. Baltimore: Johns Hopkins University Press.

Coblentz, B. E. 1990. Exotic organisms: A dilemma for conservation biology. *Conservation Biology* 4:261–65.

Coffey, M. A., and G. H. Johnston. 1997. A planning process for managing white-tailed deer in protected areas: Integrated pest management. *Wildlife Society Bulletin* 25:433–39.

Coleman, J. S., and S. A. Temple. 1993. Rural residents' free-ranging domestic cats: A survey. *Wildlife Society Bulletin* 21:381–90.

Conover, M. R. 1997a. Monetary and intangible valuation of deer in the United States. *Wildlife Society Bulletin* 25:298–305.

——. 1997b. Wildlife management by metropolitan residents in the United States: Practices, perceptions, costs, and values. *Wildlife Society Bulletin* 25:306–11.

Conover, M. R., W. C. Pitt, K. K. Kessler, T. J. DuBow, and W. A. Sanborn. 1995. Review of human injuries, illnesses, and economic losses caused by wildlife in the United States. *Wildlife Society Bulletin* 23:407–14.

Cook, R. L. 1984. Texas. In *White-tailed deer ecology and management*, ed. L. K. Halls, 457–74. Harrisburg, Pa.: Stackpole Books.

Corbett, L. K., and A. Newsome. 1975. Dingo society and its maintenance: A preliminary analysis. In *The wild canids*, ed. M. W. Fox, 369–79. New York: Van Nostrand-Reinhold.

Cowan, I. M. 1938. Geographic distribution of color phases in the red fox and black bear in the Pacific Northwest. *Journal of Mammalogy* 19:202–6.

Cox, G. 1997. *Conservation biology: Concepts and applications*. 2d ed. Dubuque, Ia.: William. C. Brown.

Coyne, M. J., G. Smith, and F. E. McAllister. 1989. Mathematic model for the population biology of rabies in raccoons in the mid-Atlantic states. *American Journal of Veterinary Research* 50:2148–54.

Crabb, W. D. 1948. The ecology and management of the prairie spotted skunk in Iowa. *Ecological Monographs* 18:201–32.

Craighead, J. J., and J. A. Mitchell. 1982. Grizzly bear. *In Wild mammals of North America*, ed. J. A. Chapman and G. A. Feldhamer, 515–56. Baltimore: Johns Hopkins University Press.

Crête, M., and C. Daigle. 1999. Management of indigenous North American deer at the end of the twentieth century in relation to large predators and primary production. *Acta Veterinaria Hungarica* 47:1–16.

Cringan, A. T. 1971. Status of the wood duck in Ontario. Transactions of the North American *Wildlife and Natural Resources Conference* 36:296–312.

Cronon, W. 1983. Changes in the land: Indians, colonists, and the ecology of New England. New York: Hill and Wang.

Crook, J. H., J. E. Ellis, and J. D. Goss-Custard. 1976. Mammalian social systems: Structure and function. *Animal Behaviour* 24:261–74.

Cutter, S. L., H. L. Renwick, and W. H. Renwick. 1991. *Exploitation, conservation, preservation: A geographic perspective of natural resource use*. 2d ed. New York: John Wiley & Sons.

Cypher, B. L., R. H. Yahner, and E. A. Cypher. 1988. Seasonal food use by white-tailed deer at Valley Forge National Historical Park, Pennsylvania, USA. *Environmental Management* 12:237–42.

Daniels, T. J. 1983a. The social organization of free-ranging urban dogs. I. Non-estrous social behavior. *Applied Animal Ethology* 10:341–63.

———. 1983b. The social organization of free-ranging urban dogs. II. Estrous groups and the mating system. *Applied Animal Ethology* 10:365–73.

Daniels, T. J., and M. Bekoff. 1989. Population and social biology of free-ranging dogs, *Canis familiaris. Journal of Mammalogy* 70:754–62.

Dauphine, T. C. 1975. The disappearance of caribou reintroduced to Cape Breton Highlands National Park. *Canadian Field-Naturalist* 89:299–310.

Davidson, W. R., F. A. Hayes, V. F. Nettles, and F. E. Kellogg, eds. 1981. *Diseases and parasites of white-tailed deer*. Miscellaneous Publication No. 7. Tallahassee, Fla.: Tall Timbers Research Station.

deCalesta, D. S. 1994. Effect of white-tailed deer on songbirds within managed forests in Pennsylvania. *Journal of Wildlife Management* 58:711–17.

deCalesta, D. S., and S. L. Stout. 1997. Relative deer density and sustainability: a conceptual framework for integrating deer management with wildlife management. *Wildlife Society Bulletin* 25:252–58.

References

285

Decker, D. J., and T. L. Brown. 1982. Fruit growers' versus farmers' attitudes toward deer in New York. *Wildlife Society Bulletin* 10:150–55.

Delaney, M. J. 1984. Old World rats and mice. In *The encyclopedia of mammals*, ed. D. Macdonald, 658–63. New York: Facts on File Publications.

Dempsey, J. A., and D. M. Keppie. 1993. Foraging patterns of eastern red squirrels. *Journal of Mammalogy* 74:1007–1013.

DeNicola, A. J., S. J. Weber, C. A. Bridges, and J. L. Stokes. 1997. Nontraditional techniques for management of overabundant deer populations. *Wildlife Society Bulletin* 25:496–99.

Derge, K. L., and R. H. Yahner. 2000. Ecology of sympatric fox squirrels (*Sciurus niger*) and gray squirrels (*S. carolinensis*) at forest-farmland interfaces of Pennsylvania. *American Midland Naturalist* 126 (in press).

Dessecker, D. R., and R. H. Yahner. 1987. Breeding bird communities associated with Pennsylvania hardwood stands. *Proceedings of the Pennsylvania Academy of Science* 61:170–73.

Diamond, J. 1985. Rats as agents of extermination. *Nature* 318:602–3.

Dickey, N. H., editor-in-chief. 1986. *Funk & Wagnalls new encyclopedia*. Vol. 8. New York: Harper and Row.

Diefenbach, D. R., and W. L. Palmer. 1997. Deer management: Marketing the science. *Wildlife Society Bulletin* 25:378–81.

Diefenbach, D. R., W. L. Palmer, and W. K. Shope. 1997. Attitudes of Pennsylvania sportsmen towards managing white-tailed deer to protect the ecological integrity of forests. *Wildlife Society Bulletin* 25:244–51.

Dixon, D., B. Cox, R. J. G. Savage, and B. Gardiner. 1988. *Dinosaurs and prehistoric animals*. New York: Macmillan.

Dixon, K. R. 1982. Mountain lion. In *Wild mammals of North America*, ed. J. A. Chapman and G. A. Feldhamer, 711–27. Baltimore: Johns Hopkins University Press.

Dodge, W. E. 1982. Porcupine. In *Wild mammals of North America*, ed. J. A. Chapman and G. A. Feldhamer, 355–66. Baltimore: Johns Hopkins University Press.

Dolan, P. G., and D. C. Carter. 1977. *Glaucomys volans. Mammalian Species* 78:1–6.

Douglas, C. W., and M. A. Strickland. 1987. Fisher. In *Wild furbearer management and conservation in North America*, ed. M. Novak, J. A. Baker, M. E. Obbard, and B. Malloch, 510–29. Toronto: Ministry of Natural Resources.

Doutt, J. K., C. A. Heppenstall, and J. E. Guilday. 1977. *Mammals of Pennsylvania*. 4th ed. Harrisburg: Pennsylvania Game Commission.

Downing, R. L. 1996. The cougar in the East. In *Proceedings of the Eastern Cougar Conference*, ed. J. W. Tischendorf and S. J. Ropski, 163–66. Fort Collins, Colo.: American Ecological Research Institute.

Dozier, H. L., M. H. Markley, and L. M. Llewellyn. 1948. Muskrat investigations on the Blackwater National Wildlife Refuge, Maryland, 1941–1945. *Journal of Wildlife Management* 12:177–90.

Dragoo, J. W., and R. L. Honeycutt. 1997. Systematics of mustelid-like carnivores. *Journal of Mammalogy* 78:426–43.

Dunn, J. P., and J. S. Hall. 1989. Status of cave-dwelling bats in Pennsylvania. *Journal of the Pennsylvania Academy of Science* 63:166–72.

Dunstone, N., and R. J. O'Conner. 1979. Optimal foraging in an amphibious mammal. I. The aqualung effect. *Animal Behaviour* 17:1182–94.

Dyck, A. P., and R. A. MacArthur. 1993. Seasonal variation in the microclimate and gas composition of beaver lodges in a boreal environment. *Journal of Mammalogy* 74:180–88.

Eagle, T. C., and J. S. Whitman. 1987. Mink. In *Wild furbearer management and conservation in North America*, ed. M. Nowak, J. A. Baker, M. E. Obbard, and B. Malloch, 614–24. Toronto: Ministry of Natural Resources.

Eagle, T. C., D. B. Siniff, J. R. Tester, R. A. Garrott, and E. D. Plotka. 1992. Efficacy of chemical contraception in feral mares. *Wildlife Society Bulletin* 20:211–16.

Eberhardt, L. L., A. K. Majorowicz, and J. A. Wilcox. 1982. Apparent rates of increase for two feral herds. *Journal of Wildlife Management* 46:367–74.

Edwards, D. A., Jr. 1996. Ecological relationships among bobcats, coyotes, and gray foxes in central Mississippi. M.S. thesis, Mississippi State University, Hattiesburg, Miss.

Edwards, W. R., S. P. Havera, R. F. Labisky, J. A. Ellis, and R. E. Warner. 1981. The abundance of cottontails in relation to agricultural land use in Illinois (U.S.A.) 1956–1978, with comments on mechanism of regulation. In *Proceedings of the World Lagomorph Conference*, ed. K. Myers and C. D. MacInnes, 761–89. Guelph, Ontario.

Eiler, J. H., W. G. Wathen, and M. R. Pelton. 1989. Reproduction in black bears in the southern Appalachian Mountains. *Journal of Wildlife Management* 53:353–60.

Eisenberg, J. F., and D. G. Kleiman. 1972. Olfactory communication in mammals. *Annual Review of Ecology and Systematics* 3:1–32.

Elder, W. H. 1965. Primeval deer hunting pressures revealed by remains from American Indian middens. *Journal of Wildlife Management* 29:366–70.

Elkinton, J. S., W. M. Healy, J. P. Buonaccorsi, G. H. Boettner, A. M. Hazzard, H. R. Smith, and A. M. Liebhold. 1996. Interactions among gypsy moths, white-footed mice, and acorns. *Ecology* 77:2332–42.

Elliott, L. 1978. Social behavior and foraging ecology of the eastern chipmunk (*Tamias striatus*) in the Adirondack Mountains. Smithsonian Contributions to Zoology, no. 65. Washington, D.C.

Erickson, D. W., and N. F. Giessman. 1989. Review of a program to alleviate local-ized deer damage. *Wildlife Society Bulletin* 17:544–48.

Erlinge, S. 1979. Adaptive significance of sexual dimorphism in weasels. *Oikos* 33:233–45.

Errington, P. L. 1948. Environmental control for increasing muskrat production. *Transactions of the North American Wildlife Conference* 13:596–609.

Esposito, J. R., and S. L. Herb. 1997. *The Nittany Lion: An illustrated tale.* Univer-sity Park: Pennsylvania State University Press.

Ewer, R. F. 1973. *The carnivores.* Ithaca, N.Y.: Cornell University Press.

Fancy, S. G. 1980. Nest-tree selection by red squirrels in a boreal forest. *Canadian Field-Naturalist* 94:198.

Feeny, P. O. 1969. Inhibitory effect of oak leaf tannins on the hydrolysis of proteins by trypsin. *Phytochemistry* 8:2119–26.

Feldhamer, G. A., L. C. Drickamer, S. H. Vessey, and J. F. Merritt. 1999. *Mam-malogy: Adaptation, diversity, and ecology.* New York: McGraw-Hill.

Fenton, M. B., and D. R. Griffin. 1997. High-altitude pursuit of insects by echolo-cating bats. *Journal of Mammalogy* 78:247–50.

Ferguson, M.A.D., and H. G. Merriam. 1978. A winter feeding relationship be-tween snowshoe hares and porcupines. *Journal of Mammalogy* 59:878–80.

Ferron, J. 1996. How do woodchucks (*Marmota monax*) cope with harsh winter conditions? *Journal of Mammalogy* 77:412–16.

Findley, J. S., and G. L. Trout. 1970. Geographic variation in *Pipistrellus hesperus*. *Journal of Mammalogy* 51:741–65.

Fish, D., and T. J. Daniels. 1990. The role of medium-sized mammals as reservoirs of *Borrelia burgdorferi* in southern New York. *Journal of Wildlife Diseases* 26:339–45.

Flyger, V., and J. E. Gates. 1982. Fox and gray squirrels. In *Wild mammals of North America*, ed. J. A. Chapman and G. A. Feldhamer, 209–29. Baltimore: Johns Hopkins University Press.

Forand, K. J., R. L. Marchinton, and K. V. Miller. 1985. Influence of dominance rank on the antler cycle of white-tailed deer. *Journal of Mammalogy* 66:58–62.

Forbes, S. H., and D. K. Boyd. 1996. Genetic structure of naturally colonizing wolves in the Central Rocky Mountains. *Conservation Biology* 10:1082–90.

———. 1997. Genetic structure and migration in native and reintroduced Rocky Mountain wolf populations. *Conservation Biology* 11:1226–34.

Forbes, S. H., and J. B. Theberge. 1996. Cross-boundary management of Algon-quin Park wolves. *Conservation Biology* 10:1091–97.

Forstén, A. 1991. Size decrease in Pleistocene-Holocene true or caballoid horses of Europe. *Mammalia* 55:407–19.

Foster, M. L., and S. R. Humphrey. 1995. Use of highway underpasses by Florida panthers and other wildlife. *Wildlife Society Bulletin* 23:95–100.

Fournier, F., and M. Festa-Bianchet. 1995. Social dominance in adult female mountain goats. *Animal Behaviour* 49:1449–59.

Fox, J. E. 1982. Adaptation of gray squirrel behavior to autumn germination by white oak acorns. *Evolution* 36:800–809.

Fox, M. W. 1978. The dog: Its domestication and behavior. New York: Garland STPM Press.

Fraser, C. M., S. Casjens, W. M. Huang, G. G. Sutton, R. Clayton, R. Lathigra, O. White, K. A. Ketchum, R. Dodson, E. K. Hickey, M. Gwinn, B. Dougherty, J.-F. Tomb, R. D. Fleischmann, D. Richardson, J. Peterson, A. R. Kerlavage, J. Quackenbush, S. Salzberg, M. Hanson, R. van Vugt, N. Palmer, M. D. Adams, J. Gocayne, J. Weidman, T. Utterback, L. Watthey, L. McDonald, P. Artiach, C. Bowman, S. Garland, C. Fujii, M. D. Cotton, K. Horst, K. Roberts, B. Hatch, H. O. Smith, and J. C. Venter. 1997. Genomic sequence of a Lyme disease spirochaete, *Borrelia burgdorferi. Nature* 390:580–86.

French, C. E., L. C. McEwen, N. D. Magruder, R. H. Ingram, and R. W. Swift. 1955. Nutritional requirements of white-tailed deer for growth and antler development. Bulletin 600. Pennsylvania Agricultural Experiment Station, University Park. 50 pp.

Fritts, S. H., E. E. Bangs, J. A. Fontaine, W. G. Brewster, and J. F. Gore. 1995. Restoring wolves to the northern Rocky Mountains of the United States. In *Ecology and conservation of wolves in a changing world*, ed. L. N. Carbyn, S. H. Fritts, and D. R. Seip, 107–26. Edmonton: Canadian Circumpolar Institute.

Fritts, S. H., and L. N. Carbyn. 1995. Population viability, nature reserves, and the outlook for gray wolf conservation in North America. *Restoration Ecology* 3:26–38.

Fritts, S. H., and W. J. Paul. 1989. Interactions of wolves and dogs in Minnesota. *Wildlife Society Bulletin* 17:121–23.

Frome, M. 1979. Panthers wanted: Alive, back East where they belong. *Smithsonian* 10:82–88.

Fuller, T. K., W. E. Berg, and D. W. Kuehn. 1985. Bobcat home range size and daytime cover-type use in northcentral Minnesota. *Journal of Mammalogy* 66:568–71.

Fuller, T. K., and L. B. Keith. 1981. Non-overlapping ranges of coyotes and wolves in northeastern Alberta. *Journal of Mammalogy* 62:403–5.

Fuller, T. K., and B. A. Sampson. 1988. Evaluation of a simulated howling survey for wolves. *Journal of Mammalogy* 52:60–63.

Gage, K. L., R. S. Ostfeld, and J. G. Olson. 1995. Nonviral vector-borne zoonoses associated with mammals in the United States. *Journal of Mammalogy* 76:695–715.

Gaines, J. S., N. C. Stenseth, M. L. Johnson, R. A. Ims, and S. Bondrup-Nielsen. 1991. A response to solving the enigma of population cycles with a multifactorial perspective. *Journal of Mammalogy* 72:627–31.

Gardner, A. L. 1973. The systematics of the genus *Didelphis* (Marsupialia: Didelphidae) in North and Middle America. Special Publication 4, Museum of Texas Tech University, Lubbock.

———. 1982. Virginia opossum. In *Wild mammals of North America*, ed. J. A. Chapman and G. A. Feldhamer, 3–36. Baltimore: Johns Hopkins University Press.

Garrott, R. A. 1995. Effective management of free-ranging ungulate populations using contraceptives. *Wildlife Society Bulletin* 23:445–52.

Garrott, R. A., D. B. Siniff, and L. L. Eberhardt. 1991. Growth rates of feral horse populations. *Journal of Wildlife Management* 55:641–48.

Garrott, R. A., D. B. Siniff, J. R. Tester, T. C. Eagle, and E. D. Plotka. 1992. A comparison of contraceptive technologies for feral horse management. *Wildlife Society Bulletin* 20:318–26.

Gashwiler, J. S. 1948. Maine muskrat investigations. *Maine Department of Inland Fish and Game Bulletin*. Augusta.

Geist, V. 1964. On the rutting behavior of the mountain goat. *Journal of Mammalogy* 45:551–68.

———. 1988. How markets in wildlife meat and parts, and the sale of hunting privileges, jeopardize wildlife conservation. *Conservation Biology* 2:15–26.

Genoways, H. H., and F. J. Brenner, editors. 1985. *Species of special concern in Pennsylvania*. Special Publication No. 11. Pittsburgh: Carnegie Museum of Natural History.

Gerstell, R. 1937. Management of the cottontail rabbit in Pennsylvania. *Pennsylvania Game News* 7(12):6–7, 12; 8(1):15–19.

Gese, E. M., T. E. Stotts, and S. Grothe. 1996. Interactions between coyotes and red foxes in Yellowstone National Park, Wyoming. *Journal of Mammalogy* 77:377–82.

Gilbert, F. F. 1973. *Parelaphostrongylus tenuis* (Dougherty) in Maine. Part I: The parasite in white-tailed deer (O. *virginianus* Zimmerman). *Journal of Wildlife Diseases* 9:136–43.

———. 1974. *Parelaphostrongylus tenuis* in Maine: II—prevalence in moose. *Journal of Wildlife Management* 8:42–46.

———. 1992. Retroductive logic and the effects of meningeal worms: A comment. *Journal of Wildlife Management* 56:614–16.

Gilbert, F. F., and M. C. Bateman. 1983. Some effects of winter shelter conditions on white-tailed deer fawns. *Canadian Field-Naturalist* 97:377–90.

Gilbert, F. F., and E. G. Nancekivell. 1982. Food habits of mink (*Mustela vison*) and otter (*Lutra canadensis*) in northeastern Alberta. *Canadian Journal of Zoology* 60:1282–88.

Gilbreath, J. 1998. 1997 marks a decade of success for the endangered red wolf. *Red Wolf Newsletter* 10(1):1–3.

Gill, D., and L. D. Cordes. 1972. Winter habitat preference of porcupines in the southern Alberta foothills. *Canadian Field-Naturalist* 86:349–55.

Gill, F. B. 1990. *Ornithology.* New York: W. H. Freeman.

Gilmore, R. M., and J. E. Gates. 1985. Habitat use by the southern flying squirrel at a hemlock–northern hardwood ecotone. *Journal of Wildlife Management* 49:703–10.

Ginsberg, H. S. 1994. Lyme disease and conservation. *Conservation Biology* 8:343–53.

Gipson, P. S., I. K. Gipson, and J. A. Sealander. 1975. Reproductive biology of wild *Canis* (Canidae) in Arkansas. *Journal of Mammalogy* 56:605–12.

Gipson, P. S., B. Hlavachick, and T. Berger. 1998. Range expansion by wild hogs across the central United States. *Wildlife Society Bulletin* 26:279–86.

Gipson, P. S., and J. A. Sealander. 1976. Changing food habits of wild *Canis* in Arkansas with emphasis on coyote hybrids and feral dogs. *American Midland Naturalist* 95:249–53.

———. 1977. Ecological relationships of white-tailed deer and dogs in Arkansas. In *Proceedings of the 1975 Predator Symposium*, ed. R. L. Phillips and C. Jonkel, 3–16. Missoula: Montana Forest and Conservation Experiment Station, University of Montana.

Glass, B. P. 1952. Factors affecting the survival of the Plains muskrat *Ondatra zibethica cinnamomina* in Oklahoma. *Journal of Wildlife Management* 16:484–91.

Godin, A. J. 1977. *Wild mammals of New England.* Baltimore: Johns Hopkins University Press.

———. 1982. Striped and hooded skunks. In *Wild mammals of North America*, ed. J. A. Chapman and G. A. Feldhamer, 674–87. Baltimore: Johns Hopkins University Press.

Goehring, H. H. 1972. Twenty-year study of *Eptesicus fuscus* in Minnesota. *Journal of Mammalogy* 53:201–7.

Goertz, J. W., R. M. Dawson, and E. E. Mowbray. 1975. Response to nest boxes and reproduction by *Glaucomys volans* in northern Virginia. *Journal of Mammalogy* 56:933–39.

Goodman, S. M. 1995. *Rattus* on Madagascar and the dilemma of protecting the endemic rodent fauna. *Conservation Biology* 9:450–53.

Goold, J. C., and S. E. Jones. 1995. Time and frequency domain characteristics of sperm whale clicks. *Journal of the Acoustical Society of America* 98:1279–91.

Götmark, F. 1992. Naturalness as an evaluation criterion in nature conservation: A response to Anderson. *Conservation Biology* 6:455–58.

Gould, E., W. McShea, and T. Grand. 1993. Function of the star in the star-nosed mole. *Journal of Mammalogy* 74:108–16.

Grant, P. R. 1972. Interspecific competition among rodents. *Annual Review of Ecology and Systematics* 3:79–106.

Grant, T. R. 1984. Monotremes. In *The encyclopedia of mammals*, ed. D. Macdonald, 818–23. New York: Facts on File Publications.

Griesemer, S. J., R. M. DeGraaf, and T. K. Fuller. 1994. Effects of excluding porcupines from established winter feeding trees in central Massachusetts. *Northeast Wildlife* 51:29–33.

Grizzell, R. A., Jr. 1955. A study of the southern woodchuck (*Marmota monax monax*). *American Midland Naturalist* 53:257–93.

Groves, C. P. 1994. Morphology, habitat, and taxonomy. In *Przewalski's horse: The history and biology of an endangered species*, ed. L. Boyd and K. A. Houpt, 39–59. Albany: State University of New York Press.

Guilday, J. E. 1958. The prehistoric distribution of the opossum. *Journal of Mammalogy* 39:39–43.

——. 1971. Biological and archaeological analysis of bones from a seventeenth century Indian village (46 PU 31), Putnam County, West Virginia. Archaeological Investigation Report No. 4. Morgantown: West Virginia Geological and Economical Society.

Hall, E. R. 1981. *The mammals of North America*. 2d ed. New York: John Wiley & Sons.

Hall, J. S. 1985. Eastern woodrat. In *Species of special concern*, ed. H. H. Genoways and F. J. Brenner, 362–65. Special Publications No. 11. Pittsburgh: Carnegie Museum of Natural History.

——. 1988. Survey of the woodrat in Pennsylvania. Final report. Harrisburg: Pennsylvania Game Commission.

Hamilton, J., W. M. Knox, and D. C. Guynn Jr. 1995. How quality deer management works. In *Quality whitetails: The why and how of quality deer management*, ed. K. V. Miller and R. L. Marchinton, 7–18. Harrisburg, Pa.: Stackpole Books.

Hamilton, W. J., Jr. 1930. The food of the Soricidae. *Journal of Mammalogy* 11:26–39.

Hammel, H. T. 1955. Thermal properties of fur. *American Journal of Physiology* 182:369–76.

Hansen, C. S. 1983. Costs of deer-vehicle accidents in Michigan. *Wildlife Society Bulletin* 11:161–66.

Hanson, R. P., and L. Karstad. 1959. Feral swine in the southeastern United States. *Journal of Wildlife Management* 23:64–74.

Harder, L. D. 1979. Winter feeding by porcupines in montane forests of southwestern Alberta. *Canadian Field-Naturalist* 93:405–10.

Harrington, F. H., and L. D. Mech. 1979. Wolf howling and its role in territory maintenance. *Behaviour* 67:207–49.

Harris, L. D., and P. B. Gallagher. 1989. New initiatives for wildlife conservation: The need for movement corridors. In *Preserving communities and corridors*, ed. G. Mackintosh, 11–34. Washington, D.C.: Defenders of Wildlife.

Harrison, D. J., J. A. Bissonette, and J. A. Sherburne. 1989. Spatial relationships between coyotes and red foxes in eastern Maine. *Journal of Wildlife Management* 53:181–85.

Harrison, D. J., and T. G. Chapin. 1998. Extent and connectivity of habitat for wolves in eastern North America. *Wildlife Society Bulletin* 26:767–75.

Hartman, G. 1994. Long-term population development of a reintroduced beaver (*Castor fiber*) in Sweden. *Conservation Biology* 8:713–17.

Haspel, C., and R. E. Calhoon. 1993. Activity patterns of free-ranging cats in Brooklyn, New York. *Journal of Mammalogy* 74:1–8.

Hayes, J. P. 1997. Temporal variation in activity of bats and the design of echolocation-monitoring studies. *Journal of Mammalogy* 78:514–24.

Hayes, J. P., and R. G. Harrison. 1992. Variation in mitochondrial DNA and the biogeographic history of woodrats (*Neotoma*) in the eastern United States. *Systematic Biology* 41:331–44.

Hayes, J. P., and M. E. Richmond. 1993. Clinal variation and morphology of woodrats (*Neotoma*) of the eastern United States. *Journal of Mammalogy* 74:204–16.

Hedrick, P. W. 1995. Gene flow and genetic restoration: The Florida panther as a case study. *Conservation Biology* 9:996–1007.

Hellgren, E. C., and M. R. Vaughan. 1989. Denning ecology of black bears in a southeastern wetland. *Journal of Wildlife Management* 53:347–53.

Hellgren, E. C., M. R. Vaughan, R. L. Kirkpatrick, and P. F. Scanlon. 1990. Serial changes in metabolic correlates of hibernation in female black bears. *Journal of Mammalogy* 71:291–300.

Henry, V. G. 1969. Predation on dummy nests of ground-nesting birds in the southern Appalachians. *Journal of Wildlife Management* 33:169–72.

Herreid, C. F., II, and K. Schmidt-Nielsen. 1966. Oxygen consumption, temperature, and water loss in bats from different environments. *American Journal of Physiology* 211:1108–12.

References

293

Herrero, S. 1970. Aspects of evolution and adaptation in American black bears (*Ursus americanus* Pallas) and brown and grizzly bears (*U. arctos* Linné.) of North America. In *Bears — Their biology and management,* 221–31. New Series Publication 23. Morges, Switzerland: International Union for Conservation of Nature and Natural Resources.

————. 1978. A comparison of some features of the evolution, ecology and behavior of black and grizzly/brown bears. *Carnivora* 1:7–17.

————. 1985. Bear attacks, their causes and avoidance. New York: Lyons and Burford.

————. 1989. The role of learning in some fatal grizzly bear attacks on people. In *Bear-people conflicts — Proceedings of a symposium on management strategies,* 9–14. Yellowknife, Northwest Territories: Northwest Territories Department of Natural Renewable Resources.

Herrero, S., and A. Higgins. 1995. Fatal injuries inflicted to people by black bear. In *Proceedings of the Fifth Western Black Bear Workshop,* ed. J. Auger and H. L. Black, 75–82. Provo, Utah: Brigham Young University Press.

————. 1998. Field use of capsicum spray as a bear deterrent. *Ursus* 10:533–37.

Hesselton, W. T., and R. M. Hesselton. 1982. White-tailed deer. In *Wild mammals of North America,* ed. J. A. Chapman and G. A. Feldhamer, 878–901. Baltimore: Johns Hopkins University Press.

Hesselton, W. T., and P. R. Sauer. 1973. Comparative physical condition of four deer herds in New York according to several indices. *New York Fish and Game Journal* 20:77–107.

Hicks, A. 1989. Whatever happened to the Allegheny woodrat? *The Conservationist* (March-April): 34–38.

Hill, E. P. 1982. Beaver. In *Wild mammals of North America,* ed. J. A. Chapman and G. A. Feldhamer, 256–81. Baltimore: Johns Hopkins University Press.

Hill, E. P., P. W. Sumner, and J. B. Wooding. 1987. Human influences on range expansion of coyotes in the Southeast. *Wildlife Society Bulletin* 15:521–24.

Hilton, H. 1978. Systematics and ecology of the eastern coyote. In *Coyotes: Biology, behavior, and management,* ed. M. Bekoff, 209–28. New York: Academic Press.

Hirth, D. H. 1977. Observations of loss of antler velvet in white-tailed deer. *Southwestern Naturalist* 22:278–80.

Hobbs, N. T. 1996. Modification of ecosystems by ungulates. *Journal of Wildlife Management* 60:695–713.

Hobson, K. A., M. C. Drever, and G. W. Kaiser. 1999. Norway rats as predators of burrow-nesting seabirds: insights from stable isotope analysis. *Journal of Wildlife Management* 63:14–25.

Hock, R. J. 1960. Seasonal variation in physiological functions of arctic ground squirrels and black bears. In *Mammalian hibernation I*, ed. C. P. Lyman and A. R. Dawe, 155–71. Cambridge: Harvard University Press.

Hockman, J. G., and J. A. Chapman. 1983. Comparative feeding habits of red foxes (*Vulpes vulpes*) and gray foxes (*Urocyon cinereoargenteus*) in Maryland. *American Midland Naturalist* 110:276–85.

Hodgdon, H. E. 1978. Social dynamics and behavior within an unexploited beaver (*Castor canadensis*) population. Ph.D. diss., University of Massachusetts, Amherst.

Hodgdon, H. E., and R. A. Lancia. 1983. Behavior of the North American beaver, *Castor canadensis*. *Acta Zoologica Fennica* 174:99–103.

Hodgdon, H. E., and J. S. Larson. 1973. Some sexual differences in behavior within a colony of marked beavers (*Castor canadensis*). *Animal Behaviour* 21:147–52.

Hone, J., and C. P. Stone. 1989. A comparison and evaluation of feral pig management in two national parks. *Wildlife Society Bulletin* 17:419–25.

Howard, W. E., and R. E. Marsh. 1982. Spotted and hog-nosed skunks. In *Wild mammals of North America*, ed. J. A. Chapman and G. A. Feldhamer, 664–73. Baltimore: Johns Hopkins University Press.

Howe, T. D., and S. P. Bratton. 1976. Winter rooting activity of the European wild boar in the Great Smoky Mountains National Park. *Castanea* 41:256–64.

Humphrey, S. R. 1982. Bats: Vespertilionidae and Molossidae. In *Wild mammals of North America*, ed. J. A. Chapman and G. A. Feldhamer, 52–70. Baltimore: Johns Hopkins University Press.

Hunter, M., Jr. 1996. Benchmarks for managing ecosystems: Are human activities natural? *Conservation Biology* 10:695–97.

Hurly, T. A., and R. J. Robertson. 1990. Variation in the food hoarding behavior of red squirrels. *Behavioral Ecology and Sociobiology* 26:91–97.

Iampietro, L. 1998. Rabies update. *Pennsylvania Game News* 70(8):18–19.

Jackson, W. B. 1982. Norway rat and allies. In *Wild mammals of North America*, ed. J. A. Chapman and G. A. Feldhamer, 1077–88. Baltimore: Johns Hopkins University Press.

Jacobson, H. A. 1995. Age and quality relationships. In *Quality whitetails: The why and how of quality deer management*, ed. K. V. Miller and R. L. Marchinton, 103–11. Harrisburg, Pa.: Stackpole Books.

Jenkins, S. R., B. D. Perry, and W. G. Winkler. 1988. Ecology and epidemiology of raccoon rabies. *Review of Infectious Diseases* 10:S620–25.

Jenkins, S. R., and W. G. Winkler. 1987. Descriptive epidemiology from an epizootic of raccoon rabies in the middle Atlantic states. *American Journal of Epidemiology* 126:429–37.

References

295

Jennings, W. L., N. J. Schneider, A. L. Lewis, and J. E. Scatterday. 1960. Fox rabies in Florida. *Journal of Wildlife Management* 24:171–79.

Jett, D. A., and J. D. Nichols. 1987. Density fluctuations in a meadow vole population at the Patuxent Wildlife Research Center. *Maryland Naturalist* 31(2):41–43.

Jobe, K. L. 1985. Implications of grizzly bear habituation to hikers. *Wildlife Society Bulletin* 13:32–37.

Johnson, K. G., and M. R. Pelton. 1979. Denning behavior of black bears in the Great Smoky Mountains National Park. *Proceedings of the Southeastern Association of Fish and Wildlife Agencies* 33:239–49.

———. 1980. Environmental relationships and the denning period of black bears in Tennessee. *Journal of Mammalogy* 61:653–60.

———. 1981. Selection and availability of dens for black bears in Tennessee. *Journal of Wildlife Management* 45:111–19.

Johnson, M. L., and S. Johnson. 1982. Voles. In *Wild mammals of North America*, ed. J. A. Chapman and G. A. Feldhamer, 326–54. Baltimore: Johns Hopkins University Press.

Johnson, S. A., K. A. Berkley, and J. E. Fisher. 1997. 1996 Allegheny woodrat monitoring program. Mimeo. Indiana Division of Fish and Wildlife, Bloomington.

Johnson, S. A., and R. F. Madej. 1993. A 1991–92 survey of recent occurrences of the eastern woodrat in Indiana. Mimeo. Indiana Division of Fish and Wildlife, Bloomington.

Johnson, W. C., and C. S. Adkisson. 1986. Airlifting in oaks. *Natural History* 95:40–47.

Johnston, D. H., and M. Beauregard. 1969. Rabies epidemiology in Ontario. *Bulletin of the Wildlife Diseases Association* 5:357–70.

Johnston, D. H., D. R. Voigt, C. D. MacInnes, P. Bachmann, K. F. Lawson, and C. E. Rupprecht. 1988. An aerial baiting system for the distribution of attenuated or recombinant rabies vaccines for foxes, raccoons, and skunks. *Review of Infectious Diseases* 10:S660–64.

Jones, C., R. S. Hoffman, D. W. Rice, M. D. Engstrom, R. D. Bradley, D. J. Schmidly, C. A. Jones, and R. J. Baker. 1997. Revised checklist of North American mammals north of Mexico, 1997. Occasional Papers No. 173. Lubbock: Museum of Texas Tech University.

Jones, J. M., and A. Woolf. 1983. Relationship between husbandry practices and coyote use of swine in west central Illinois. *Wildlife Society Bulletin* 11:133–35.

Kasbohm, J. W., M. R. Vaughan, and J. G. Kraus. 1995. Food habits and nutrition of black bears during a gypsy moth infestation. *Canadian Journal of Zoology* 73:1771–75.

———. 1996. Effects of gypsy moth infestation on black bear reproduction and survival. *Journal of Wildlife Management* 60:408–16.

References

Katahira, L. K., P. Finnegan, and C. P. Stone. 1993. Eradicating feral pigs in montane mesic habitat at Hawaii Volcanoes National Park. *Wildlife Society Bulletin* 21:269–74.

Kaufmann, J. H. 1982. Raccoons and allies. In *Wild mammals of North America*, ed. J. A. Chapman and G. A. Feldhamer, 567–85. Baltimore: Johns Hopkins University Press.

Kazacos, K. R. 1982. Contaminative ability of *Baylisascaris procyonis* infected raccoons in an outbreak of cerebrospinal nematodiasis. *Proceedings of the Helminthological Society of Washington* 49:155–57.

Keiper, R. R. 1976. Social organization of feral ponies. *Proceedings of the Pennsylvania Academy of Science* 50:69–70.

Keith, L. B. 1974. Some features of population dynamics in mammals. *Proceedings of the International Congress of Game Biologists* 11:17–58.

Keith, L. B., J. R. Cary, O. J. Rongstad, and M. C. Brittingham. 1984. Demography and ecology of a declining snowshoe hare population. *Wildlife Monographs* 90:1–43.

Keith, L. B., and L. A. Windberg. 1978. A demographic analysis of the snowshoe hare cycle. *Wildlife Monographs* 58:58–70.

Kenward, R. E., and J. L. Holm. 1989. What future for British red squirrels? *Biological Journal of the Linnean Society* 38:83–89.

Kerby, G. 1984. The cat family. In *The encyclopedia of mammals*, ed. D. Macdonald, 26–27. New York: Facts on File Publications.

Kile, T. J., and R. L. Marchinton. 1977. White-tailed deer rubs and scrapes: spatial, temporal and physical characteristics and social role. *American Midland Naturalist* 97:257–66.

Kimball, T. L., and R. E. Johnson. 1978. The richness of American wildlife. In *Wildlife and America*, ed. H. P. Brokaw, 3–17. Washington, D.C.: Council on Environmental Quality.

Kingdon, J. 1984. The zebra's stripes: An aid to group cohesion? In *The encyclopedia of mammals*, ed. D. Macdonald, 486–87. New York: Facts on File Publications.

Kirkby, R. J. 1977. Learning and problem-solving in marsupials. In *The biology of marsupials*, ed. B. Stonehouse and D. Gilmore, 193–208. Baltimore: University Park Press.

Kirkland, G. L., Jr. 1977. Responses of small mammals to the clearcutting of northern Appalachian forests. *Journal of Mammalogy* 58:600–609.

Kirkpatrick, J. F., I. K. M. Liu, and J. W. Turner Jr. 1990. Remotely-delivered immunocontraception in feral horses. *Wildlife Society Bulletin* 18:326–30.

Kirsch, J. A. W. 1977. The six-percent solution: Second thoughts on the adaptedness of the Marsupialia. *American Scientist* 65:276–98.

Kleiman, D. 1966. Scent-marking in the Canidae. *Symposium of the Zoological Society of London* 18:166–77.

Knudsen, G. J. 1962. Relationship of beaver to forests, trout and wildlife in Wisconsin. Technical Bulletin 25. Wisconsin Conservation Department.

Kolenosky, G. B. 1971. Hybridization between wolf and coyote. *Journal of Mammalogy* 52:446–49.

Kordek, W. S., and J. S. Lindzey. 1980. Preliminary analysis of female reproductive tracts from Pennsylvania black bears. Bear Biology Association Conference Serial Publication 3:159–62.

Korschgen, L. J. 1957. Food habits of the coyote in Missouri. *Journal of Wildlife Management* 21:424–35.

Krebs, C. J. 1996. Population cycles revisited. *Journal of Mammalogy* 77:8–24.

Krebs, C. J., M. S. Gaines, B. L. Keller, J. H. Myers, and R. H. Tamarin. 1973. Population cycles in small rodents. *Science* 179:35–41.

Krebs, J. W., R. C. Holman, U. Hines, T. W. Strine, E. J. Mandel, and J. E. Childs. 1992. Rabies surveillance in the United States during 1991. *Journal of the American Veterinary Medical Association* 201:1836–48.

Krebs, J. W., J. S. Smith, C. E. Rupprecht, and J. E. Childs. 1997. Rabies surveillance in the United States during 1996. *Journal of the American Veterinary Medical Association* 211:1525–39.

———. 1998. Rabies surveillance in the United States during 1997. *Journal of the American Veterinary Medical Association* 213:1713–28.

Krebs, J. W., T. W. Strine, and J. E. Childs. 1993. Rabies surveillance in the United States during 1992. *Journal of the American Veterinary Medical Association* 203:1718–31.

Krebs, J. W., T. W. Strine, J. S. Smith, C. E. Rupprecht, and J. E. Childs. 1994. Rabies surveillance in the United States during 1993. *Journal of the American Veterinary Medical Association* 205:1695–1709.

———. 1995. Rabies surveillance in the United States during 1994. *Journal of the American Veterinary Medical Association* 207:1562–75.

Krebs, J. W., T. W. Strine, J. S. Smith, D. L. Noah, C. E. Rupprecht, and J. E. Childs. 1996. Rabies surveillance in the United States during 1995. *Journal of the American Veterinary Medical Association* 209:2031–44.

Krebs, J. W., M. L. Wilson, and J. E. Childs. 1995. Rabies—Epidemiology, prevention, and future research. *Journal of Mammalogy* 76:681–94.

Kuehn, D. W. 1989. Winter foods of fishers during a snowshoe hare decline. *Journal of Wildlife Management* 53:688–92.

Kuenzi, A. J., and M. L. Morrison. 1998. Detection of bats by mist-nest and ultrasonic sensors. *Wildlife Society Bulletin* 26:307–11.

Kunz, T. H., E. L. P. Anthony, and W. T. Rumage III. 1977. Mortality of little brown bats following multiple pesticide applications. *Journal of Wildlife Management* 41:476–83.

Kurta, A. 1995. *Mammals of the Great Lakes Region.* Ann Arbor: University of Michigan Press.

Kuwert, E., C. Merieux, H. Koprowski, and K. Bokel, eds. 1985. *Rabies in the tropics.* New York: Springer-Verlag.

Lacher, T. E., Jr., and M. A. Mares. 1996. Availability of resources and use of space in eastern chipmunks, *Tamias striatus. Journal of Mammalogy* 77:833–49.

Lacki, M. J., and R. A. Lancia. 1983. Changes in soil properties of forests rooted by wild boar. *Proceedings of the Annual Conference of the Southeastern Association of Fish and Wildlife Agencies* 37:228–36.

———. 1986. Effects of wild pig on beech growth in Great Smoky Mountains National Park. *Journal of Wildlife Management* 50:655–59.

Landers, J. L., R. J. Hamilton, A. S. Johnson, and R. L. Marchinton. 1979. Foods and habitat of black bears in southeastern North Carolina. *Journal of Wildlife Management* 43:143–53.

Lancia, R. A., and H. E. Hodgdon. 1983. Observations on the ontogeny of behavior of hand-reared beavers (*Castor canadensis*). *Acta Zoologica Fennica* 174:117–19.

Larivière, S., and M. Crête. 1993. The size of eastern coyotes (*Canis latrans*): A comment. *Journal of Mammalogy* 74:1072–74.

Lavender, D. 1967. Some American characteristics of the American Fur Company. In *Aspects of the fur trade: Selected papers of the 1965 North American Fur Trade Conference*, 30–39. St. Paul: Minnesota Natural History Society.

Lawrence, B. 1945. Brief comparison of the short-tailed shrew and reptile poisons. *Journal of Mammalogy* 26:393–96.

Lawrence, B. D., and J. A. Simmons. 1982. Echolocation in bats: The external ear and perception of the vertical positions of targets. *Science* 218:481–83.

Lawson, B., and R. Johnson. 1982. Mountain sheep. In *Wild mammals of North America*, ed. J. A. Chapman and G. A. Feldhamer, 1036–55. Baltimore: Johns Hopkins University Press.

Layne, J. N. 1954. The biology of the red squirrel, *Tamiasciurus hudsonicus loquax* (Bangs), in central New York. *Ecological Monographs* 24:227–67.

Lee, D. S., and J. B. Funderburg. 1982. Marmots. In *Wild mammals of North America*, ed. J. A. Chapman and G. A. Feldhamer, 176–91. Baltimore: Johns Hopkins University Press.

Leege, T. A. 1968. Natural movements of beavers in southeastern Idaho. *Journal of Wildlife Management* 32:973–76.

References

Lefebvre, L. W., N. R. Holler, and D. G. Decker. 1985. Efficacy of aerial application of a 2% zinc phosphide bait on roof rats in sugarcane. *Wildlife Society Bulletin* 13:324–27.

Lehman, N., A. Eisenhawer, K. Hansen, D. L. Mech, R. O. Peterson, and R. K. Wayne. 1991. Introgression of coyote mitochondrial DNA into sympatric North American gray wolf populations. *Evolution* 45:104–19.

Lehner, P. N. 1982. Differential vocal response of coyotes to group howl and group yip-howl playbacks. *Journal of Mammalogy* 63:675–79.

Leighton, A. H. 1932. Notes on the beaver's individuality and mental characteristics. *Journal of Mammalogy* 12:117–26.

Leonard, D. E. 1981. Bioecology of the gypsy moth. In *The gypsy moth: Research toward integrated pest management,* ed. C. C. Doane and M. L. McManus, 9–29. Technical Bulletin 1584. Washington, D.C.: U.S. Department of Agriculture–Forest Service.

Leslie, D. M., Jr., and K. J. Jenkins. 1985. Rutting mortality among male Roosevelt elk. *Journal of Mammalogy* 66:163–64.

Lidicker, W. Z., Jr. 1988. Solving the enigma of microtine cycles. *Journal of Mammalogy* 69:225–35.

Liebhold, A. M., J. A. Halverson, and G. A. Elmes. 1992. Gypsy moth invasion in North America: A quantitative analysis. *Journal of Biogeography* 19:513–20.

Lindzey, F. G., and E. C. Meslow. 1976. Winter dormancy in black bears in southwestern Washington. *Journal of Wildlife Management* 40:408–15.

Linscombe, G., N. Kinler, and R. J. Aulerich. 1982. Mink (*Mustela vison*). In *Wild mammals of North America,* ed. J. A. Chapman and G. A. Feldhamer, 629–43. Baltimore: Johns Hopkins University Press.

Litvaitis, J. A. 1993. Influence of historic land use on early successional vertebrates. *Conservation Biology* 7:866–73.

Litvaitis, J. A., A. G. Clark, J. H. Hunt. 1986. Prey selection and fat deposits of bobcats (*Felis rufus*) during autumn and winter in Maine. *Journal of Mammalogy* 67:389–92.

Litvaitis, J. A., and R. Villafuerte. 1996. Factors affecting the persistence of New England cottontail metapopulations: The role of habitat management. *Wildlife Society Bulletin* 24:686–93.

Lorimer, C. G., and L. E. Frelich. 1994. Natural disturbance regimes in old-growth northern hardwoods: Implications for restoration efforts. *Journal of Forestry* 92(1):33–38.

Lowery, G. H., Jr. 1974. *The mammals of Louisiana and its adjacent waters.* Baton Rouge: Louisiana State University Press.

Lugo, A. E. 1990. Removal of exotic organisms. *Conservation Biology* 4:345.

Lund, R. C. 1997. A cooperative, community-based approach for the management of suburban deer populations. *Wildlife Society Bulletin* 25:488–90.

Lundrigan, B. 1996. Morphology of horns and fighting behavior in the Family Bovidae. *Journal of Mammalogy* 77:462–75.

Lutz, J., and L. Lutz. 1996. The eastern puma—An update from the Eastern Puma Research Network. In *Proceedings of the Eastern Cougar Conference*, ed. J. W. Tischendorf and S. J. Ropski, 127–38. Fort Collins, Colo.: American Ecological Research Institute.

MacCleery, D. W. 1992. *American forests: A history of resiliency and recovery.* Publication No. FS-540. USDA-Forest Service, Washington, D.C.

MacDonald, D. W. 1976. Food caching by red foxes and some other carnivores. *Zeitschrift für Tierpsychologie* (Berlin) 42:170–85.

MacDonald, K., E. Matsui, R. Stevens, and M. B. Fenton. 1994. Echolocation calls and field identification of the eastern pipistrelle (*Pipistrellus subflavus*: Chiroptera: Vespertilionidae), using ultrasonic bat detectors. *Journal of Mammalogy* 75:462–65.

Macintosh, N. W. G. 1975. The origin of the dingo: An enigma. In *The wild canids*, ed. M. W. Fox, 87–106. New York: Van Nostrand-Reinhold.

Maclean, G. S. 1981. Torpor patterns and microenvironment of the eastern chipmunk, *Tamias striatus. Journal of Mammalogy* 62:64–73.

Maehr, D. S. 1990. The Florida panther and private lands. *Conservation Biology* 4:167–70.

Maehr, D. S., and G. B. Caddick. 1995. Demographics and genetic introgression in the Florida panther. *Conservation Biology* 9:1295–98.

Maehr, D. S., and J. A. Cox. 1995. Landscape features and panthers in Florida. *Conservation Biology* 9:1008–19.

Mahan, C. G., and R. H. Yahner. 1992. Microhabitat use by red squirrels in central Pennsylvania. *Northeast Wildlife* 49:49–56.

Mahan, C. G., M. A. Steele, M. J. Patrick, and G. L. Kirkland Jr. 1999. The status of the northern flying squirrel (*Glaucomys sabrinus*) in Pennsylvania. *Journal of the Pennsylvania Academy of Science* 73:15–21.

Mahyhew, I. G., A. Delahunta, J. R. Georgi, and D. G. Aspros. 1976. Naturally occurring cerebrospinal parelaphostrongylosis. *Cornell Veterinary* 66:56–72.

Major, J. T., and J. A. Sherburne. 1987. Interspecific relationships of coyotes, bobcats, and red foxes in western Maine. *Journal of Wildlife Management* 51:606–16.

Manfredo, M. J., H. C. Zinn, L. Sikorowski, and J. Jones. 1998. Public acceptance of mountain lion management: A case study of Denver, Colorado, and nearby foothills areas. *Wildlife Society Bulletin* 26:964–70.

Mankin, P. C., and R. E. Warner. 1999. Responses of eastern cottontails to intensive row-crop farming. *Journal of Mammalogy* 80:940–49.

Marchinton, R. L., and D. H. Hirth. 1984. Behavior. In *White-tailed deer ecology and management*, ed. L. K. Halls, 129–68. Harrisburg, Pa.: Stackpole Books.

Marchinton, R. L., K. V. Miller, and J. S. McDonald. 1995. Genetics. In *Quality whitetails: The why and how of quality deer management*, ed. K. V. Miller and R. L. Marchinton, 169–89. Harrisburg, Pa.: Stackpole Books.

Marden, J. H., and M. G. Kramer. 1994. Surface-skimming stoneflies: A possible intermediate stage in insect flight evolution. *Science* 266:427–30.

——. 1995. Locomotor performance of insects with rudimentary wings. *Nature* 377:332–34.

Marquis, D. A. 1981. Effect of deer browsing on timber in Allegheny hardwood forests of northwestern Pennsylvania. U.S. Department of Agriculture Forest Service Research Paper NE-475. Broomall, Pa.

Marti, C. D., and M. N. Kochert. 1995. Are red-tailed hawks and great horned owls diurnal-nocturnal dietary counterparts? *Wilson Bulletin* 107:615–28.

Martin, I. G. 1981. Venom in the short-tailed shrew (*Blarina brevicauda*) as an insect mobilizing agent. *Journal of Mammalogy* 62:189–92.

Mattfield, G. F. 1984. Eastern hardwood and spruce/fir forest. In *White-tailed deer ecology and management*, ed. L. K. Halls, 305–30. Harrisburg, Pa.: Stackpole Books.

Matthews, J. R., originating editor. 1991. *The official World Wildlife Fund guide to endangered species of North America.* Vol. 1. Washington, D.C.: Beacham Publishing.

Mattson, D. J., R. R. Knight, and B. M. Blanchard. 1992. Cannibalism and predation on black bears by grizzly bears in the Yellowstone Ecosystem, 1975–1990. *Journal of Mammalogy* 73:422–25.

Mayer, J. J., and I. L. Brisbin Jr. 1991. *Wild pigs in the United States: Their history, comparative morphology, and current status.* Athens: University of Georgia Press.

McCabe, R. E., and T. R. McCabe. 1984. Of slings and arrows: An historical retrospection. In *White-tailed deer ecology and management*, ed. L. K. Halls, 19–72. Harrisburg, Pa.: Stackpole Books.

McCaffery, K. R., J. Tranetzki, and J. Piechura. 1974. Summer foods of deer in northern Wisconsin. *Journal of Wildlife Management* 38:215–19.

McCord, C. M., and J. E. Cardoza. 1982. Bobcat and lynx. In *Wild mammals of North America*, ed. J. A. Chapman and G. A. Feldhamer, 728–66. Baltimore: Johns Hopkins University Press.

McCracken, C., D. A. Rose, and K. A. Johnson. 1995. *Status, management, and commercialization of the American black bear* (Ursus americanus). Washington, D.C.: TRAFFIC USA/World Wildlife Fund.

McCullough, D. R. 1982. Behavior, bears, and humans. *Wildlife Society Bulletin* 10:27–33.

McGinnis, H. J. 1996. Reports of pumas in Pennsylvania, 1890–1981. In *Proceedings of the Eastern Cougar Conference*, ed. J. W. Tischendorf and S. J. Ropski, 92–125. Fort Collins, Colo.: American Ecological Research Institute.

McGinnis, H., and J. L. George. 1980. The eastern coyote—Pennsylvania's not-so-new animal. *Pennsylvania Game News* 51(6):17–22.

McGowan, E. M. 1993. Experimental release and fate study of the Allegheny woodrat (*Neotoma magister*). Final report, appendix I. Endangered Species Unit, New York State Department of Environmental Conservation, Delmar.

McLean, R. G. 1970. Wildlife rabies in the United States: Recent history and current concepts. *Journal of Wildlife Diseases* 6:229–35.

McManus, J. J. 1974. Activity and thermal preference of the little brown bat, *Myotis lucifugus*, during hibernation. *Journal of Mammalogy* 55:844–46.

McNaught, D. A. 1987. Wolves in Yellowstone?—Park visitors respond. *Wildlife Society Bulletin* 15:518–21.

McShea, W. J., and G. Schwede. 1993. Variable acorn crops: Responses of white-tailed deer and other consumers. *Journal of Mammalogy* 74:999–1006.

Mech, L. D. 1970. *The wolf: The ecology and behavior of an endangered species.* New York: Natural History Press.

———. 1995. The challenge and opportunity of recovering wolf populations. *Conservation Biology* 9:270–78.

Mech, L. D., S. H. Fritts, and D. Wagner. 1995. Minnesota wolf dispersal to Wisconsin and Michigan. *American Midland Naturalist* 133:368–70.

Melquist, W. E., and A. E. Dronkert. 1987. River otter. In *Wild furbearer management and conservation in North America*, ed. M. Nowak, J. A. Baker, M. E. Obbard, and B. Malloch, 626–41. Toronto: Ministry of Natural Resources.

Melquist, W. E., and M. G. Hornocker. 1983. Ecology of river otters in west central Idaho. *Wildlife Monographs* 83:1–60.

Melquist, W. E., J. S. Whitman, and M. C. Hornocker. 1981. Resource partitioning and coexistence of sympatric mink and river otter populations. In *Proceedings of the Worldwide Furbearer Conference*, ed. J. A. Chapman and D. Pursley, 187–220. Frostburg, Md.

Mengak, M. T. 1998. Woodrat studies. Mimeo. Virginia Department of Game and Inland Fisheries, Richmond.

Merritt, J. E. 1987. *Guide to the mammals of Pennsylvania.* Pittsburgh: University of Pittsburgh Press.

Messier, F., and C. Barrette. 1985. The efficiency of yarding behaviour by white-tailed deer as an antipredator strategy. *Canadian Journal of Zoology* 63:785–89.

Miller, F. L. 1982. Caribou. In *Wild mammals of North America*, ed. J. A. Chapman and G. A. Feldhamer, 923–59. Baltimore: Johns Hopkins University Press.

Miller, J. E. 1983. Control of beaver damage. *Proceedings of the Eastern Wildlife Damage Control Conference* 1:177–83.

Miller, K. V., R. L. Marchinton, K. J. Forand, and K. L. Johansen. 1987. Dominance, testosterone levels, and scraping activity in a captive herd of white-tailed deer. *Journal of Mammalogy* 68:812–17.

Miller, K. V., R. L. Marchinton, and J. J. Ozoga. 1995. Deer sociobiology. In *Quality whitetails: The why and how of quality deer management*, ed. K. V. Miller and R. L. Marchinton, 118–28. Harrisburg, Pa.: Stackpole Books.

Miller, R. S. 1967. Pattern and process in competition. *Advances in Ecological Research* 4:1–74.

Miller, S. G., S. P. Bratton, and J. Hadidian. 1992. Impacts of white-tailed deer on endangered plants. *Natural Areas Journal* 12:67–74.

Mills, J. 1994. Asian dedication to the use of bear bile as medicine. In *Proceedings of the International Symposium on the Trade of Bear Parts for Medicinal Use*, ed. D. A. Rose and A. L. Gaski, 4–16. Washington, D.C.: TRAFFIC USA/ World Wildlife Fund.

Mitchell, B. 1982. Pennsylvania's elk herd. *Pennsylvania Game News* 53(12):14–18.

Mladenoff, D. J., and T. A. Sickley. 1998. Assessing potential gray wolf restoration in the northeastern United States: A spatial prediction of favorable habitat and potential population levels. *Journal of Wildlife Management* 62:1–10.

Mladenoff, D. J., T. A. Sickley, R. G. Haight, and A. P. Wydeven. 1995. A regional landscape analysis and prediction of favorable gray wolf habitat in the northern Great Lakes Region. *Conservation Biology* 9:279–94.

Moen, A. N., and C. W. Severinghaus. 1981. The annual weight cycle and survival of white-tailed deer in New York. *New York Fish and Game Journal* 28:162–77.

Moore, G. C., and J. S. Millar. 1984. A comparative study of colonizing and longer established eastern coyote populations. *Journal of Wildlife Management* 48:691–99.

Moore, W. G., and R. L. Marchinton. 1974. Marking behavior and its social function in white-tailed deer. In *The behavior of ungulates and its relation to management*, ed. V. Geist and F. Walther, 447–56. IUCN Publication 24. Morges, Switzerland: International Union for Conservation of Nature and Natural Resources.

Moran, R. J. 1973. *The Rocky Mountain elk in Michigan*. Michigan Department of Natural Resources, Research and Development Report No. 267.

Morrison, P. 1960. Some interrelations between weight and hibernation function. *Bulletin of the Museum of Zoology* 124:75–91.

Morton, S. R., H. F. Recher, S. D. Thompson, and R. W. Braithwaite. 1982. Comments on the relative advantages of marsupial and eutherian reproduction. *American Naturalist* 120:128–34.

Morton, T. 1883. *New English Canaan*. With introductory matter and notes by C. F. Adams Jr. Vol. 14. Boston: Prince Society.

Mowat, G., B. G. Slough, and S. Boutin. 1996. Lynx recruitment during a snowshoe hare population peak and decline in southwest Yukon. *Journal of Wildlife Management* 60:441–52.

Mower, K. J., T. W. Townsend, and W. J. Tyznik. 1997. White-tailed deer damage to experimental apple orchards in Ohio. *Wildlife Society Bulletin* 25:337–43.

Müller-Schwarze, D. 1972. Social significance of forehead rubbing in blacktailed deer (*Odocoileus hemionus columbianus*). *Animal Behaviour* 20:788–97.

Müller-Schwarze, D., S. Heckman, and B. Stagge. 1983. Behavior of free-ranging beaver (*Castor canadensis*) at scent marks. *Acta Zoologica Fennica* 174:111–13.

Munson, P. J., and J. H. Keith. 1984. Prehistoric raccoon predation on hibernating *Myotis*, Wyandotte Cave, Indiana. *Journal of Mammalogy* 65:152–55.

Munthe, K., and J. H. Hutchinson. 1978. A wolf-human encounter on Ellesmere Island, Canada. *Journal of Mammalogy* 59:876–78.

Muul, I. 1968. Behavioral and physiological influences on the distribution of the flying squirrel, *Glaucomys volans*. Miscellaneous Publications No. 134. University of Michigan, Ann Arbor. 66 pp.

Naiman, R. J., C. A. Johnston, and J. C. Kelley. 1988. Alteration of North American streams by beaver. *BioScience* 38:753–62.

Nassar, R., and J. Mosier. 1991. Projections of pet populations from census demographic data. *Journal of the American Veterinary Medical Association* 198:1157–59.

National Geographic Society. 1981. *Book of mammals*. 2 volumes. Washington, D.C.: Special Publication Division, National Geographic Society.

Neal, T. J. 1968. A comparison of two muskrat populations. *Iowa State Journal of Science* 43:193–210.

Negus, N. C., P. J. Berger, and L. Forsland. 1977. Reproductive strategy of *Microtus montanus*. *Journal of Mammalogy* 58:347–53.

Nelson, R. A., D. L. Steiger, and T. D. I. Beck. 1983. Neuroendocrine and metabolic interactions in the hibernating black bear. *Acta Zoologica Fennica* 174:137–41.

Neumann, R. L. 1967. Metabolism in the eastern chipmunk (*Tamias striatus*) and the southern flying squirrel (*Glaucomys volans*) during winter and summer. In *Mammalian hibernation III*, ed. K. C. Fisher, A. R. Darve, C. P. Lyman, E. Schönbaum, and F. E. South Jr., 64–74. New York: American Elsevier Publishing.

Nevo, E. 1979. Adaptive convergence and divergence of subterranean mammals. *Annual Review of Ecology and Systematics* 10:269–308.

Newcombe, C. L. 1930. An ecological study of the Allegheny cliff rat (*Neotoma pennsylvanica* Stone). *Journal of Mammalogy* 11:204–11.

Nicoll, M. E. 1984. Solenodons. In *The encyclopedia of mammals*, ed. D. Macdonald, 748–49. New York: Facts on File Publications.

Nielsen, D. G., M. J. Dunlap, and K. V. Miller. 1982. Pre-rut rubbing by white-tailed bucks: Nursery damage, social role, and management options. *Wildlife Society Bulletin* 10:341–48.

Northern Rocky Mountain Wolf Recovery Team. 1985. *Northern Rocky Mountain wolf recovery plan.* Washington, D.C.: U.S. Fish and Wildlife Service.

Novak, M. 1987. Beaver. In *Wild furbearer management and conservation in North America*, ed. M. Nowak, J. A. Baker, M. E. Obbard, and B. Malloch, 282–312. Toronto: Ministry of Natural Resources.

Nowak, R. M. 1978. Evolution and taxonomy of coyotes and related *Canis*. In *Coyotes: Biology, behavior, and management*, ed. M. Bekoff, 3–16. New York: Academic Press.

——. 1979. *North American Quaternary Canis.* Monograph No. 6. Lawrence: Museum of Natural History, University of Kansas.

——. 1992. The red wolf is not a hybrid. *Conservation Biology* 6:593–95.

——. 1999. *Walker's mammals of the world.* 2 vols. 6th ed. Baltimore: Johns Hopkins University Press.

Nudds, T. D. 1992. Retroductive logic and the effects of meningeal worms: A reply. *Journal of Wildlife Management* 56:617–19.

O'Brien, S. J., M. E. Roelke, L. Marker, A. Newman, C. A. Winkler, D. Meltzer, L. Colly, J. F. Evermann, M. Bush, and D. E. Wildt. 1985. Genetic basis for species vulnerability in the cheetah. *Science* 227:1428–34.

O'Brien, S. J., M. E. Roelke, N. Yuhki, K. W. Richards, W. E. Johnson, W. L. Franklin, A. E. Anderson, O. L. Bass, R. C. Belden, and J. S. Martenson. 1990. Genetic introgression within the Florida panther *Felis concolor coryi. National Geographic Research* 6:485–94.

Obbard, M. E., J. G. Jones, R. Newman, A. Booth, A. J. Satterthwaite, and G. Linscombe. 1987. In *Wild furbearer management and conservation in North America*, ed. M. Nowak, J. A. Baker, M. E. Obbard, and B. Malloch, 1007–34. Toronto: Ministry of Natural Resources.

Ofcarcik, R. P., and E. E. Burns. 1971. Chemical and physical properties of selected acorns. *Journal of Food Science* 36:576–78.

Okoniewski, J. C. 1982. A fatal encounter between an adult coyote and three conspecifics. *Journal of Mammalogy* 63:679–80.

Olsen, S. J., and J. W. Olsen. 1977. The Chinese wolf, ancestor of New World dogs. *Science* 197:533–35.

Ostfeld, R. S. 1997. The ecology of Lyme-disease risk. *American Scientist* 85:338–46.

Ostfeld, R. S., M. C. Miller, and K. R. Hazler. 1996. Causes and consequences of tick (*Ixodes scapularis*) burdens on white-footed mice (*Peromyscus leucopus*). *Journal of Mammalogy* 77:266–73.

Ough, W. D. 1982. Scent marking by captive raccoons. *Journal of Mammalogy* 63:318–19.

Ozoga, J. J. 1985. Marks of excellence. *Michigan Sportsman* 10:44–46.

———. 1989a. Temporal pattern of scraping behavior in white-tailed deer. *Journal of Mammalogy* 70:633–36.

———. 1989b. Induced scraping activity in white-tailed deer. *Journal of Wildlife Management* 53:877–80.

Ozoga, J. J., L. J. Verme, and C. S. Bienz. 1982. Parturition behavior and territoriality in white-tailed deer: Impact on neonatal mortality. *Journal of Wildlife Management* 46:1–11.

Packer, C. 1983. Sexual dimorphism: The horns of African antelopes. *Science* 221:1191–93.

Palmer, W. L., G. M. Kelly, and J. L. George. 1982. Alfalfa losses to white-tailed deer. *Wildlife Society Bulletin* 10:259–60.

Palmer, W. L., J. M. Payne, R. G. Wingard, and J. L. George. 1985. A practical fence to reduce deer damage. *Wildlife Society Bulletin* 13:240–45.

Panuska, J. A. 1959. Weight patterns and hibernation in *Tamias striatus*. *Journal of Mammalogy* 40:554–66.

Paquet, P. C. 1992. Prey use strategies of sympatric wolves and coyotes in Riding Mountain National Park, Manitoba. *Journal of Mammalogy* 73:337–43.

Paradiso, J. L., and R. M. Nowak. 1982. Wolves. In *Wild mammals of North America*, ed. J. A. Chapman and G. A. Feldhamer, 460–74. Baltimore: Johns Hopkins University Press.

Paragi, T. F., W. B. Krohn, and S. M. Arthur. 1994. Using estimates of fisher recruitment and survival to evaluate population trend. *Northeast Wildlife* 51:1–11.

Parker, W. T., and M. K. Phillips. 1991. Application of the experimental population designation to recovery of endangered red wolves. *Wildlife Society Bulletin* 19:73–79.

Parmalee, P. W. 1953. Food habits of the feral house cat in east-central Illinois. *Journal of Wildlife Management* 17:375–76.

Patenaude, F. 1984. The ontogeny of behavior of free-living beavers (*Castor canadensis*). *Zeitschrift für Tierpsychologie* (Berlin) 66:33–44.

Patton, D. R., and J. R. Vahle. 1986. Cache and nest characteristics of the red squirrel in an Arizona mixed-coniferous forest. *Western Journal of Forestry* 1:48–51.

Payne, N. F. 1982. Colony size, age, and sex structure of Newfoundland beaver. *Journal of Wildlife Management* 46:655–61.

Payne, N. F., and R. P. Peterson. 1986. Trends in complaints of beaver damage in Wisconsin. *Wildlife Society Bulletin* 14:303–7.

Payne, R. S., and S. McVay. 1971. Songs of humpback whales. *Science* 17:585–97.

Pearson, O. P. 1942. On the cause and nature of a poisonous action produced by the bite of a shrew *Blarina brevicauda. Journal of Mammalogy* 23:159–66.

Peek, J. M., M. R. Pelton, H. D. Picton, J. W. Schoen, and P. Zager. 1987. Grizzly bear conservation and management: A review. *Wildlife Society Bulletin* 15:160–69.

Pelton, M. R. 1982. Black bear. In *Wild mammals of North America*, ed. J. A. Chapman and G. A. Feldhamer, 504–14. Baltimore: Johns Hopkins University Press.

———. 1986. Habitat needs of black bears in the East. In *Wilderness and natural areas in eastern United States: A management challenge*, ed. D. L. Kulhavy and R. N. Conner, 49–53. Nacogdoches, Texas: Center for Applied Studies, School of Forestry, S. F. Austin University.

———. 1990. Black bears in the Southeast: To list or not to list? *Eastern Workshop on Black Bear Research and Management* 10:155–61.

Pelton, M. R., C. D. Scott, and G. M. Burchardt. 1976. Attitudes and opinions of persons experiencing property damage and/or injury by black bears in the Great Smoky Mountains National Park. In *Bears—Their biology and management*, ed. M. R. Pelton, J. W. Lenfer, and G. E. Folk Jr., 157–67. New Series Publication 40. Morges, Switzerland: International Union for Conservation of Nature and Natural Resources.

Pelton, M. R., and F. T. Van Manen. 1994. Distribution of black bears in North America. *Eastern Workshop on Black Bear Research and Management* 12:133–38.

———. 1997. Status of black bears in the southeastern United States. In *Proceedings of the Second International Symposium on the Trade of Bear Parts*, ed. D. F. Williamson and A. L. Gaski, 31–44. Washington, D.C.: TRAFFIC USA/World Wildlife Fund.

Perry, H. R., Jr. 1982. Muskrats. In *Wild mammals of North America*, ed. J. A. Chapman and G. A. Feldhamer, 282–325. Baltimore: Johns Hopkins University Press.

Person, D. K., and D. H. Hirth. 1991. Home range and habitat use of coyotes in a farm region of Vermont. *Journal of Wildlife Management* 55:433–41.

Peters, R. P., and L. D. Mech. 1975. Scent-marking in wolves. *American Scientist* 63:628–37.

Peterson, R. O. 1977. *Wolf ecology and prey relationships on Isle Royale*. Monograph Series No. 11. U.S. National Park Service.

Peterson, R. O., and R. E. Page. 1988. The rise and fall of Isle Royale wolves, 1975–1986. *Journal of Mammalogy* 69:89–99.

Petras, M. L., and J. C. Topping. 1981. Studies of natural populations of *Mus*. VI. Sizes of populations inhabiting corn cribs in southwestern Ontario. *Journal of Mammalogy* 62:146–53.

Pettigrew, J. D. 1986. Flying primates? Megabats have the advanced pathway from eye to midbrain. *Science* 231:1304–6.

Phillips, D. W. 1979. Muskrat population dynamics on a controlled wetland in southern Saskatchewan. M.S. thesis, University of Regina, Regina, Saskatchewan.

Pine, D. S., and G. L. Gerdes. 1973. Wild pigs in Monterey County, California. *California Fish and Game* 59:126–37.

Planz, J. V., E. G. Zimmerman, T. A. Spradling, and D. R. Akins. 1996. Molecular phylogeny of the *Neotoma floridana* species group. *Journal of Mammalogy* 77:519–35.

Platt, W. J. 1974. Metabolic rates of short-tailed shrews. *Physiological Zoology* 47:75–90.

Poole, E. L. 1940. A life history sketch of the Allegheny woodrat. *Journal of Mammalogy* 21:249–70.

Post, D. M., O. J. Reichman, and D. E. Wooster. 1993. Characteristics and significance of the caches of eastern woodrats (*Neotoma floridana*). *Journal of Mammalogy* 74:688–92.

Powell, D. S., and J. E. Barnard. 1982. Gypsy moth's impact on the timber resource. In *Proceedings of Coping with the Gypsy Moth*, ed. S. R. Cochran, J. C. Finley, and M. J. Baughman, 72–83. Penn State Forestry Issues Conference, Pennsylvania State University, University Park.

Powell, D. S., and T. J. Considine Jr., 1982. An analysis of Pennsylvania's forest resources. Resource Bulletin NE-69. Broomall, Pa.: U.S. Department of Agriculture—Forest Service, Northeastern Forest Experiment Station.

Powell, R. A. 1979. Fishers, population models, and trapping. *Wildlife Society Bulletin* 7:149–54.

———. 1981. Hunting behavior and food requirements of the fisher (*Martes pennanti*). In *Proceedings of the Worldwide Furbearer Conference*, ed. J. A. Chapman and D. Pursley, 883–917. Frostburg, Md.

Powell, R. A., and R. B. Brander. 1977. Adaptations of fishers and porcupines to their predator prey system. In *Proceedings of the 1975 Predator Symposium*, ed. R. L. Phillips and C. Jonkel, 45–53. Missoula: Montana Forest and Conservation Experiment Station, University of Montana.

Powell, R. A., and W. J. Zielinski. 1983. Competition and coexistence in mustelid communities. *Acta Zoologica Fennica* 174:223–27.

Powell, R. A., J. W. Zimmermann, D. E. Seaman, and J. F. Gilliam. 1996. Demographic analyses of a hunted black bear population with access to a refuge. *Conservation Biology* 10:224–34.

Preston, E. M. 1973. Computer simulated dynamics of a rabies-controlled fox population. *Journal of Wildlife Management* 37:501–512.

Pullen, T. M., Jr. 1975. Observations on construction activities of beaver in east-central Alabama. *Journal of the Alabama Academy of Science* 46:14–19.

Ragni, B., and E. Randi. 1986. Multivariate analysis of craniometric characteristics in European wild cat, domestic cat, and African wild cat (genus *Felis*). *Zeitschrift für Säugetierkunde* 51:243–51.

Rainey, D. G. 1956. Eastern woodrat, *Neotoma floridana*: Life history and ecology. University of Kansas Publications, Museum of Natural History 8:535–646.

Ralls, K. 1976. Mammals in which females are larger than males. *Quarterly Review of Biology* 51:245–76.

———. 1977. Sexual dimorphism in mammals: Avian models and unanswered questions. *American Naturalist* 111:917–38.

Randi, E., and B. Ragni. 1991. Genetic variability and biochemical systematics of domestic and wild cat populations (*Felis silvestris*: Felidae). *Journal of Mammalogy* 72:79–88.

Raskevitz, R. F., A. A. Kocan, and J. H. Shaw. 1991. Gastropod availability and habitat utilization by wapiti and white-tailed deer sympatric on range enzootic for meningeal worm. *Journal of Wildlife Diseases* 27:92–101.

Reardon, R. 1995. *Entomophaga maimaiga* in North America: A review. *Gypsy Moth News* (October): 3–4.

Reese, K. P., and J. D. Hair. 1976. Avian species diversity in relation to beaver pond habitats in the Piedmont Region of South Carolina. *Proceedings of the Annual Conference of the Southeastern Association of Fish and Wildlife Agencies* 30:437–47.

Regan, R. J., J. V. Gwynn, and G. R. Woods. 1995. The Northeast. In *Quality whitetails: The why and how of quality deer management*, ed. K. V. Miller and R. L. Marchinton, 238–50. Harrisburg, Pa.: Stackpole Books.

Reichman, O. J. 1975. Relation of desert rodent diets to available resources. *Journal of Mammalogy* 56:731–51.

Reid-Sanden, F. L., J. G. Dobbins, J. S. Smith, and D. B. Fishbein. 1990. Rabies surveillance in the United States during 1989. *Journal of the American Veterinary Medical Association* 197:1571–83.

Renouf, D., and M. B. Davis. 1982. Evidence that seals may use echolocation. *Nature* 300:635–37.

Reynolds, R. J., J. F. Pagels, and M. L. Fies. 1998. Demographic features of the northern flying squirrel, *Glaucomys sabrinus* (Shaw) (Mammalia: Sciuridae), in Virginia. Mimeo. Virginia Department of Game and Inland Fisheries, Verona.

Richard, P. B. 1964. Les materiaux de construction du castor (*Castor fiber*), leur signification pour ce rongdur. *Zeitschrift für Tierpsychologie* (Berlin) 21:592–601.

Riege, D. A. 1991. Habitat specialization and social factors in distribution of red and gray squirrels. *Journal of Mammalogy* 72:152–62.

Roberts, T. S. 1937. How two captive young beavers constructed a food pile. *Minnesota Academy of Science* 45:1107–18.

Robinson, D. E., and E. D. Brodie Jr. 1982. Food hoarding behavior in the short-tailed shrew *Blarina brevicauda*. *American Midland Naturalist* 108:369–75.

Robitaille, J. A., and J. Bovet. 1976. Field observations on the social behaviour of the Norway rat, *Rattus norvegicus* (Berkenhout). *Biology of Behaviour* 1:289–308.

Rogers, L. L. 1980. Inheritance of coat color and changes in pelage coloration in black bears in northeastern Minnesota. *Journal of Mammalogy* 61:324–27.

Rogers, L. L., and S. C. Durst. 1987. Evidence that black bears reduce peripheral blood flow during hibernation. *Journal of Mammalogy* 68:867–78.

Rolley, R. E. 1987. Bobcat. In *Wild furbearer management and conservation in North America*, ed. M. Nowak, J. A. Baker, M. E. Obbard, and B. Malloch, 670–81. Toronto: Ministry of Natural Resources.

Ronald, K., J. Selley, and P. Healey. 1982. Seals. In *Wild mammals of North America*, ed. J. A. Chapman and G. A. Feldhamer, 769–827. Baltimore: Johns Hopkins University Press.

Rosatte, R. C. 1987. Advances in rabies research and control: Applications for the wildlife profession. *Wildlife Society Bulletin* 504–11.

Rosatte, R. C., M. J. Power, and C. D. MacInnes. 1992. Trap-vaccinate-release and oral vaccination for rabies control in urban skunks, raccoons and foxes. *Journal of Wildlife Diseases* 28:562–71.

Rose, D. A. 1994. Status, management, and commercialization of the American black bear, part I. In *Proceedings of the International Symposium on the Trade of Bear Parts for Medicinal Use*, ed. D. A. Rose and A. L. Gaski, 48-53. Washington, D.C.: TRAFFIC USA/World Wildlife Fund.

Rosenzweig, M. L. 1966. Community structure in sympatric carnivora. *Journal of Mammalogy* 47:602–12.

Rothman, R. J., and L. D. Mech. 1979. Scent-marking in lone wolves and newly formed pairs. *Animal Behaviour* 27:750–60.

Roy, M. S., E. Geffen, D. Smith, and R. K. Wayne. 1996. Molecular genetics of pre-1940 red wolves. *Conservation Biology* 10:1413–24.

Rue, L. L., III. 1969. The world of the red fox. New York: Lippincott.

References

Ruedas, L. A., R. C. Dowler, and E. Aita. 1989. Chromosomal variation in the New England cottontail, *Sylvilagus transitionalis. Journal of Mammalogy* 70:860–64.

Rutherford, W. H. 1955. Wildlife and environmental relationships of beavers in Colorado forests. *Journal of Forestry* 53:803–6.

Ryder, O. A. 1993. Przewalski's horse: Prospects for reintroduction into the wild. *Conservation Biology* 7:13–15.

Samuel, D. E., and B. B. Nelson. 1982. Foxes. In *Wild mammals of North America*, ed. J. A. Chapman and G. A. Feldhamer, 475–90. Baltimore: Johns Hopkins University Press.

Samuel, W. M., M. J. Pybus, D. A. Welch, and C. J. Wilke. 1992. Elk as a potential host for meningeal worm: Implications for translocation. *Journal of Wildlife Management* 56:629–39.

Sargeant, A. B., and S. H. Allen. 1989. Observed interactions between coyotes and red foxes. *Journal of Mammalogy* 70:631–33.

Sargeant, A. B., S. H. Allen, and J. O. Hastings. 1987. Spatial relations between sympatric coyotes and red foxes in North Dakota. *Journal of Wildlife Management* 51:285–93.

Sargeant, A. B., G. A. Swanson, and H. A. Doty. 1973. Selective predation by mink, *Mustela vison*, on waterfowl. *American Midland Naturalist* 89:208–14.

Sauer, P. R. 1984. Physical characteristics. In *White-tailed deer ecology and management*, ed. L. K. Halls, 73–90. Harrisburg, Pa.: Stackpole Books.

Saunders, B. P. 1974. Meningeal worm in white-tailed deer in northwestern Ontario and moose population densities. *Journal of Wildlife Management* 37:327–30.

Sawyer, T. G., R. L. Marchinton, and C. W. Berisford. 1982. Scraping behavior of female white-tailed deer. *Journal of Mammalogy* 63:696–97.

Sawyer, T. G., R. L. Marchinton, and K. V. Miller. 1989. Response of female white-tailed deer to scrapes and antler rubs. *Journal of Mammalogy* 70:431–33.

Schmitz, O. J., and G. B. Kolenosky. 1985. Hybridization between wolf and coyote in captivity. *Journal of Mammalogy* 66:402–5.

Schmitz, O. J., and D. M. Lavigne. 1987. Factors affecting body size in sympatric Ontario *Canis. Journal of Mammalogy* 68:92–99.

Schoening, H. W. 1956. Rabies. In *The yearbook of agriculture 1956: Animal diseases*, 195–202. Washington, D.C.: U.S. Government Printing Office,

Schooley, R. L., C. R. McLaughlin, G. J. Matula Jr., and W. B. Krohn. 1994. Denning chronology of female black bears: Effects of food, weather, and reproduction. *Journal of Mammalogy* 75:466–77.

Schowalter, D. B., and J. R. Gunson. 1979. Reproductive biology of the big brown bat (*Eptesicus fuscus*) in Alberta. *Canadian Journal of Zoology* 93:48–54.

References

Schubert, C. A., R. C. Rosatte, C. D. MacInnes, and T. D. Nudds. 1998. Rabies control: An adaptive management approach. *Journal of Wildlife Management* 62:622–29.

Schullery, P. 1980. *The bears of Yellowstone.* Yellowstone National Park, Wyo.: Yellowstone Library and Museum Association.

Schulte, B. A. 1998. Scent marking and responses to male castor fluid by beavers. *Journal of Mammalogy* 79:191–203.

Schwartz, M. 1997. *A history of dogs in the early Americas.* New Haven: Yale University Press.

Scott, D. P., and R. H. Yahner. 1989. Winter habitat and browse use by snowshoe hares, *Lepus americanus,* in a marginal habitat in Pennsylvania. *Canadian Field-Naturalist* 103:560–63.

Scott, J. D., and T. W. Townsend. 1985. Characteristics of deer damage to commercial tree industries of Ohio. *Wildlife Society Bulletin* 13:135–43.

Scribner, K. T., M. H. Smith, and P. E. Johns. 1989. Environmental and genetic components of antler growth in white-tailed deer. *Journal of Mammalogy* 70:284–91.

Sedjo, R. A. 1991. Forest resources: Resilient and serviceable. In *America's renewable resources: Historical trends and current challenges,* ed. K. D. Frederick and R. A. Sedjo, 81–120. Washington, D.C.: Resources for the Future.

Seegmiller, R. F., and R. D. Ohmart. 1981. Ecological relationships of feral burros and desert bighorn sheep. *Wildlife Monographs* 78:1–58.

Seidensticker, J., M. A. O'Connell, and A. J. T. Hohnsingh. 1987. Virginia opossum. In *Wild furbearer management and conservation in North America,* ed. M. Nowak, J. A. Baker, M. E. Obbard, and B. Malloch, 247–63. Toronto: Ministry of Natural Resources.

Seidensticker, J. C., IV, M. G. Hornocker, W. V. Wiles, and J. P. Messick. 1973. Mountain lion social organization in the Idaho Primitive Area. *Wildlife Monographs* 35:1–60.

Serfass, T. 1998. Fishers—They're back. *Pennsylvania Game News* 69(2):25–28.

Serfass, T. L., R. P. Brooks, and L. M. Rymon. 1993. Evidence of long-term survival and reproduction by translocated river otters, *Lutra canadensis. Canadian Field-Naturalist* 107:59–63.

Serfass, T. L., R. P. Brooks, T. J. Swimley, L. M. Rymon, and A. H. Hayden. 1996. Considerations for capturing, handling, and translocating river otters. *Wildlife Society Bulletin* 24:25–31.

Serfass, T. L., R. P. Brooks, W. M. Tzilkowski, and D. H. Mitcheltree. 1994. Fisher reintroduction in Pennsylvania: Feasibility and review. School of Forest Resources, Pennsylvania State University, University Park.

Serfass, T. L., M. J. Lovallo, R. P. Brooks, A. H. Hayden, and D. M. Mitcheltree. 1999. Status and distribution of river otters in Pennsylvania following a reintroduction project. *Journal of the Pennsylvania Academy of Science* 73:10–14.

Serfass, T. L., R. L. Peper, M. T. Whary, and R. B. Brooks. 1993. River otter (*Lutra canadensis*) reintroduction in Pennsylvania: Prerelease care and clinical evaluation. *Journal of Zoo and Wildlife Medicine* 24:28–40.

Seton, E. T. 1909. *Life histories of northern mammals.* Vol. 1. New York: Scribner's.

Severinghaus, C. W., and E. L. Cheatum. 1956. Life and times of the white-tailed deer. In *The deer of North America*, ed. W. P. Taylor, 57–186. Harrisburg, Pa.: Stackpole Books.

Severinghaus, C. W., and R. W. Darrow. 1976. Failure of elk to survive in the Adirondacks. *New York Fish and Game Journal* 23:98–99.

Shaffer, M., and B. G. Rehnberg. 1999. Tree selection for antler rubbing by white-tailed deer (*Odocoileus virginianus*) in an agricultural region of southern Pennsylvania. *Journal of the Pennsylvania Academy of Science* 72:83–85.

Sharov, A., J. Mayo, and D. Leonard. 1998. Results from the gypsy moth Slow the Spread Pilot Project. *Gypsy Moth News* 44:3–6.

Shaw, W. T. 1936. Moisture and its relation to the cone-storing habit of the western pine squirrel. *Journal of Mammalogy* 17:337–49.

Sherry, D. F. 1989. Food storing in the Paridae. *Wilson Bulletin* 101:289–304.

Short, H. L. 1976. Composition and squirrel use of acorns of black and white oak groups. *Journal of Wildlife Management* 40:479–83.

Shrauder, P. A. 1984. Appalachian Mountains. In *White-tailed deer ecology and management*, ed. L. K. Halls, 331–44. Harrisburg, Pa.: Stackpole Books.

Sievert, P. R., and L. B. Keith. 1985. Survival of snowshoe hares at a geographic range boundary. *Journal of Wildlife Management* 49:854–66.

Sikes, R. K. 1970. Rabies. In *Infectious diseases of wild animals*, ed. J. W. Davis, L. H. Karstad, and D. O. Trainer, 31–33. Proceedings of the National Rabies Symposium. Ames: Iowa University Press.

Simms, D. A. 1979. North American weasels: Resource utilization and distribution. *Canadian Journal of Zoology* 57:504–20.

Singer, F. J., W. T. Swank, and E. E. C. Clebsch. 1984. Effects of wild pig rooting in a deciduous forest. *Journal of Wildlife Management* 48:464–73.

Skelly, J. M., D. D. Davis, W. Merrill, and E. A. Cameron, eds. 1989. Diagnosing injury to eastern forest trees. Agricultural Information Services, Pennsylvania State University, University Park.

Slade, L. M., and E. B. Godfrey. 1982. Wild horses. In *Wild mammals of North America*, ed. J. A. Chapman and G. A. Feldhamer, 1089–98. Baltimore: Johns Hopkins University Press.

Slough, B. G. 1978. Beaver food cache structure and utilization. *Journal of Wildlife Management* 42:644–46.

Smallwood, P. D. 1992. Temporal and spatial scales in foraging ecology: Testing hypotheses with spiders and squirrels. Ph.D. diss., University of Arizona, Tucson.

Smith, C. C. 1968. The adaptive nature of social organization in the genus of tree squirrels *Tamiasciurus. Ecological Monographs* 38:31–63.

Smith, C. C., and O. J. Reichman. 1984. The evolution of food caching by birds and mammals. *Annual Review of Ecology and Systematics* 15:329–51.

Smith, D. W., and S. H. Jenkins. 1997. Seasonal change in body mass and size of tail of northern beavers. *Journal of Mammalogy* 78:869–76.

Smith, H. R. 1985. Wildlife and the gypsy moth. *Wildlife Society Bulletin* 13:166–74.

———. 1989. Predation: Its influence on population dynamics and adaptive changes in morphology and behavior of the Lymantriidae. In *A comparison of features of New and Old World tussock moths,* ed. W. E. Willner and K. A. McManus, 469–88. General Technical Report NE-123. Washington, D.C.: U.S. Department of Agriculture.

Smith, J. D., and G. Madkour. 1980. Penial morphology and the question of chiropteran phylogeny. In *Proceedings of the 5th International Bat Research Conference,* ed. D. E. Wilson and A. L. Gardner, 347–65. Lubbock: Texas Tech Press.

Smith, J. S. 1989. Rabies virus epitopic variation: Use in ecologic studies. *Advances in Virus Research* 36:215–53.

Smith, T. S. 1998. Attraction of brown bears to red pepper spray deterrent: Caveats for use. *Wildlife Society Bulletin* 26:92–94.

Snyder, R. L., and J. J. Christian. 1960. Reproductive cycle and litter size of the woodchuck. *Ecology* 41:647–56.

Snyder, R. L., D. E. Davis, and J. J. Christian. 1961. Seasonal changes in the weights of woodchucks. *Journal of Mammalogy* 42:297–312.

Sonenshine, D. E., and E. L. Winslow. 1972. Contrasts in distribution of raccoons in two Virginia localities. *Journal of Wildlife Management* 36:838–47.

Sovada, M. A., A. B. Sargeant, and J. W. Grier. 1995. Differential effects of coyotes and red foxes on duck nest success. *Journal of Wildlife Management* 59:1–9.

Speakman, J. R., P. I. Webb, and P. A. Racey. 1991. Effects of disturbance on the energy expenditure of hibernating bats. *Journal of Applied Ecology* 58:1087–1104.

Spielman, A. 1988. Lyme disease and human babesiosis: Evidence incriminating vector and reservoir hosts. In *The biology of parasitism,* ed. P. T. Englund and A. Sher, 147–65. New York: Alan R. Liss.

Stafford, K. C., III. 1993. The epizootiology of Lyme disease. *Northeast Wildlife* 50:181–89.

Stebbings, R. E. 1984. Bats. In *The encyclopedia of mammals,* ed. D. Macdonald, 786–803. New York: Facts on File Publications.

Steele, M. A., L. Z. Hadj-Chikh, and J. Hazeltine. 1996. Caching and feeding decisions by *Sciurus carolinensis*: Responses to weevil-infested acorns. *Journal of Mammalogy* 77:305–14.

Stephenson, A. B. 1969. Temperatures within a beaver lodge in winter. *Journal of Mammalogy* 50:134–36.

Storm, G. L. 1965. Movements and activities of foxes as determined by radio tracking. *Journal of Wildlife Management* 29:1–12.

Storm, G. L., R. D. Andrews, R. L. Phillips, R. A. Bishop, D. B. Siniff, and J. R. Tester. 1976. Morphology, reproduction, dispersal, and mortality of midwestern red fox populations. *Wildlife Monographs* 49:1–82.

Storm, G. L., D. F. Cottam, and R. H. Yahner. 1995. Movements and habitat use by female deer in historic areas at Gettysburg, Pennsylvania. *Northeast Wildlife* 52:49–57.

Storm, G. L, and C. H. Halvorson. 1967. Effect of injury by porcupines on radial growth of ponderosa pine. *Journal of Forestry* 65:740–43.

Storm, G. L., W. K. Shope, and W. M. Tzilkowski. 1993. Cottontail population response to forest management using clearcutting and short rotations. *Northeast Wildlife* 50:91–99.

Storm, H. 1972. *Seven arrows.* New York: Ballantine Books.

Stout, G. G. 1982. Effects of coyote reduction on white-tailed deer productivity on Fort Sill, Oklahoma. *Wildlife Society Bulletin* 10:329–32.

Strickland, M. A., C. W. Douglas, M. Novak, and N. P. Hunziger. 1982. Fisher. In *Wild mammals of North America,* ed. J. A. Chapman and G. A. Feldhamer, 586–98. Baltimore: Johns Hopkins University Press.

Stromayer, K. A. K., and R. J. Warren. 1997. Are overabundant deer herds in the eastern United States creating alternate stable states in forest plant communities? *Wildlife Society Bulletin* 25:227–34.

Stroud, D. C. 1982. Population dynamics of *Rattus rattus* and *R. norvegicus* in a riparian habitat. *Journal of Mammalogy* 63:151–54.

Suga, N. 1990. Biosonar and neural computation in bats. *Scientific American* 262:60–68.

Svendsen, G. E. 1978. Castor and anal glands of the beaver (*Castor canadensis*). *Journal of Mammalogy* 59:618–20.

——. 1980a. Seasonal change in feeding patterns in beaver in southeastern Ohio. *Journal of Wildlife Management* 44:285–90.

——. 1980b. Patterns of scent-mounding in a population of beaver (*Castor canadensis*). *Journal of Chemical Ecology* 6:133–48.

———. 1982. Weasels. In *Wild mammals of North America*, ed. J. A. Chapman and G. A. Feldhamer, 613–28. Baltimore: Johns Hopkins University Press.

Sweeney, J. M., and J. R. Sweeney. 1982. Feral hog. In *Wild mammals of North America*, ed. J. A. Chapman and G. A. Feldhamer, 1099–1113. Baltimore: Johns Hopkins University Press.

Swihart, R. K., and M. R. Conover. 1990. Reducing deer damage to yews and apple trees: Testing Big Game Repellent, Ropel, and soap as repellents. *Wildlife Society Bulletin* 18:156–62.

Swihart, R. K., and R. H. Yahner. 1982. Eastern cottontail use of fragmented farmland habitat. *Acta Theriologica* 27:257–73.

Tamarin, R. H. 1977. Dispersal in island and mainland voles. *Ecology* 58:1044–54.

Temple, S. A. 1990. The nasty necessity: Eradicating exotics. *Conservation Biology* 4:113–15.

Tenneson, C., and L. W. Oring. 1985. Winter food preferences of porcupines. *Journal of Wildlife Management* 49:28–33.

Thewissen, J. G. M., and S. K. Babcock. 1992. The origin of flight in bats. *BioScience* 42:340–45.

Thomas, D. W. 1995. Hibernating bats are sensitive to nontactile human disturbance. *Journal of Mammalogy* 76:940–46.

Thomas, D. W., W. B. Fenton, and R. M. R. Barclay. 1990. Winter energy budgets and cost of arousals for hibernating little brown bats, *Myotis lucifugus*. *Journal of Mammalogy* 71:475–79.

Thomas, K. R. 1974. Burrow systems of the eastern chipmunk *(Tamias striatus pipilans* Lowery) in Louisiana. *Journal of Mammalogy* 55:454–59.

Thompson, D. C. 1978. The social system of the grey squirrel. *Behaviour* 64:305–28.

Thorington, R. W., Jr. 1984. Flying squirrels are monophyletic. *Science* 225:1048–50.

Thorington, R. W., Jr., K. Darrow, and C. G. Anderson. 1998. Wing tip anatomy and aerodynamics in flying squirrels. *Journal of Mammalogy* 79:245–50.

Thorington, R. W., Jr., and L. R. Heaney. 1981. Body proportions and gliding adaptations of flying squirrels. *Journal of Mammalogy* 62:101–14.

Thurber, D. K., W. R. McClain, and R. C. Whitmore. 1994. Indirect effects of gypsy moth defoliation on nest predation. *Journal of Wildlife Management* 58:493–500.

Thurber, J. M., and R. O. Peterson. 1991. Changes in body size associated with range expansion in the coyote (*Canis latrans*). *Journal of Mammalogy* 72:750–55.

Tietje, W. D., B. O. Pelchat, and R. L. Ruff. 1986. Cannibalism of denned black bears. *Journal of Mammalogy* 67:762–66.

Tietje, W. D., and R. L. Ruff. 1980. Denning behavior of black bears in boreal forest of Alberta. *Journal of Wildlife Management* 44:858–70.

References

Todd, A. W., L. B. Keith, and C. A. Fischer. 1981. Population ecology of coyotes during a fluctuation of snowshoe hares. *Journal of Wildlife Management* 45:629–40.

Tomasi, T. E. 1978. Function of venom in the short-tailed shrew, *Blarina brevicauda*. *Journal of Mammalogy* 59:852–54.

———. 1979. Echolocation by the short-tailed shrew, *Blarina brevicauda*. *Journal of Mammalogy* 60:751–59.

Toweill, D. E., and J. E. Tabor. 1982. River otter. *In Wild mammals of North America*, ed. J. A. Chapman and G. A. Feldhamer, 688–703. Baltimore: Johns Hopkins University Press.

Towne, C. W., and E. N. Wentworth. 1950. *Pigs from cave to cornbelt*. Norman: University of Oklahoma Press.

Tucker, P. K., and D. J. Schmidly 1981. Studies of a contact zone among three chromosomal races of *Geomys bursarius* in east Texas. *Journal of Mammalogy* 62:258–72.

Turner, J. W., Jr., and J. F. Kirkpatrick. 1991. New developments in feral horse contraception and their potential application to wildlife. *Wildlife Society Bulletin* 19:350–59.

Twichell, A. R. 1939. Notes on the southern woodchuck in Missouri. *Journal of Mammalogy* 20:71–74.

Two charged in illegal bear gallbladder trading. 1999. *Pennsylvania Game News* 70(3):45–46.

Tyndale-Biscoe, C. H. 1973. *Life of marsupials*. New York: American Elsevier Publishing.

Tyser, R. W., and C. A. Worley. 1992. Alien flora in grasslands adjacent to road and trail corridors in Glacier National Park, Montana (USA). *Conservation Biology* 6:253–62.

Usher, M. B., T. J. Crawford, and J. L. Banwell. 1992. An American invasion of Great Britain: The case of the native and alien squirrel (*Sciurus*) species. *Conservation Biology* 6:108–15.

Vahle, J. R., and D. R. Patton. 1983. Red squirrel cover requirements in Arizona mixed conifer forests. *Journal of Forestry* 81:14–15, 22.

Van Buskirk, J., and R. S. Ostfeld. 1995. Controlling Lyme disease by modifying the density and species composition of tick hosts. *Ecological Applications* 5:1133–40.

Van Dierendonck, M. C., and M. F. Wallis de Vries. 1996. Ungulate reintroductions: Experiences with the takhi or Przewalski horse (*Equus ferus przewalskii*) in Mongolia. *Conservation Biology* 10:728–40.

Van Dyke, F. G., and R. H. Brocke. 1987. Searching technique for mountain lion sign at specific locations. *Wildlife Society Bulletin* 15:256–59.

Van Dyke, F. G., R. H. Brocke, H. G. Shaw, B. B. Ackerman, T. P. Hemker, and

F. G. Lindzey. 1986. Reactions of mountain lions to logging and human activity. *Journal of Wildlife Management* 50:95–102.

Vander Wall, S. B. 1990. Food hoarding in animals. Chicago: University of Chicago Press.

Vaughan, M. R., and L. B. Keith. 1981. Demographic response of experimental snowshoe hare populations to overwinter food shortage. *Journal of Wildlife Management* 45:354–80.

Vaughan, T. A., J. M. Ryan, and N. J. Czaplewski. 2000. *Mammalogy*. 4th ed. New York: Saunders College Publishing.

Vecellio, G. M., R. H. Yahner, and G. L. Storm. 1994. Crop damage by deer at Gettysburg Park. *Wildlife Society Bulletin* 22:89–93.

Verme, L. J. 1969. Reproductive patterns of white-tailed deer related to nutritional plane. *Journal of Wildlife Management* 33:881–87.

Vézina, A. F. 1985. Empirical relationships between predator and prey size among terrestrial vertebrate predators. *Oecologia* 67:555–65.

Vilà, C., P. Savolainen, J. E. Maldonado, I. R. Amorim, J. E. Rice, R. L. Honeycutt, K. A. Crandall, J. Lundeberg, and R. K. Wayne. 1997. Multiple and ancient origins of the domestic dog. *Science* 276:1687–89.

Vilà, C., and R. K. Wayne. 1999. Hybridization between wolves and dogs. *Conservation Biology* 13:195–98.

Voigt, D. R., and W. E. Berg. 1987. Coyote. In *Wild furbearer management and conservation in North America*, ed. M. Nowak, J. A. Baker, M. E. Obbard, and B. Malloch, 342–57. Toronto: Ministry of Natural Resources.

Voigt, D. R., and B. D. Earle. 1983. Avoidance of coyotes by red fox families. *Journal of Wildlife Management* 47:852–57.

Vtorov, I. P. 1993. Feral pig removal: Effects on soil microarthropods in a Hawaiian rain forest. *Journal of Wildlife Management* 57:875–80.

Waddell, T. E., and D. E. Brown. 1984. Weights and color of black bears in the Pinaleño Mountains, Arizona. *Journal of Mammalogy* 65:350–51.

Wagner, K. K., R. H. Schmidt, and M. R. Conover. 1997. Compensation programs for wildlife damage in North America. *Wildlife Society Bulletin* 25:312–19.

Waldo, C. M., and G. B. Wislocki. 1951. Observations on the shedding of the antlers of Virginia deer (*Odocoileus virginianus borealis*). *American Journal of Anatomy* 88:351–96.

Waller, D. M., and W. S. Alverson. 1997. The white-tailed deer: A keystone herbivore. *Wildlife Society Bulletin* 25:217–26.

Walro, J. M., and G. E. Svendsen. 1982. Castor sacs and anal glands of the North American beaver (*Castor canadensis*): Their histology, development, and relationship to scent communication. *Journal of Chemical Ecology* 8:809–19.

References

Wang, L. C., and J. W. Hudson. 1971. Temperature regulation in normothermic and hibernating eastern chipmunk, *Tamias striatus*. *Comparative Biochemistry and Physiology* 38A:59–90.

Warner, R. E. 1985. Demography and movements of free-ranging domestic cats in rural Illinois. *Journal of Wildlife Management* 49:340–46.

Warren, R. J. 1995. Should wildlife biologists be involved in wildlife contraception research and management? *Wildlife Society Bulletin* 23:441–44.

———. 1997. The challenge of deer overabundance in the twenty-first century. *Wildlife Society Bulletin* 25:213–14.

Wathen, W. G., G. F. McCracken, and M. R. Pelton. 1985. Genetic variation in black bears from the Great Smoky Mountains National Park. *Journal of Mammalogy* 66:564–67.

Wayne, R. K., D. A. Gilbert, N. Lehman, K. Hansen, A. Eisenhawer, D. Girman, R. O. Peterson, L. D. Mech, P. J. P. Gogan, U. S. Seal, and R. J. Krumenaker. 1991. Conservation genetics of the endangered Isle Royale gray wolf. *Conservation Biology* 5:41–51.

Wayne, R. K., and S. M. Jenks. 1991. Mitochondrial DNA analysis implying extensive hybridization of the endangered red wolf *Canis rufus*. *Nature* 351:565–68.

Wayne, R. K., N. Lehman, M. W. Allard, and R. L. Honeycutt. 1992. Mitochondrial DNA variability of the gray wolf: Genetic consequences of population decline and habitat fragmentation. *Conservation Biology* 6:559–69.

Webster, L. T. 1942. *Rabies*. New York: Macmillan.

Weeks, H. P., Jr. 1995. Mineral supplementation for antler production. In *Quality whitetails: The why and how of quality deer management*, ed. K. V. Miller and R. L. Marchinton, 155–68. Harrisburg, Pa.: Stackpole Books.

Weigl, P. D. 1978. Resource overlap, interspecific interactions and the distribution of the flying squirrels, *Glaucomys volans* and *G. sabrinus*. *American Midland Naturalist* 100:83–96.

Weir, B. J., and I. W. Rowlands. 1973. Reproductive strategies of mammals. *Annual Review of Ecology and Systematics* 4:139–63.

Weller, M. W. 1978. Management of freshwater marshes for wildlife. In *Ecological processes and management potential*, ed. R. E. Good, D. F. Whigham, and R. L. Simpson, 267–84. New York: Academic Press.

Weller, M. W., and C. E. Spatcher. 1965. Role of habitat in the distribution an abundance of marsh birds. Special Report 43, Iowa Agricultural and Home Economics Experiment Station, Ames.

Whitaker, J. O., Jr. 1972. Food habits of bats from Indiana. *Canadian Journal of Zoology* 50:877–83.

Whitaker, J. O., Jr., and S. L. Gummer. 1992. Hibernation of the big brown bat, *Eptesicus fuscus*, in buildings. *Journal of Mammalogy* 73:312–16.

Whitaker, J. O., Jr., and W. J. Hamilton, Jr. 1998. *Mammals of the eastern United States*. 3d ed. Ithaca, N.Y.: Cornell University Press.

Whitaker, J. O., Jr., C. Maser, and L. E. Keller. 1977. Food habits of bats of western Oregon. *Northwest Science* 51:46–55.

White, D., Jr., K. C. Kendall, and H. D. Picton. 1999. Potential energetic effects of mountain climbers on foraging grizzly bears. *Wildlife Society Bulletin* 27:146–51.

Widmann, R. H. 1994. New survey of Pennsylvania's forests shows continued increases in timber volume, but oaks decrease. *Pennsylvania Forests* (Spring): 8–11.

Wielgus, R. B., and F. L. Bunnell. 1995. Tests of hypotheses for sexual segregation in grizzly bears. *Journal of Wildlife Managemen* 59:552–60.

Williams, L. M., and M. C. Brittingham. 1997. Selection of maternity roosts by big brown bats. *Journal of Wildlife Management* 61:359–68.

Williams, L. R., and G. H. Cameron. 1984. Demography of dispersal in Attwater's pocket gopher (*Geomys attwateri*). *Journal of Mammalogy* 65:67–75.

Williams, T. C., L. C. Ireland, and J. M. Williams. 1973. High altitude flights of the free-tailed bat, *Tadarida brasiliensis*, as observed with radar. *Journal of Mammalogy* 54:807–21.

Williams-Whitmer, L. M. 1994. Maternity roost selection and the use of bat boxes by displaced colonies of big brown and little brown bats. M.S. thesis, Pennsylvania State University, University Park.

Wilson, M. L. 1986. Reduced abundance of adult *Ixodes dammini* (Acari: Ixodidae) following destruction of vegetation. *Journal of Economic Entomology* 79: 693–96.

Wilson, M. L., and R. D. Deblinger. 1993. Vector management to reduce the risk of Lyme disease. In *Ecology and environmental management of Lyme disease*, ed. H. S. Ginsberg, 126–56. New Brunswick, N.J.: Rutgers University Press.

Wilsson, L. 1962. Observations on the dambuilding behaviour of the beaver (*Castor fiber* L.). Contribution No. AF 61(O52)-195. University of Stockholm, Sweden.

———. 1971. Observations and experiments on the ethology of the European beaver (*Castor fiber* L.). *Viltrevy* 8:115–266.

Wislocki, G. B. 1956. Further notes on antlers in female deer of the genus *Odocoileus*. *Journal of Mammalogy* 37:231–35.

Witmer, G. W., M. J. Pipas, and A. Hayden. 1995. Some observations on coyote food habits in Pennsylvania. *Journal of the Pennsylvania Academy of Science* 69:77–80.

Wood, G. W., and R. H. Barrett. 1979. Status of wild pigs in the United States. *Wildlife Society Bulletin* 7:237–46.

References

Wood, G. W., and R. E. Brenneman. 1977. Research and management of feral hogs on Hobcaw Barony. In *Research and management of wild hog populations: Proceedings of a symposium*, ed. G. W. Wood, 23–53. Clemson, S.C.: Belle W. Baruch Forest Science Institute, Clemson University.

Wood, G. W., and D. N. Roark. 1980. Food habits of feral hogs in coastal South Carolina. *Journal of Wildlife Management* 44:506–511.

Wooding, J. B. 1984. Coyote food habits and the spatial relationship of coyote and red foxes in Mississippi and Alabama. M.S. thesis, Mississippi State University, Mississippi State, Hattiesburg, Miss.

Wooding, J. B., J. A. Cox, and M. R. Pelton. 1994. Distribution of black bears in the southeastern Coastal Plain. *Proceedings of the Annual Conference of Southeastern Association of Fish and Wildlife Agencies* 48:270–75.

Wooding, J. B., and T. S. Hardisky. 1992. Denning by black bears in northcentral Florida. *Journal of Mammalogy* 73:895–98.

Woolf, A., and G. F. Hubert Jr. 1998. Status and management of bobcats in the United States over three decades: 1970s-1990s. *Wildlife Society Bulletin* 26:287–93.

Woolf, A., C. A. Mason, and D. Kradel. 1977. Prevalence and effects of *Parelaphostrongylus tenuis* in a captive wapiti population. *Journal of Wildlife Diseases* 13:149–54.

Wright, R. G. 1992. Wildlife research and management in the national parks. Urbana: University of Illinois Press.

Yahner, R. H. 1975. The adaptive significance of scatter hoarding in the eastern chipmunk. *Ohio Journal of Science* 75:176–77.

———. 1978a. The adaptive nature of the social system and behavior in the eastern chipmunk, *Tamias striatus. Behavioral Ecology and Sociobiology* 3:397–427.

———. 1978b. Burrow system and home range use by eastern chipmunks, *Tamias striatus*: Ecological and behavioral considerations. *Journal of Mammalogy* 59:324–29.

———. 1980. Burrow system use by red squirrels. *American Midland Naturalist* 103:409–11.

———. 1987. Feeding-site selection by red squirrels, *Tamiasciurus hudsonicus*, in a marginal habitat in Pennsylvania. *Canadian Field-Naturalist* 101:586–89.

———. 1988. Small mammals associated with even-aged aspen and mixed-oak forest stands in central Pennsylvania. *Journal of the Pennsylvania Academy of Science* 62:122–26.

———. 1992. Dynamics of a small mammal community in a fragmented forest. *American Midland Naturalist* 127:381–91.

———. 1997. Long-term dynamics of bird communities in a managed forested land-scape. *Wilson Bulletin* 109:595–613.

———. 1998. Butterfly and skipper use of nectar sources in forested and agricultural landscapes of Pennsylvania. *Journal of the Pennsylvania Academy of Science* 71:104–8.

———. 2000. *Eastern deciduous forest: Ecology and wildlife conservation.* 2d ed. Minneapolis: University of Minnesota Press.

Yahner, R. H., and C. G. Mahan. 1996. Effects of egg type on depredation of arti-ficial ground nests. *Wilson Bulletin* 108:129–36.

Yahner, R. H., and H. R. Smith. 1991. Small mammal abundance and habitat rela-tionships on deciduous forested sites with different susceptibility of gypsy moth defoliation. *Environmental Management* 15:113–20.

Yahner, R. H., and G. E. Svendsen. 1978. Effects of climate on the circannual rhythm of the eastern chipmunk, *Tamias striatus. Journal of Mammalogy* 59:109–17.

Yurco, F. J. 1990. The cat and ancient Egypt. *Field Museum of Natural History Bulletin* 61:15–23.

Zagata, M. D., and A. N. Moen. 1974. Antler shedding by white-tailed deer in the Midwest. *Journal of Mammalogy* 55:656–59.

Zimen, E. 1984. Wolves. In *The encyclopedia of mammals,* ed. D. Macdonald, 58–59. New York: Facts on File Publications.

INDEX

Burro, 217, 221–22
Burrow system (burrow), 22–25, 37, 47, 58, 60, 63–65, 67, 93–94, 98

Cache, food, 20, 60, 62, 64, 67, 79, 83, 94–96
California, 74, 214, 228, 230
Canada, 15, 71, 74, 88, 91, 95, 108, 136–37, 154–55, 178, 184, 186, 194, 205, 208–9, 214, 244, 256
Canid, 9, 128–30, 136, 139, 145, 148–49, 153, 177, 190, 201, 247
Canine, 129, 159, 182, 200, 217, 232, 261
Caribou, 9, 137, 232–33, 249, 259, 261; woodland, 231, 250
Carnassials, 128–29, 159, 176, 182, 195, 200
Carnivora, 8, 9, 128, 158, 175, 181, 199
Carnivore, 17, 61, 128, 153, 158, 164, 174, 182, 195, 201, 205–6, 259
Carp, 192
Carrion, 55–56
Carrying capacity, 54, 111, 244
Castoreum, 91
Castoridae, 7, 81
Cat, 4, 9, 113, 150, 199–201, 207–8; African wild, 202–5; European wild, 202–5; feral (domestic), 9, 11, 200–5; sabertoothed, 201
Catfish, 192
Catskill Mountains, 186
Cattail, 110, 112
Cattle, 257; Texas longhorn, 257
Cavity, tree, 58, 70, 72–73, 78, 98, 119, 173, 176
Cedar, white, 207
Cenozoic era, 3
Central America, 205, 231
Cervid, 9, 231–33, 244, 256 , 259
Cheetah, 200–1
Cherry: black, 102; flowering, 242
Chesapeake Bay, 185
Chestnut, American, 102, 168; blight, 102, 168
Chickadee, black-capped, 61
China, 158, 175, 220, 232, 260
Chipmunk, 58, 59, 150; eastern, 7, 57–58, 60–64, 67, 78, 93, 95, 192
Chiroptera, 6–7, 27, 29
Chitty hypothesis, 108
Chordata, 4
Chromosome, 50
Climate, 14, 25, 71, 96, 197, 249
Coati, white-tailed, 175

Colony, beaver, 85, 88, 90–91, 94–96
Colorado, 66, 100, 214, 228
Commensal species, 103–5, 230
Communication, 38, 90–93, 144–46, 182, 251, 253, 255
Connecticut, 100, 113
Conservation, 43, 49, 51, 53, 71, 73, 76, 86, 88, 90, 100–2, 139, 153–54, 157, 167–70, 184, 187, 200, 202, 204, 207–8, 230, 237, 250; status, 100, 153, 207
Continental drift, 4, 14
Contraception, in wild horses, 222–23
Convention on International Trade in Endangered Species of Wild Fauna and Flora (CITES), 206
Copperhead, 19
Corridor, 212
Cottontail, 190, 193, 204; Appalachian, 5, 7, 46, 49–53, 100; eastern, 7, 45–46, 49–52, 54, 77, 206; New England, 7, 46, 49–53
Coy-dog, 142–43
Coy-wolf, 143
Coyote, 8, 54–56, 93, 128–29, 132, 135–46
Crabapple, 242
Crayfish, 192
Crepuscular behavior, 47, 83, 91, 98, 129, 159, 201
Cretaceous period, 4
Cuckoo: black-billed, 118; yellow-billed, 118
Cursorial behavior, 129, 159, 200, 217, 233

Dam, beaver, 83–84, 88–90, 94
Darwin, Charles, 13, 132
DDT, 41, 74
Deer, 4, 9, 56, 137–38, 142, 211–13, 223, 231–33, 257–58; barking (muntjac), 232, 260; Chinese water, 232, 249; mule, 4, 209, 249–51; Père David's, 232; roe, 260; sika, 9, 231–32; tufted, 232; whitetailed, 4, 9, 77, 89, 114–16, 137, 155, 157, 190, 201, 207, 209, 213, 229, 231–55, 259, 261
Delaware, 16, 22, 29, 45, 71, 81, 97, 158, 168, 179, 200, 205, 231
Delayed implantation, 159, 182–83, 196
Den: bank, 83, 90, 94, 110; bear, 159, 171–74; skunk, 196
Dentition, 13
Desert, 1, 19, 57, 135, 190, 220, 222, 258
Diaphragm, 2

Forest cutting (logging), 72, 88, 136, 139, 212, 237

Forest fragmentation, 101–2, 143, 186, 206, 249

Forest-management practice, 51–52; even-aged system, 51

Forest maturation, 53, 102

Forest regeneration, 88, 233, 239, 241

Fossorial, 2

Fox, 128, 177, 179; bat-eared, 129; competition between red and gray, 140; gray, 8, 129, 139–40, 142, 150; red, 8, 61, 75, 129–30, 138–42, 150–51, 190

Frog, 229

Functional response, 55–56

Fungus, 72, 78, 118, 226

Gemsbok, 258

Gene flow, 212

Genetic variation (diversity), 26, 49, 132, 154, 168, 210, 212

Genetics, 246

Georgia, 100, 151, 167, 177

Germination, 62

Gestation, 12, 14, 29, 48, 59, 85, 98, 108, 159, 176, 183, 196, 201, 218, 226, 233, 258

Gettysburg National Military Park, 234, 241

Glacier, 61, 71

Glacier National Park, 74, 154, 161, 163

Glands: anal, 91–92, 182; castor, 82, 91–92, 145; mammary, 2–3; musk, 198; scent, 18, 145, 253, 255; submaxillary, 19; venom-producing, 20

Gliding, 33, 68–70, 72

Global warming (climate change), 73

Goat: feral (domestic), 9, 213, 256–57; mountain, 262

Gorilla, 188

Goshawk, 68

Grand Teton National Park, 154

Grape, wild, 168

Grassland, 17, 47, 58, 66, 192, 195, 218, 256

Great Cypress Swamp, 208

Great Dismal Swamp, 173

Great Smoky Mountains National Park, 161, 168, 172, 229, 241

Greater Yellowstone Area, 154–55

Growing season, 66

Grouse, ruffed, 52, 55, 86

Hare, 4, 7, 45–48, 54, 137–38; European, 7,
45–46; snowshoe, 7, 46, 54–56, 126, 206, 242

Hawaii, 224, 228, 257

Hawaii Volcanoes National Park, 230

Hawk: Cooper's, 68; red-tailed, 67

Hawthorn, 242

Health, 187, 204, 229, 239, 243–44, 247, 259

Hemlock, eastern, 102, 125–26, 210

Herbivore, 26, 33, 59, 61, 83, 98, 122, 219, 233

Hibernation, 2, 30–31, 41–42, 60, 65–67, 93–94, 122, 159, 171–73, 188, 195

Hoarding: larder, 60–64, 78–80, 93–94, 101; scatter, 60–63, 80

Home range, 61, 64, 211–12

Horse, 4, 197, 216–23; draft, 220; feral, 9, 75, 217, 218–23; forest, 220; Przewalski's wild (takhi), 220; tarpan, 220

Howling, 144–48, 155, 157

Hudson Bay Company, 54

Humans, early, 14, 131–33, 219, 239

Humans attacked by: black bear, 163–64; coyote, 138; gray wolf, 149; grizzly bear, 163–64; mountain lion, 214–15

Hunting, 49, 87–88, 133, 139, 147, 149, 153–54, 169, 201–2, 204–7, 209, 211–14, 221, 223, 228–30, 235–38, 247

Huxley, Thomas, 13

Hybridization, 142–43, 202, 227–28

Hystricidae, 120

Idaho, 131, 154, 165, 211

Illinois, 136, 207

Impala, 256–57

Inbreeding, 210

Incisor, 17, 19, 82

Incus, 2

Indiana, 15, 101, 136

Inner ear: birds and reptiles, 2; mammals, 2–3

Insect, 3, 19, 23, 29, 31–37, 39–40, 60–61, 126, 140, 236

Insectivora, 6, 16, 20, 25

Insectivore, 17, 20, 23, 33, 61, 98, 188: ancestor, 32

Introduced species, 49, 54, 75, 88, 126, 134, 139, 143–44, 153–57, 169, 184–87, 215, 221, 228, 231, 238, 250

Invertebrate, 20, 23, 60–61, 89, 118, 129, 187, 191, 226

Isle Royale National Park, 154

Jackal, 128, 132
Jackrabbit: black-tailed, 7, 46, 54; white-tailed, 7, 46–47
Jaguar, 200–1
Jay, blue, 61

K-strategist, 108
Kangaroo, 26; great red, 188
Kansas, 228
Kentucky, 15
Keratin, 216

Lactation, 3, 13, 172, 174
Lagomorpha, 5, 7, 45
Lake, 82–83, 94, 110, 191
Lake Superior, 154
Lemming, 107; southern bog, 8
Lemur, 33; flying, 33, 68
Leporid(ae), 4, 7, 45, 46, 53, 54, 57, 107, 110, 201
Lichen, 72
Lifespan, 85, 124, 130, 159, 201, 218, 226, 258
Lion: African, 199–201; mountain, 153, 187, 200–1, 206, 208–15, 237
Litter size, 12, 18, 23, 25, 29–30, 48, 55–56, 59, 85, 99, 108, 124, 130, 159, 163, 168, 183, 196, 201, 218, 226, 233, 258
Livestock, 103, 138, 157, 213–14, 229, 236, 239
Lodge: beaver, 83–84, 89–90, 93–95; muskrat, 110
Louisiana, 110, 185
Louse, 103
Lynx, 9, 54–55, 200, 205–6

Maine, 50, 71, 155–56, 178, 212, 248
Mallard, 142
Malleus, 2
Mammalia, 4
Manatee, 25
Maple, 83, 125; red, 102, 251; sugar, 95
Marmot, 58–59, 66; Olympic, 66; yellow-bellied, 66
Marsh, 110–12, 191
Marsupial, 5, 11, 25
Marsupium, 12–13
Marten, American, 9, 182, 193
Maryland, 6–10, 16, 71, 95, 107, 121, 167, 178–79, 184–85, 191, 194, 210, 217, 221, 223

Massachusetts, 50, 113, 117, 206
Mast, 59, 64, 168
Megachiroptera, 29, 33
Melanin, 166
Mephitid(ae), 9, 128, 181, 183, 194–95
Mesozoic era, 3
Metabolic rate (metabolism), 20, 31, 94, 96, 172
Metapopulation, 51–52
Metatheria, 5, 13–16
Mexico, 5, 14, 96, 121, 149, 194–95
Michigan, 126, 154, 185, 250
Microchiroptera, 29, 33–35
Midden, 78–80
Migration, 2, 30, 60, 94, 203, 233
Mimicry, 165
Mink, 9, 89, 181, 183, 191–92
Minnesota, 47, 56, 80, 147, 153, 166, 195, 210, 250
Miocene epoch, 217
Mississippi River, 160, 165–66
Mist-net, 36
Mitochondrial DNA, 131, 194
Molar, tribosphenic, 13
Mole, 4, 22–24, 61; eastern, 6, 24; golden, 25; hairy-tailed, 6, 13, 17, 22; marsupial, 25; star-nosed, 6, 23; true, 25
Molossidae, 32
Monogamy, 85, 188
Monotremata, 20
Monster, Gila, 19
Montana, 74, 154
Moose, 9, 53, 137, 155, 231–32, 236, 249–50, 257, 260–61
Moose sickness, 248–49
Mortality, 134, 211, 249
Moth, 39; gypsy, 101, 117–19, 168
Mouse, 7, 8, 16–17, 19, 22, 97, 107, 130, 140, 150, 192, 203–4, 206; Arizona pocket, 190; cotton, 7, 98; deer, 8, 191; eastern harvest, 7, 98; golden, 8; house, 8, 97–98, 103–5; meadow jumping, 8; white-footed, 8, 97, 114–19, 191; wood-land jumping, 8
Mowing to reduce ticks, 115
Muntjac, Reeve's, 260–61
Murid(ae), 7, 8, 97–99, 124
Muskox, 258
Muskrat, common, 8, 14, 53, 89, 98, 110–12
Mustelid(ae), 9, 128, 181, 182–84, 186, 188–92, 195, 201, 210

Myocastoridae, 8
Myotis: eastern small-footed, 6; gray, 6; Indiana, 5, 6, 41; little brown, 6, 29, 32, 36, 39, 40, 42; northern, 6, 41; southeastern, 6

National forest, 169, 230
National park, 138, 154, 161, 230
National Park Service, 154, 161, 170
Native American, 86–87, 121, 132, 149, 160, 208, 221, 228, 235
Nematode, parasitic, 73, 248–49
Nest: box, 73; leaf, 58, 78; tree, 58
New England, 72, 136, 168
New Hampshire, 52, 126, 156, 185–86
New Jersey, 6–10, 46, 100, 113, 139, 167, 178–79, 207
New World, 97, 103–4, 149, 175, 203, 228
New York, 6–10, 46, 50, 88, 100, 102, 113, 117, 126, 136, 151, 155, 166–67, 178–79, 184–86, 191, 200, 205, 210–12, 231, 246, 248, 250
Nocturnal mammals, 3, 35, 47, 58, 67–68, 83, 91, 98, 118, 129, 144, 159, 182, 195, 201, 224, 255
North Carolina, 71–72, 143–44, 167, 169, 173, 185, 228, 230, 238
Notoryctemorphia, 25
Numerical response, 55–56
Nuthatch, white-breasted, 61
Nutria, 8, 110
Nutrition (in deer), 246–47, 259

Oak, 61, 64, 101–2; black, 61–62; chestnut, 61; northern red, 61; scarlet, 61; white, 61–62
Ocean, 1
Ochotonidae, 45
Ohio, 6–10, 15, 71, 95, 136, 139, 168, 179, 184–85, 207, 224, 228, 242
Oilbird, 37
Old World, 29, 97–98, 103, 105, 107, 149, 175, 202–3, 227, 230
Olfactory bowl, 146–47
Olfactory sense (olfaction), 25, 33, 37, 62, 77, 82, 85, 91–93, 122, 129, 133, 144–45, 159, 182, 196–98, 251, 253
Oligocene epoch, 26, 216
Omnivore, 1, 98, 129, 159, 176, 196
Ontario, 80, 136–37, 244, 250
Opossum: common, 14; Virginia, 6, 11–15, 75

Orchard, 240, 242
Osceola National Forest, 173
Otter, 181; giant, 182; northern river, 9, 182–85, 187, 191–92
Owl, great horned, 67, 193
Ozone depletion, 74

Pangea, 4
Panther, Florida, 208, 210–11
Parasite, 118, 247–50
Parental care, 3
Pariah, 134
Patagium, 28
Pelage, 2, 17, 23, 46, 58, 81–82, 92, 165–67, 172, 182, 191, 193, 195, 197–98, 200, 203, 205–6, 217, 220, 227–28, 232, 253, 258
Pennsylvania, xi, 6–10, 41, 49–50, 52–53, 56, 64, 66, 71, 88–89, 100, 102, 113, 117, 126, 136, 138–39, 153, 166–67, 170, 173, 178–79, 184–86, 191, 194–95, 209–11, 234, 238–39, 242, 248–50
Pennsylvania Game Commission, 43
Perissodactyla, 9, 216–17
Pesticide (insecticide), 39, 41, 119, 184
Phalanger, 68
Pheromone, 145
Physiology, winter, 50, 170–71, 174
Pig (hog): Eurasian (European) wild (boar), 224, 227–28; feral, 9, 15, 143, 213, 224, 227–30
Pika: American, 45; collared, 45
Pike, 192
Pine, 125
Pinnae, 17
Pinniped, 37–38
Pipistrele, eastern, 7, 29, 31, 41
Placenta, 13–14
Plant succession, 102, 256
Plantigrade, 159, 176
Platypus, duck-billed, 5, 19–21
Pleistocene epoch, 26, 61, 136, 162, 219
Pliocene epoch, 26
Poaching, 169–70
Pokeweed, 168
Pollination, 27
Polygyny, 188, 244, 261
Pond: beaver, 82–83, 88–90, 94; muskrat, 110–12
Pony, 220–21
Poplar, tulip, 95

Index

331

Stand, clearcut, 51–52, 56, 70
Stapes, 2
Steppe, 26
Stonefly, 33
Stream, 1, 17, 20, 82–83, 89, 91, 110, 191
Stress, 108–9, 167
Stunning, 38
Suburbia (residential area), 49, 114, 176–77, 204, 213, 223, 238, 243
Suid(ae), 9, 224–26, 231, 256
Survival, 64, 154, 163, 168–71, 174, 187, 210, 212; winter, 41, 54
Swamp, 206
Swiftlet, cave, 37

Tactile organ, 23
Tactile sense, 25, 144
Tail, prehensile, 12
Talpidae, 6, 22
Tannin, 61–62
Taproot, 62
Teal, blue-winged, 142
Tennessee, 71–72, 100, 167, 169, 172
Territory (territoriality), 47, 60–61, 63, 66, 77–80, 87, 91, 93, 98, 108, 110, 140–41, 144, 146, 148, 189–90, 258
Tertiary period, 216
Testosterone, 245, 259, 261
Texas, 100, 104, 185, 210–12, 214, 228, 238
Theria, 5
Threatened species, 5–6, 8, 10, 206–7
Tick: deer, 114–16; wood (dog), 114
Timber industry, 126, 239
Tornado, 236
Torpor, 2, 31, 42, 171, 195
Trade: bear parts, 170; beaver, 87
Tragus, 36
Trapping, 87–89, 149, 179, 185–86, 202, 207, 228–30
Triassic period, 3–4
Trout, 192; brook, 89
Tundra, 1, 159, 233, 258
Turkey, wild, 185, 229, 236

Ultrasonic bat detectors, 36–37
Ungulate, 26, 226, 232–33, 258–59; even-toed, 9, 216, 224, 256; odd-toed, 9, 216–17
Urbanization, 53, 58, 90, 134, 138, 168, 176–77, 204, 206, 211, 238
Ursid(ae), 8, 128, 158–60, 167, 190

U.S. Fish and Wildlife Service, 170, 207
U.S. Forest Service, 222

Vaccine: contraception, 222; Lyme disease, 116; rabies, 151–52, 180, 204
Valley Forge National Historical Park, 234
Value: aesthetic, 41, 89–90, 127, 134, 146, 153, 155, 186–87, 205–7, 219, 223, 236, 238–39, 247, 250, 257; ecological, 41, 138, 229–30, 256; economic, 39, 86–88, 105, 125–26, 169–70, 179–80, 185, 207, 222–23, 229–30, 236–43, 251, 257; recreational, 213, 219, 230, 238, 247; religious, 203, 208
Vehicular collision, 169, 211, 239
Venom, 19–21, 60
Vertebrate, 1, 19, 61, 77–78, 91, 114, 118, 191, 226, 229
Vespertilionidae, 6, 27, 29, 188
Viper, pit, 19
Virginia, 5–10, 16, 29, 45–46, 72–73, 97, 100, 167, 169, 173, 178–79, 185–86, 191, 194, 210, 217, 221, 223–24, 241
Visual sense (vision), 33, 91, 129, 133, 144, 159, 182, 198, 251, 260
Vole, 7–8, 16, 22, 53, 97, 107–10, 112, 192–93; beach, 108; meadow, 8, 17, 98, 108; montane, 107; prairie, 8, 108; rock, 8; southern red-backed, 8, 98; spacing behavior, 108–9; woodland, 8, 24, 98, 108

Wampum, 87
Wasp, 19
Water quality, 184
Waterfowl, 89, 112
Weasel, 181, 187, 191, 210; competition between, 190–92; least, 9, 182–83, 191–93; long-tailed, 9, 181–82, 191–93
Weather, 2, 64, 108, 185
West Indies, 16, 45, 97, 228
West Virginia, 6–10, 72, 166–67, 177–79, 184–86, 194, 210, 224, 228, 230, 257
Whale: baleen, 25; humpback, 38; killer, 189; sperm, 38, 188; toothed, 25, 37–38
Wild Horse and Burro Act, 222
Wildflower, 241–42, 247
Wildlife agency, 88, 126, 157, 169–70, 207, 213–14, 237, 243, 247, 250
Willow, 83
Winter lethargy, 171–74